George Jones
why baby why

George Jones
why baby why

Jim Brown

QUARRY
MUSIC
BOOKS

The publisher gratefully acknowledges the
support of the Book Publishing Industry
Development Program of the Department
of Canadian Heritage.

George Jones: *Why Baby Why* is a serious
critical and biographical study of the music
and career of George Jones. The quotation of lyrics
from songs written or performed by George Jones
illustrates the biographical information and
critical analysis presented by the author and
thus constitutes fair use under existing copyright
conventions. The authors of all lyrics cited in the
text are duly credited.

Order No. QP 00810
ISBN 1-55082-243-8

Editorial development, design, type, and
imaging by Quarry Press Inc.,
Kingston, Ontario, Canada.

Published by Quarry Press Inc.,
PO Box 1061, Kingston, ON
K7L 4Y5 Canada,
www. quarrypress.com

Printed and bound in the United States of America
by Vicks Lithograph and Printing Corporation,
Utica, New York.

Distributed in the following territories by:
General Distribution Services
325 Humber College Blvd,
Etobicoke, ON M9W 7C3, Canada
Music Sales Limited
257 Park Avenue South, New York, NY 10010 USA
Music Sales Limited
8/9 Frith Street, London W1D 3JB England
Music Sales Pty. Limited
120 Rothschild Street, Rosebery, Sydney, NSW 2018, Australia

Contents

"I didn't get into this business even thinking about money, what I would do, and where I would go. I just wanted my guitar in my hands and to keep going. I just wanted to sing."
— George Jones

You know this old world is full of singers
But just a few are chosen
To tear your heart out when they sing.
— Who's Gonna Fill Their Shoes
(*Troy Seals & Max D. Barnes*)

Part One

The Cold Hard Truth

1
The Greatest
Country Singer in the World

Considering that George Jones learned to sing from an instruction manual written in Purgatory and brought back to Earth by Jimmie Rodgers and Hank Williams, his very existence as a walking, talking, touring, recording artist in the third millennium is a miracle. But George has seldom been distracted from the one thing he loves to do, and, even though his world has fallen to pieces several times, he just keeps on singing. His continued presence on the country music scene, not to mention an unending flow of high quality records, has given more and more credence with each passing year to Lefty Frizzell's assessment (first stated for the benefit of his teenaged nephew Jimmy who had made fun of George's vocal style) that George Jones "may be the best country singer of all time."

George Jones has set the standard in country music for the past three decades. First inspired by Roy Acuff and Bill Monroe when he heard them on the *Grand Ole Opry* broadcasts, George became hooked on the bluesy, yodel-inflected vocals that Hank Williams sang. He liked Lefty Frizzell's records, too. Although you can hear the influence of all four of these great country music pioneers in George's voice, he forged a style of his own.

While George Jones has cut hundreds of great country records which merit critical recognition, even admiration, most of what has been written about him harkens back to a bleak period of seven troubled years, from the time Tammy Wynette divorced him and he added cocaine abuse to his predilection for binge drinking, until George kicked his drug habit, quit boozing, and got back to the basics of life. These seven short years — out of a career that began when George was a teenager busking on the streets of Beaumont, Texas in the late 1940s — have fascinated a legion of sensationalist writers. Long after Jones had successfully rehabilitated himself, some writers still found it difficult not to dwell on his worst of times. As recently as 1992 some commentators felt that George Jones was not worthy of being inducted into the Country Music Hall of Fame because he was, they said, being rewarded for a career of bad behavior and not for being the greatest living country singer. Seemingly obsessed with George Jones' unworldly gypsy lifestyle, rather than inspired by the wonder of his gift for singing, these people have often used Jones as a whipping boy, citing George as another music business casualty who wasted his talents on fast-living. Some people just can't seem to forgive ole George. You just have to wonder why.

But right from the start-up in the mid-50s, when George first hit the national country charts with a song asking *Why Baby Why*, he has created more questions than answers, none more fascinating than his sense of kinship with his true mentor, Hank Williams. An entire generation of young singers who followed in his footsteps appear to have been more than merely influenced by the music of Hank and haunted by the disturbing image of Luke the Drifter discovered by his chauffeur on the back seat of his pale blue Cadillac — stiff and blue and dead at the age of 29. Faron Young, Johnny Horton, Merle Kilgore, Johnny Cash, Carl Perkins, Waylon Jennings, Jerry Lee Lewis, Roy Orbison, Buddy Holly, and Elvis all took their cue from Hank, even yodeling Bill Haley, the Philadelphia-based pioneer who began to rock his country in the 1950s. George Jones was a charter member of this club. During George's worst of times, he was discovered by friends seated on the rear-seat upholstery of a yellow Cadillac hanging out with a life-size cut-out of Hank Williams, drinking a case of Jim Beam, bottle by bottle, just fixing to die like Hank had died.

While he was still a teenager, George had spoken with Hank after a radio show performance, and while playing the Opry and the *Louisiana Hayride*, George had also met most of the singers who were involved in tragic accidents during the years that followed Hank's death, including Johnny Horton (who married Hank's widow before he died) and Carl Perkins (who was critically injured in the 1956 car accident that claimed his brother's life). George had toured with Perkins and Horton on a bill with Johnny Cash and Elvis in 1955, then met another outlaw singer named Waylon Jennings when Waylon was working as a disc jockey at KOYL in Odessa, Texas. Jones and Jennings and Cash became fast friends, and all three just kept on keeping on — no matter what dangerously mad exploits they got themselves into.

Much has been written about this bad boy George — in related autobiographies like Tammy Wynette's *Stand by Your Man* and Johnny Cash's *Man in Black*, in two unauthorized biographies of George released in 1984 by Dolly

Carlisle and Bob Allen, and in a host of Jones-bashing newspaper and magazine articles written by dogged journalists fixed upon seeing him as their very own made-in-the-Hank-Williams-mold tragic hero, even predicting his imminent death. No question, George Jones struggled with his personal demons during the 1970s, but he was also victimized by a rabble of shady managers, agents, and promoters who manipulated media opinion of Jones from time to time for their own purposes. That George Jones has survived all of this turmoil without manipulating or maligning anyone represents a moral triumph of monumental proportions, surpassed only by his musical achievement.

A few years ago, George wrote his own autobiography, *I Lived To Tell It All*, with respected author Tom Carter, where he gives full dollar value by reciting his outrageous road stories. While he tries to correct the distorted picture of him painted by Dolly Carlisle and Bob Allen, responding to allegations made in Tammy Wynette's book and dispelling myths about his behavior based on hearsay in the media, he also struggles to make peace with nearly everyone, including former wives and managers. Showing a true generosity of spirit, he does seem to have found closure with a wide spectrum of folks.

There is no doubt that George Jones lived much of the first 50 years of his life in the fast-lane, but if what he has done was "wasting" talent, perhaps more recording artists should have let it all hang out because now that all the facts and figures have come in, at the beginning of the second century of country music, George Jones figures to be the number one country singer of all time. He's at least high on the list of the Top 10 along with Hank Williams, Johnny Cash, Conway Twitty, Merle Haggard, Webb Pierce, Dolly Parton, Buck Owens, Willie Nelson, and Waylon Jennings. George loves to sing and country fans love to listen. However obscured by controversy, the wonder of his music shines through his life.

2
The George Jones Show

George Jones sits back on the comfortable leather sofa. There is a smile on his face, and, as his gaze follows the stories being bantered back and forth by his guests, Loretta Lynn and Billy Ray Cyrus, his intense hazel eyes are darkly visible through his trademark tinted eyeglasses.

Billy Ray is telling Loretta that he did meet her husband Mooney Lynn — whom Loretta affectionately refers to as "Doo" (which is short for Doolittle) — before Doo passed away. It was at a time before Cyrus' smash breakthrough hit *Achy Breaky Heart* when Billy Ray had been passing by the Lynns' property and had dropped off an early record, handing it to Doo for Loretta, who was on tour at the time.

When Billy Ray says that the record he'd left with Doo had been kind of slow, George interjects, recalling that "Stonewall Jackson told me one time that he had a song that started off slow and just sort of tapered off . . ."

Billy Ray and his guitarist perform the song, singing the harmonies and strumming their acoustic guitars. It *is* slow, a ballad, but it's better than Billy Ray has humbled it to be.

George Jones seems at ease here on this television studio set that has been fixed up to simulate his living room, including a photo gallery of country performers apparently moved from his home to the studio. When Billy Ray mentions how cool it is that George has all these pictures of his fellow country music stars hanging on the wall there in the studio, Jones quips, "They robbed me. I was walking down the hall and pictures were goin' off the wall. . . ." The camera pans the studio wall and the black and white 8 X 10 photos to let the viewing audience see what he is talking about, coming to rest on a photo of Loretta which, through a trick of studio lighting, seems to glow. It's the only color shot displayed, and now a further special effect takes us to a second set location where Loretta and a band perform *She's Got You*. There's some magic here as Loretta recreates one of her friend and mentor Patsy Cline's hits, linking the present to the past. Loretta, like George, has roots that run deep.

It is a Saturday night in February of the year 2000 and the *George Jones Show* is a re-run being shown on TNN after the Opry broadcast. This "George Jones & Friends" format is co-produced by Billy Galium and George's wife, Nancy Jones. With Jones chatting amiably with his guests, then segueing to live sequences that have been filmed separately, the formula works better than times in the past when George didn't always put his best foot forward in high pressure situations on network television programs like *The Tonight Show* or the televised Country Music Association (CMA) Awards shows. The idea here is to bring veterans together with some of the more promising artists in an intimate setting that is far removed from the glitz and glitter style of production often favored by TV producers.

George and his guests next watch a film clip of a four-year-old Billy Ray, then move on to an anecdote that Loretta tells of a time when she and George were at a circus midway and rode the "Mad Mouse" together. "I tried to forget it as fast as I could," George quips.

His third guest, a quiet, dark-haired, young woman seated beside Billy Ray, is Sara Evans. Sara now mentions her own record, *Three Chords And The Truth*, and says it's about a woman who has just heard a George Jones record. She strums her guitar and sings, "I'd never heard that song before, but I knew each word by heart . . . He changed my mind with three chords and the truth."

George beams at her and says, "You're the kind we need!"

After Loretta performs *My Blue Kentucky Girl* with the band, George closes the show with *Who's Gonna Fill Their Shoes*, his personalized tribute to ole Hank, Marty, and Lefty and everybody else from Roy Acuff to Merle Haggard. The song begins with Jones asking his audience to imagine what it would be like living "without all your radio heroes." He seems to bite back tears as he sings, "The heart of country music beats in Luke the Drifter . . ." and hooks it with, "Lord, who's gonna fill their shoes?" As George sings tribute to his music heroes, especially Hank Williams, this emotionally charged moment is laced with the additional irony that in recent times these heroes have been banished from the radio airwaves. All of them, including George Jones.

Although George may not be in the Top 10 these days, he is popping up all over the place. He's touring from the West Coast to the East Coast and he's on TV and he's smiling a whole lot. Both his recent studio album, COLD HARD TRUTH, and the radio single *Choices* have been nominated for Grammy awards. A few nights later, George would win his second Grammy for Best Performance by a Country Male Vocalist. At age 68, there were still a whole lot of people who regarded him as the world's greatest living country singer. "The Rolls Royce of country singers," critics have commented. He's still got that amazing vocal gift, an ability to sing so emotionally well that he is said to have made Texas oil men weep. But there was a time when that voice mysteriously sounded like Donald Duck quacking George Jones songs.

3
Deedoodle Duck

I n his early publicity pictures, George Jones still has that crew-cut he first got
when he went into the Marine Corp. Most of the other singers in the 1950s
had gone to duck-tail haircuts and side-burns, slicking their pompadours back
with gobs of Brill Cream. Not George Jones. I wondered if the Beatles had Jones
in mind when they wrote that line, *"Here comes ole flat-top, cruisin' up slowly
…"* When George met Tammy Wynette, a hairdresser before she became a
Nashville star, he began to let his hair grow out again, and, for a while in the
1970s, he wore it long with side-burns …

That's how this chapter began, but before I could complete the sentence
the door bell chimed. I glanced at my wrist-watch — four-thirty in the a.m. Who
could it be at this late hour? Surely not the pizza guy. Pizza companies usually
don't deliver much after three. Not in North Vancouver on a weeknight. Besides,
my two roommates were sound asleep. The house had been silent for hours.

The bell rang again.

I had better see who it is, I decided, before they wake up the whole house-
hold. I got up from my word-processor, did a quick "save" while standing there
in the den, and, as the battered Toshiba portable groaned into performing that
function, I stepped through the living room. Better flip on the porch light, I
thought, so you can see who the unexpected visitor is. I put my hand to the
knob and cautiously pulled the door open.

There in the full glare of the porch light was a guy dressed in a duck suit.
He had a guitar in his hands and he began to sing: *"I think … she … still cares …"*

I gawked as this bizarre apparition then began to speak in urgent Donald
Duck-like phrases. I couldn't make much sense out of what he was saying. He
was jabbering away too rapidly to be understood. Plus, I was nervous. There had
been an alarming number of home invasions in Vancouver in the days just
before Halloween. You read about them nearly every day in the newspapers.
Then, as my thoughts raced on, I noticed the guy standing behind the duck.

An older man, he wore a fedora and a crumpled three-piece suit. Looked like an off-duty cop. His shoes were black and polished to a high sheen. He kind of reminded me of someone but I couldn't decide exactly who. When he spoke, he sounded like Walter Brennan reciting lines of cheesy dialog from an episode of *The Real McCoys*. There was just a crinkly hint of a smile at the corners of his mouth.

"He wants to know why you're doin' it."

"I don't get you," I said.

"The book. Why you're writin' it . . ."

I said, "I don't believe any of this. Are you guys trick or treating or what? If you are, you are two days early."

"You'd better tell him," said the man. "He can be awfully darned persistent."

The duck dug a pint-sized flask out of a jacket pocket and took a slug. The guitar dangled from a gaudy strap hung around its neck. The duck hiccuped and said, "*White Lightnin'*!"

I said, "Well, we think there's a whole lot of people who want to know more about George Jones, the singer."

This sent the duck into near hysteria. It backed away into the curving row of rose bushes that led to the driveway and hitched the guitar back into position. Its companion shrugged and shifted his feet. The duck began to sing: "*I stopped loving . . . you to-da-a-a-ay . . .*"

I flinched. This *was* serious. When I was writing the book *Country Women in Music*, my songwriter pal Ralph Murphy had told me that songwriters often write in the third person. They avoid the first person during the creative process because many songwriters, due to their shy nature, are more comfortable composing in the third person. More distancing. When they get serious, they realize they have to craft it into the first person for a singer to get their message across in concert situations. This duck was re-writing George Jones' hits from the third to the first. I had better pay attention.

"He seems like a nice little fella," I said to the man standing in the shadows, trying to humor him. "But he can't sing worth squat. Not when he quacks like that."

"You don't want to get him upset," said the old man. "Why don't you just tell him what he wants to know?"

"What? — about the book?"

"That's it." He chuckled a sly "hee-hee" chuckle. He seemed to be enjoying this. In fact, he was tickled half to death.

"How 'bout I tell *you?*" I said. "*He* seems busy."

"That could work."

"Well," I began, "there's a couple of books already out by people who were trying real hard, written in 1984, but they don't tell the whole story, plus, they're not exactly . . . accurate, and there's a whole lot of water that's flowed under the bridge since they were written."

No comment from either the man or the duck.

The duck had moved on to *I Don't Need Your Rockin' Chair*. It seemed to be two-stepping some, doing a little dance, and moving 'round in the shadows as it sang and strummed. The old man just stood there, yet, when I kept my eyes focused on him, he seemed to shape-shift in and out of well-known Hollywood actor profiles. He was Jack Nicholson, then he was Clint, then a smiling, conciliatory Gene Hackman. Behind all of these, I sensed a darker, gaunter figure who generated each successive manifestation. It was not the ghost of Christmas past, present, *or* future.

"There's Tammy Wynette's book *Stand by Your Man*. But she didn't . . . um, well, she told quite a few fibs about George . . . let's just say she wasn't exactly kind. And there's George's own book," I continued, "the one he wrote with Tom Carter, *I Lived To Tell It All*."

"Uh-huh."

"It's a dandy."

"*So,*" quacked the duck, sidling into the lit space just beyond the porch, "*why are you writing your book?*"

"People want to read more stuff. They want to read what a writer has to say, as well as what George had to say four or five years ago. Plus, I intend to put in some additional material about what else was going on in each decade, you know, pull in some of the comments that people have made and paint a wider canvas."

No comment from either visitor.

"I've always liked his stuff, right from *Why Baby Why*. When I was in high school, I had a band and we played *White Lightning*, in 1960 . . . that, and Bob Mitchum's *Thunder Road*, which had lyrics set to the melody of the *Hans Gruber Schottische*, a round dance something like a polka . . ." I shrugged and added, "It was before *Gator* and those *Smokey and the Bandit* movies came out . . ."

The duck had begun to mutter to itself. It seemed to be thinking out loud. I looked past the two figures on the porch step to the driveway where a shiny metallic-gray, late-model Cadillac sat parked beneath a streetlight, its motor idling discreetly. The figure at the wheel appeared to be wearing a gorilla suit. I blinked and squinted. Yep, *big* monkey man.

The old man shrugged and said, "George, y'know, he kinda got hisself in with the wrong crowd at one point in his life . . ."

"Just for a few years," I said. "Everybody was doing blowcaine in those days. Lawyers, construction workers, disco dancers, not just country singers. It was during the time the Colombian cartels flooded the streets of North America with their product. Several famous Hollywood directors were nearly snowed under by the blizzard."

"Uh-huh."

"He's over all that, now? Isn't he."

"Pretty much, except he enjoys a cold glass of beer or wine, now and then. Not very often."

"He said that in his book."

The duck was silent, but still supremely agitated. The man shuffled his feet. I felt the need to end this. If I didn't deal with these characters, right here and now, they would be back. I was sure of that. George had dealt with them when they had invaded his life. Why, I wondered, had they shown up on my doorstep weeks after I'd begun to research and write my book? Two figments of George's imagination ringing my door bell at four in the morning. That was the key to sending them on their way. Which, of course, was absurd. How could they really be here? That duck suit didn't look like a costume, though — the duck looked real. It appeared to be a flesh and blood and feathers duck dressed in a Nudie Cohn-designed khaki tunic with little applique treble cleft emblems and musical notes and a military cap. It was *like* the Disney creation, but it was not wearing a sailor suit. It was wearing a custom-tailored U.S. Marine jacket. Which was impossible. However, I had already learned during my early research on George Jones that things had gotten pretty crazed for those few bad years. This quickly, I had become susceptible to the singer's own past hallucinations. They were standing on my front porch confronting me. By immersing myself in his music and his life, I was now experiencing some weird kind of contact high.

"Look," I said, "I'm not going to dredge up dirt on George and Tammy and the Jones Boys. No sensational reports of arrests, lawsuits, and alleged wrong-doings. I'm interested in the music. He made a whole lot of records, most of them pretty darned good ones. Nobody seems to talk about the music very much, not in most of the books that have written about him. That's what I do.

I write about music and the people who make it."

The duck said something, speaking in low confidential tones to the old man.

"What?" I said.

"He wants to know if you're going to write about the gorillas."

"Sure, some. I'm not going to leave the bad guys out completely. But the book isn't about them, it's about George and his music."

The duck leaned toward its companion and murmured. It seemed nearly pacified.

"He wants to know if you're going to write about . . . him."

"I haven't thought it through that far. How does he feel about it?"

The duck turned its sorrowful eyes back to me. It quacked some indecipherable phrase. Had it said, "I'm a people?"

"Yeah, sure you are," I ventured. "You're George's alter-ego, but you're also him, too, and famous as all get out, and you can't get around that. You've become a part of the lives of a whole lot of folks. People really like your music. They haven't forgotten how good it is, even if they can't hear it on the radio much these days. Forget about the radio guys . . ."

"You don't want to bring them up much," said the old man. "Or you'll get him all worked up again."

"Okay, okay. But I'm freezing to death out here." It was true, I was in my pyjamas. There were slippers on my feet. I yawned. "Thanks for dropping by. I'll take your visit under advisement."

The duck said, *"Play it cool, man, Play it cool."* They both turned and walked off toward the Cadillac. The gorilla got out, and, for a moment, I heard the blare of a country station on the car stereo. Alan Jackson's *Don't Rock The Jukebox.* The duck and the old man got in, the gorilla shut the rear door, then got behind the wheel. The Caddy pulled back into the dark October night. . . .

That dream was only one of many to disturb my sleep during the time that I spent writing this book. Sure, it *was* a dream, but dreams can be every bit as real as everyday events — until you wake up. The gorillas appeared in other dreams, only they weren't cartoon characters, but hard-nosed, bad-ass dudes who weren't playing parlor games. For the first time in many years, I found myself dealing with nightmares from which I woke bathed in sweat. I would dream and awaken and the next chapter would be going through my head as if while I was sleeping my thought processing had sorted things out. There were plenty of them to be sorted through.

What, I wondered, was I to make of all the cartoon stuff? Hank's favorite reading had been comic books. George had been nicknamed "The Possum" in the '50s. A possum had been a character in a popular cartoon strip in those days, *Pogo*; along with Al Capp's *Lil' Abner* with all that stuff about Lower Slobovia, Shmooes, and Dogpatch, this possum and his alligator pal and these hillbilly characters like Mammy and Pappy Yokum, Lil' Abner, Daisy Mae, Sadie Hockins, and General Bullmoose had been as real as life. They had sometimes drunk homebrew that was called kickapoo joy juice. The everyday events in their deep South lives had been effective vehicles for the cartoonists to lampoon current events in biting political satire, while, at the same time, being darned funny to read, too. When I was in high school, they even had a Sadie Hockins' Dance. My teen band had played it once. And there were those Thumper Jones records that George had put out, named after the cartoon rabbit in the Disney film *Bambi*. Of course, that, too, had been made into a cartoon strip in the "funny papers" for a while. In 1977, George had come out with *Old King Kong*, a merry romp through the annals of monster movies that compares his love for his woman with the likes of Kong and Godzilla. Then, in the midst of his cocaine addiction phase, George began to sing like Donald Duck.

I had read that the first time this had happened had been triggered by the nervous trepidation he had felt when he faced an audience of assembled music business types for a show his handlers had arranged at the Exit-In club in Nashville. Jones had felt that they weren't there so much to listen to him sing as to judge him. And that may have been the case. However, once the duck had been let loose, it took on a persona, Deedoodle Duck, and it hung around until George finally kicked his substance dependency. At one time, when he became trapped in a looped journey, driving from Florence up the highway to Nashville, around the curve of Tammy Wynette's mansion driveway and back down the same highway to Florence, and back through the loop, again, and again, the duck and an old man who resembled Walter Brennan had argued and debated life's many perplexities. They spoke through George's vocal chords and taunted him endlessly. And that time when he sat in his Cadillac with a life-size cut-out of Hank Williams for companionship while listening to cassette tapes of Hank on auto-reverse, the duck and the old man had been there then, too, not amused by George's pathetic attempt at duplicating Hank's legendary exit from this life. You see, some men have more capacity for whiskey than others, and, try as he did, George Jones could not drink enough to do himself in. It wasn't due to lack of effort. Because he didn't take to injecting cocaine, he also couldn't snort enough to put him out of his misery. And he was miserable. He couldn't help it if he was still in love with Tammy. He just hurt because she didn't love him like she used to do.

The deeper I delved into George Jones's legacy, the more I came to understand how George had survived. George escaped into the music, and, when things got unbearably tough, he would sometimes escape one dimension further, into cartoon characters, splintered fractions of himself that could not feel the pain that wracked his body and tortured his soul. I found myself reaching for the music more often than I reached for reference material. After a while, I knew just what George Jones cuts to put on the stereo to pull myself out of a mood or power myself through a chapter. I'm not much of a singer, not one at all, really, but I do play guitar some, and I would haul out my Martin D-28 and run through one of the songs. George didn't write all that many of his classic numbers, but those that he did write and the others that he chose to record have an integral consistency: with few exceptions those songs heal you as you strum the chords and hum or sing the melodies. Of course, it works far better if you let George do the singing.

4
Choices

On George Jones' COLD HARD TRUTH, some songs take on double and triple meanings. *Choices*, the opening cut, captures George's life-long predicament as he catwalks us back through the half-century and more of his career, right back to 1931. It's one of those "my left hand don't always do what my right hand wants to, I done myself wrong" songs. For George Jones, choosing "wrong" from "right" has not only inspired his singing but also prolonged his career, if not promoting his good health. But he's not preaching; he's lamenting.

> I've had choices
> Since the day that I was born
> There were voices
> That told me right from wrong
> If I had listened
> No I wouldn't be here today
> Living and dying
> With the choices I've made . . .

Choices (by Mike Curtis & Billy Yates)

The track begins with the plaintive mewling of Stuart Duncan's fiddle, which evokes old-timey feelings as Duncan sets the scene for George Jones' vocal entry. During the first verse, the band track is sparse, just Glenn Worff's bass, a rhythmic splashing of the drummer's brushes on a cymbal, and a simply picked acoustic guitar, then George stretches out into his notes as if he's Nolan Ryan loosening up to pitch a nine-inning game. Duncan comes in again near the end of that verse, filling with his fiddle in the background, the drummer fortifying the rhythm with his kick and snare. In the second verse Paul Franklin glides into view, his distinctive pedal steel guitar style jazzier than Duncan's traditional fiddle but married to the feel of Jones' phrasing, nevertheless. By the finish of the second verse, Brent Mason has entered the mix, and the gentle barking of his lower register electric guitar licks rhythm along with Hargus "Pig" Robbins' open-ended piano notes. It's just a six-piece band, the kind you might hear on any night that a touring Nashville act played your local theater in the past 50 years, but these veteran session players go about their task with such restraint, such good taste.

In the liner notes, Jones thanks his producer, Keith Stegall, likens him to long-time Jones' producer Billy Sherrill, and calls Keith a "little genius." Stegall's genius is that in 1999 he had the ability to preside over a session that is so thoroughly traditional that it brings tears to your eyes. There's really nothing extra or modern or — thank heavens — contemporary added to the pure intent of delivering a country song here: no forceps, no anaesthetic, no caesarean section. The music issues forth easily. It is difficult not to compare the sparkling zest of the up-tempo numbers like *Real Deal, Sinners & Saints,* and *Ain't Love Like That* with the bulk of Top 40 pablum that one hears on country radio today. George's music here is so good you may never go back to that radio stuff. And the ballads, well, no one can sing a ballad quite like the Possum. This is country music as it was and as it can be. Country music as it lives in the heart and soul of George Jones.

As the tracks move forward to *You Never Know Just How Good You've Got It,* you check the liner notes again to see who those background singers are. John Wesley Ryles, Larry Marrs, Vince Gill, and Patty Loveless. Not exactly The Jordanaires, but collectively they sing like angels in a country choir. This combination is especially moving on the finale, *When The Last Curtain Falls,* a moment that has not come, yet, even though Jones was critically injured and in a coma for a while right after the tracks were laid down.

In March 1999, when that near-fatal automobile accident took place, I was on a bus traveling from Ottawa to Toronto, a nightmarish journey through a sudden blizzard which left many vehicles turned over in the ditch, with the added thrill of someone hurling a rock from an overpass into the windshield, leaving a long crack across the Greyhound drivers' field of vision. I arrived at the airport hotel, checked in, turned on the hotel-room television set and learned the chilling news. A newscast announcer was telling the TV audience that George Jones had been talking on his cellular phone while driving home and had run into a bridge abutment near Franklin, Tennessee. The Possum was in critical condition. There was footage of emergency vehicles, plenty of red and blue flashing lights, and, of course, clips of Jones from the station's archives. It was a slow news day, as they say, and the item was updated hourly until I shut the TV down and fell into an uneasy sleep. Little did I know then that I would become fascinated by the fact that George Jones seemed to have more lives than a cat and more hits than anyone who had ever sung country.

In the days that followed, the country music world waited for news that Jones had pulled through; he always had before. He had survived numerous collisions, marriages, bankruptcy, a time when his bingeing had put his health and sanity in supreme jeopardy, and triple bypass heart surgery. But, this time, he was in a coma and many people offered up their prayers that he would make it through this latest in a lifetime of crises. I added my own prayers to the group effort and waited, too. I wondered if Jones had completed recording his first album for Asylum Records. I knew that he'd begun the project a few weeks before the accident.

"The basic tracks for ten songs had been completed," Evelyn Shriver reveals in the liner notes for COLD HARD TRUTH. "George sang live with the band but had planned several additional recording sessions for 'final' vocals where he would have the opportunity to really finesse his parts. Big plans for photo sessions and a video were put aside. All that mattered now was would George Jones live to hear the final record."

Reuters newswire service issued terse packets of information during the vigil: "Jones, 67, was airlifted to Vanderbilt University Medical Center after his sport utility vehicle hit a bridge south of Nashville, police said. Dr John Morris, head of the trauma unit at the hospital, told NBC affiliate WSMV-TV that Jones has been unconscious since the accident and the next two to four days should be critical. 'He is on a ventilator but we expect this to be temporary,' Morris said. Jones' injuries were described as a collapsed lung, blood in the right chest, and a ruptured liver."

After lying unconscious in hospital for 11 days, the Possum opened his eyes and began to journey down the long, hard road to full recovery. His fans breathed a collective sigh of relief. As it turned out, he hadn't done that badly at singing live with the band. And, with a supreme effort from Keith Stegall to complete the project while Jones was convalescing, first the single, Choices, and then the whole album were both released. Evelyn Shriver called the making of COLD HARD TRUTH a "little miracle." Shriver had signed Jones to Asylum Records because she believed in him and had encouraged him to "do the record he would have made 20 years ago if he had been sober."

The alleged discovery — by police officers attending the accident scene — of an open bottle of vodka in Jones' vehicle had fueled the usual controversy that had accompanied most of his record releases throughout the years. Then it was rumored that he was being sued by state authorities for damage to their bridge. Go figure. Tom Carter begins his introduction to I Lived To Tell It All, his 1996 book collaboration with George Jones, with the story of how he filled up his car with three loads of paperwork from accumulated lawsuits that Jones had been involved in over the years. Some things never change. And George, apparently, may still take a nip from the bottle, now and then, even though he is a recovered substance abuser, most of the time, except when he makes the mistake of piloting his SUV on a rainy night in Nashville and finds himself reliving his past. These are the choices George Jones has made.

⊷⊱5⊰⊶
Ain't No Trains to Nashville

To find another perspective on the music of George Jones that might reveal the "cold hard truth," I traveled from my home in North Vancouver through the Rocky Mountains to Bentley, Alberta, where Canadian country legend Dick Damron makes his home a few miles from the location of his family homestead. I had worked with Damron on his autobiography, *The Legend and the Legacy*. After Damron cut a couple of rockabilly sides at a local radio station in the late 1950s, he began recording country music in 1961 at Starday Studios in Nashville with producer Tommy Hill, the same label George had first signed with a few years earlier. He went on to record more than 20 Nashville albums throughout his Canadian Country Music Hall of Fame career. His breakout hit was *Countryfied*, a Canadian number one for both Damron and George Hamilton IV and a Top 40 U.S. charter for Hamilton.

Like George Jones, Damron has never really veered from his country roots, and, like Jones, he was cast off country radio in the early 1990s just when he was recording some of the best records he had ever made. Yet the very moment that Damron and I were about to feed on Jones' latest Asylum Records release, Damron himself was seeing a bit of a resurgence. He was at number 13 and number 15 on the MP3.com internet site chart with *Ain't No Trains To Nashville* and *Susan Flowers,* two of the tracks from Lonnie Ratliff's Westwood International Records compilation CD *Still Countrified,* a "best of" Dick Damron CD that had first sparked new interest in Europe where Damron had regularly played the Wembley International Country Music Festival along with George Jones and Marty Robbins during the 1970s and '80s. On the new internet playlist at "General Country" on the MP3 site, Damron was receiving acknowledgment, mainly through *Ain't No Trains To Nashville,* a song that when it was released in 1989 had predicted a coming dearth of creativity at country radio because programming would be through a "man with a digital computer" who no longer wanted to hear songs about Jesus, trains, or pickup trucks.

Ironically, Damron had been sabotaged at his own record label BMG/RCA Canada when the label had adopted a computerized approach to mailing out singles. *Ain't No Trains To Nashville* had been number 9 with a bullet on the Canadian charts when the label had issued the next single, through that same computer, and torpedoed the record's progress up the chart. The track was then listed by *Billboard* as the "Pick of the Week," but the label made no move to market the single or Damron's THE LEGEND & LEGACY album in the United States. It had just about broken the Bentley-based singer's heart. When Damron's brother, Howard Damron, died in a helicopter crash that same year, Damron had almost folded his tent, and only come back with gospel music (his WINGS ON THE WIND won both the Alberta Recording Industry Association and the Texas Proud awards as Gospel Album of the Year in 1992) . . . and later in the decade his autobiography. Throughout this period working with Damron, I nursed a hurt for him and Canadian cowboy singer Ian Tyson, along with Willie Nelson, Waylon Jennings, Johnny Cash, and . . . George Jones, all of whom were no longer being playlisted on country radio — despite the fact that all of them were putting out recordings that contained some of the best singing and best songs that they had done during the past 50 years. It was a shame.

Damron had recorded with Joe Bob Barnhill's A-team players like Fred Carter Jr., Greg Galbraith, Mark Casstevens, Hal Rugg, Weldon Myrick, Rob Hajacos, Glenn Worf, and Clyde Brooks for many years. His veteran ears can hear a whole lot of what is going on and not going on. He liked this new George Jones album a whole lot, enough to listen to it twice through before he grew restless, switched on his satellite dish, and tuned in to a vintage Wilburn Brothers TV show on Willie's new network.

After getting settled in Damron's kitchen, I had pulled out COLD HARD TRUTH. The first cut, *Choices,* written by Billy Yates and Mike Curtis, went by with a nod from Damron who merely said, "*That's* the track!" Then, the title track, *The Cold Hard Truth,* began. I knew that this song had been written by Jamie O'Hara, the songwriter who had put his talent together with Kieran Kane in The O'Kanes during the new traditionalist revival of the 1980s. Along the way, Damron cocked his ear: "Listen to that bass track . . . Do you hear that tick-tack guitar track in there? *That* sounds like the kind of thing that Harold Bradley would play." When the third track, *Sinners & Saints,* began, Damron leaned back in his kitchen chair, ran his hands through thinning, silvered hair and said, "You know, it's such a shame. George is singing better than he ever has on records, and now they won't play him on the radio . . . Listen to his phrasing! Listen to how rich his voice is!"

Damron wasn't talking dollars and cents. He was speaking of the fact that now, even though he is a senior citizen, George Jones' re-found health and happiness have provided the Possum with the opportunity to sing better than most of the times he'd gone into those helter-skelter recording sessions armed with a flask of moonshine in his rear pocket and an attitude formed from the times he'd been victimized by managers, record labels, and promoters who had taken him for every dollar they could, gorillas who then put the blame on him when he couldn't handle the pressure. Luke the Drifter and the Possum, legends and cartoons, singing ducks and self-interested gorillas — all of the above is part of the simple yet complex life of George Jones. It's the COLD HARD TRUTH.

Starday Records publicity photo from the late 1950s.

George with the Jones Boys performing on From Nashville with Music, *1969.*

Mr and Mrs Country Music, George Jones and Tammy Wynette, perform on Country Music Hit Parade.

George salutes his fans.

Garth Brooks presents George with the Academy of Country Music Pioneer Award.

Part Two

The Legacy of
Luke the Drifter

The Big Hurt

The Possum was born George Glenn Jones in a log cabin near Saratoga, Texas on the 12th of September, 1931. His father, George Washington Jones, was a hell-raiser long before he married Clara Patterson, the daughter of a preacher known as "Uncle Litt." He continued his excesses throughout the marriage. George senior was, nevertheless, a hardworking family provider who only occasionally drank up the week's food money before he made it home on Friday night. This was an old story — the men drank their troubles away, while the women held on to their religion in order to keep their families together — but this way of life seems to have been true for country singers in particular.

The Jones clan had left Alabama in the 1840s because they couldn't make ends meet in the backwoods there. Sometime after Texas became a state in the union, George's great grandfather Frank Jones had relocated to the rainforest wilderness of east Texas, known as the "Piney Woods" or the "Big Thicket." During the Civil War, Frank Jones enlisted in the Confederate army, and along with everyone else in the South, suffered the humiliation of defeat. As men will do, he passed on his tales of the conflict to his offspring in a legacy of pride and hate that grew and smouldered and festered in people's memories as the biggest hurt of all. It was a hurt that would survive into succeeding generations of Jones boys.

George's father, George Washington Jones, had always been a hard-working man and a decent provider — when he could find work. Life in the Big Thicket region of east Texas was tough, though; the area was unforgiving, and the lot of a laboring man in those days just wasn't a hopeful proposition. As the years went by and the situation got tougher, George Washington Jones nursed his hurt with whiskey, sometimes lashing out at the nearest object or person, it hardly seemed to matter who or what, at the time. And in his frustration and failing sense of self-worth, George Washington Jones passed the big hurt on down the line, one more time.

In the 1930s, '40s, and '50s, the rural way of life in the South was gradually giving way to city-dwelling due to the sheer impact of the drought and depression years. But the displaced felt a deep wrong in their hearts over the loss of the farming land that their ancestors had come from Europe to the "land of opportunity" to work. Many of the farming families of the rural South moved west to seek work in California, Oregon, or Washington State or to cities up north where they could find work. But they brought with them their love of the traditional music that was known as hillbilly, country & western, and, finally, just country music. At first, the displaced and dispossessed were not a happy bunch. Of course, there were plenty of reasons for their state of mind. Rural families had been treated like the dirt they tilled. Their lives were kept poor by quotas for planting cash crops like tobacco. And their chance for a better life was stifled at every turn by a bureaucracy that owed its allegiance to rich city folks and even richer New York bankers. If they made any money at all, they were taxed to death. And if they made their own whiskey, they were hunted down like criminals during and after the years of prohibition. As Earl 'Peanut' Montgomery would say in song,

> The dirt was clay and was the color of the blood in me
> A twelve-acre farm on a ridge in south Tennessee
> We left our sweat all over that land
> Behind a mule we watched grow old, row after row
> Tryin' to grow corn and cotton
> On ground so poor that grass won't grow

Where Grass Won't Grow (Earl Montgomery)

America had been billed as the land of opportunity, and, at first, there *were* opportunities, especially out west as the frontier pushed across the continent. But as the map filled in there were merely opportunities for subsistence-level existence, and working the land seemed the least respected vocation in the new world. Conditions did not necessarily improve for those who grew and picked the cotton or tobacco. In fact, tobacco farmers were harassed by federal agents almost as often as moonshiners were. There were strict quotas for planting tobacco, quotas that meant most farmers and their families were limited to a poverty level existence. As time went by, many of those farmers and their families were run off the land, displaced and dispossessed. Their ancestors held that hurt inside themselves for generations down the line.

Some historians have looked at the American Civil War as an economic conflict between the industrialized North and the agrarian-based economy of the Old South. The Confederate states wanted to break away from control and taxation, just as the original 13 states had rebelled against control and taxation from London and enforced implementation of those unfair trade practices by the British army and navy. Whatever reasons the decision-makers in either the north or the south had for squaring off and doing battle, the poor folk, farmers mostly — or tradesmen or boys too young to have entered the workplace — were the men who lay dead on the killing fields.

Just as African American survivors of the Antebellum South and the Reconstruction eras began to sing the blues, so poor white survivors sang hillbilly songs about the pain and injustice of their lives. Ray Charles, who recorded one of the most remarkable country albums of the century in 1962 with MODERN SOUNDS IN COUNTRY & WESTERN MUSIC, recognized this sympathy between country and the blues. As Charles once told Ralph Emery in *The View from Nashville*, "Country music is a lot like blues. It's simple, honest, and you don't have to be a genius to get it. If I was to direct someone to real country music, I'd send them to George Jones. I've been a fan of his since the early '60s. George has that real earthy sound of what I feel, like Hank Williams or Hank Snow. I'm not against modernization, and I don't want to be misunderstood. But I love that country sound in itself, the pureness of it without a room full of musicians. We should never let this sound — the sounds of the hills and mountains — slip away, no more than I think we should allow the genuine old-fashioned-type Muddy Waters blues slip away. Why? We Americans don't have nothing else, musically speaking. We don't have Bach and Beethoven or Tchaikovsky or Sibelius. They're other countries' music. But Muddy Waters, George Jones — we *own* that music! We can go to the bank with *that*."

During the WWII years, families like the Jones had to go where the work was, to places like Beaumont, Texas, where oil rigs were sprouting up where only years before a proud forest had stood, and where there was work in the shipyards. As the years went by the population was driven headlong toward an uncertain future. In the cities, people's independence disappeared. There were no gardens to feed families, no cows to milk, and, after a while, there were even laws against raising chickens inside city limits. During this period, people were making babies like never before, children who would grow up in crazy times, their lives molded to television models like the Nelson Family on the *Ozzie & Harriet Show* and where the hillbilly way of life was mocked on the *Beverly*

Hillbillies. Their uncertainty was continued by a nuclear weapons buildup and a new war, the Cold War, that never seemed to end. In the 1960s the rate of change would become so rapid that a full-blown cultural revolution would take place and age-old values would be turned upside down. As each generation of young boys grew into men there always seemed to be a war to be fought and tears to be shed over the graves of those who died too young. In the '60s some young men began to burn their draft cards. Others were put on planes and ships and sent to the killing fields in Vietnam.

True to this pattern, after George Washington Jones and Clara were married, George senior worked as a logger, then built up a successful route as a truck driver peddling ice for a Mr Pickerall, a Depot Town icemaker, before the Great Depression drove him to more desperate pursuits. George senior then turned to logging, again, but on a freelance basis. Along with many other desperate men, he would enter the Big Thicket, then owned by absentee landlords and bankers in New York, and cut down a tree and haul it into town where it would be made into barrel staves. After a while, the landowners began to harass and prosecute the freelancers, and George senior saw another of his options disappear into the rich-get-richer and the poor-get-poorer equation that America was becoming.

In many ways, the Big Thicket was a remnant of the American frontier, a wild and untamed region populated by the descendants of outlaws and people who had fled the encroachment of civilization. Like the inhabitants of the hills and hollers of the east Tennessee mountains, these people lived according to their own moral code. However, the piney forest was also a vast resource that would not remain ignored by those who exploited the land, a resource that seemed inexhaustible until it was cut down by companies run by investors from up North. A lot of the pine trees were first cut during the final years of the 19th century and early 20th century. A whole lot more were cut during the booming wartime years. As the population of Beaumont and Houston increased, the remaining resource was quickly harvested to build wood-frame houses to accommodate the newly-arrived population. With the discovery of oil in the region, the swampy wilderness, which had at one time been a kind of Sherwood Forest hideaway for the wood-be Robin Hoods of the day, was further laid to waste by new gangs of roughnecks and oil-riggers.

The quickly changing times meant that the Jones family's relatively serene, poverty-stricken, rural existence was over. The loss of the land to the lumber companies, real estate tycoons, and oil barons was part of the big hurt felt by everyone, including George Washington Jones. Men like him were uprooted one last time. In the industrial wasteland surrounding Beaumont, men like George senior lost whatever dignity they still clung to. Before that happened, he was driven outside the law one last time during the 1930s.

George Washington Jones had been distilling whiskey and making beer for his own consumption. With no remaining options left, he began to sell his moonshine just to bring in a few dollars. Now and then, when the authorities staged a crackdown on the shine trade, he would be forced to seek refuge in the wilderness, again. Sometimes he would share his whiskey and beer with gangs of ruffians who came to steal it. And other times he would drink with the 'revenuers' themselves. Not all of the cops that came to bust him were unsympathetic to what he did. When the boom times came 'round again, he moved his family to Beaumont and returned to laboring. Like many of the outlaws who had sought refuge in the Big Thicket, he was driven to operate outside the law only as a last resort.

The Jones family relocated several times before George Glenn was born. He was the eighth and last of Clara and George Washington Jones' children. George Glenn was raised mostly on rural properties outside of Saratoga and Kountze. He spent his summers with his sister, Helen, and her husband on their farm, so he really was a country boy, even though by the time he was a teenager the family was forced to relocate, that final time, to the Maritime housing project in Beaumont, where the wartime economy drew oil-drilling crews and shipbuilders into a makeshift settlement that was as rough and ready as any of the frontier towns had been during the previous century.

George's older brother-in-law, whom he affectionately called Uncle Dub, was a forceful influence, teaching him the values of hard work and discipline, whereas at home his father's peripatetic behavior sometimes provided mixed signals. Though he may have hated his father for his weaknesses, George clung to both of his parents. They were family, all he had, and not every situation they dealt him was bad. They provided for him, which was more than many children of that era could say of the adults who brought them into this world. And they loved him, which was most important of all.

Both of George's parents were musically inclined. His mother played the piano and organ at the local church, and his dad played some on the guitar. Uncle Litt came around and along with his own children sang the traditional hymns and gospel songs that were part of his regular church services. Young George took to the music, quickly learning the lyrics and melodies to almost every song he heard. He had displayed interest in music as early as the age of three when he coaxed notes from a battered old guitar that had only one string. In 1938 when the family acquired a battery-powered radio, George was keen to tune in to the Opry broadcasts where Roy Acuff and Bill Monroe were the young boy's favorites. His memory of those times is vivid. "Saturday nights were the only nights my parents would ever allow one of the kids to lay in bed with them," George recalls in the authorized video biography *George Jones: Same Ole Me*. "My daddy would let me lay in bed between 'em and listen to the *Grand Ole Opry*, and I would tell my mother, I would say, 'Mama you wake me up, if I fall to sleep when Roy Acuff or Bill Monroe comes on.' And, sure enough, I'd go to sleep and she'd wake me up."

George began singing at the local church in Kountze, where he hooked up with Brother Burl and Sister Annie, Pentecostal preachers and singers, and absorbed more of the gospel influences that would later enrich the harmonies on his recordings. He also credits this husband and wife team with helping him overcome some of his initial shyness. George's father recognized that his interest in music needed some helping out and took him on the train to Beaumont where he bought George his first guitar. George learned guitar chords from Sister Annie and the rudiments of entertaining while playing with her and Brother Burl at revival meetings. "I learned my first chords on the guitar after my daddy finally bought me one when I was about nine years old. I loved music so much. I went to this church. Sister Annie and Brother Burl Stephens," George explains in *Same Ole Me*. "She taught me my first chords on the guitar like C, G and D and things like that. I started hangin' out over there more often, you know, and we played songs like *Lily Of The Valley*. We used to do all the real old gospel songs."

George's first direct influences came from gospel singers and his first performances were at church functions. But it would not be long before George discovered that people were willing to pay him to sing. In *George Jones: The Saga of an American Singer*, Bob Allen suggests that it was George's father who had more profane plans than mere gospel singing and soon set his son up on a street corner in Beaumont to sing for spare change. George tells the story a different way in his authorized video biography. "It was a Sunday. There wasn't too much traffic downtown, just a few people went a-shoppin'. I was just sittin' there playin' my gi-tar, *Precious Jewel* and *The Wabash Cannonball* and all them things like that, and a little handful of people would just gather and listen, since they didn't have anything else to do, you know. I wound up leavin' there with about 27 dollars. That's more money than I'd ever seen in my life. Here I am doin' somethin' that I like more than anything in the world, and then I found out that there were other people that might like it. When I found that out, that just put it all over the top."

According to Allen, when George senior stole away to purchase a bottle of liquor with the first few dollars that passers-by donated, young George kept on playing and made his own grubstake, $24 dollars. According to Jones and Carter in their book *I Lived To Tell It All*, George went himself on a bus to Beaumont, alone, singing to the driver and the passengers because he had no money to pay the fare, and discovered the art of busking completely by accident. From then on, both versions of the story agree on what happened next.

George squandered that first grubstake away before the day was out, buying himself food and soda pop and playing the pinball machines in a nearby arcade. It was more money than George's sister, Helen, could make in a whole year, but it was gone in a few hours, and it became a pattern of behavior George could never explain, yet one that plagued him for many years. That he could have bought food and clothing for his family never entered his young head, just as it did not always enter his daddy's head when he had coins a-jingling in his pocket. Later on, George would be more thoughtful and help his mother out with the family groceries.

According to Bob Allen, the father-son relationship had an even darker side than this single example of exploitation. Allen describes the times when George was a mere slip of a boy and his father would come home drunk and haul his son out of bed and demand the child sing the soothing gospel songs he had learned from Clara and her father, Uncle Litt, and the 'secular songs' he had learned while listening to the Opry. If the boy was too sound asleep or reluctant to sing right away, the father would haul down his pants and beat him with his leather belt. Sometimes this would take place on the front porch of the family home. As Bob Allen describes these scenes of the moody father, full of "whiskey and meanness," having drunk up the grocery money, arriving home, "the children would shiver in their iron bedsteads as he came down the road singing *More Pretty Girls Than One* . . . at the top of his raspy, whiskey-soaked voice. Ranting and raving like a crazy man, he would violently throw open the front door, nearly tearing it from its hinges. Cursing, hollering and blaspheming, he would break furniture and throw things around. He'd roust his wife and small children up out of their beds and raise his hand up against them and sometimes slap them. . . ." For young George, he reserved special treatment, as Allen continues. "Old George, with malevolence in his eyes and whiskey on his breath, would come storming into the room. Waving his thick leather belt, he would yank his youngest son out of bed and push him outside onto the porch. With the sharp slap of the belt to his son's backside, he'd then holler at him: 'Goddamnit, sing!' . . . With tears streaming down his face, the boy would sing. His voice would soar and tremble with the gospel fervor of Uncle Litt's prayers and Holiness music as he sang the mournful secular songs of Roy Acuff and Bill Monroe, which Old George particularly loved to hear. But there was yet a new edge in his voice as he sang these songs: the fiercely repressed yet clearly discernible timbre of tearful outrage and anger over the helplessness of his predicament — outrage and anger which he could not otherwise vent." The next morning, the old man wouldn't remember what he had done, and the family was merely grateful that his ugly mood had passed.

By today's standards, what the father allegedly did to the son is a criminal offence. Back in the 1930s, however, such activity went unchallenged by neighbors. Clara and her other children were so intimidated by George senior's, actions that the best they could think of doing was — when they heard the father's drunken approach — to waken the boy and push him half-asleep out a bathroom window and encourage him to hide himself away from his father's wrath. In further response to George senior's abusive behavior, Dub Scroggins married George's older sister Helen to get her away from the beatings that ensued whenever Clara or any of the children opposed the old man's will. There was no such escape on the immediate horizon for little George.

While presented by Allen in the melodramatic language characteristic of many celebrity biographies, here in this anecdote we glimpse a precedent for patterns of behavior that would dog George Jones throughout his life. Many times as an adult, George would disappear for days, then return home to meet his wife of the day at the door, shamefaced and seeking forgiveness. If he turned the furniture upside down now and then, it was only when he was drunk, and he would sleep it off, not remembering what he had done. George Jones would not shake this demon until decades later when he sought out therapy.

And years later when exploited and abused by managers, agents, and promoters, George Jones would find himself incapable of remembering his lyrics, resorting to performing versions of his songs as if they were sung by Donald Duck. His father had been his physical superior and he'd been held hostage and whipped if he fell silent. At points in his career when he was held hostage to perform shows for which he was seldom paid the fair amount, and sometimes not paid at all, and still other shows he told his handlers he didn't want to have them book, George would become a 'no show'. In fact, anyone who built him up to a moment of anxiety and invited a roomful of media along could expect the pressure to cause 'No-Show Jones' to climb through some washroom or dressing room window and flee.

Yet George Jones still loved his father. These revealing yet sordid episodes from his childhood are not among those that George himself chose to remember in any detail in his autobiography. George puts forward the proposition that his father only turned to drink after his favorite daughter, his first-born, Ethel, died from a fever at age seven, a few years before little George was born.

George forgives his father his trespasses as he would have us forgive him his. He focuses instead on the good times he shared with his father, bouncing around together in an old pickup truck that had no springs, or the times when he would strum his guitar and the whole family would fill their tiny house with the warming harmonies of old-time gospel songs. Somewhere between the two sets of memories, George's own and the ones Bob Allen recreated after speaking to George's neighbors and relatives, the truly accurate picture of the family history lies.

There was no doubt that young George had a gift for singing. Even before he had a guitar, he would stand on the porch of the family home strumming a broom and pretending he was singing at the Opry. Roy Acuff was his first hero. Acuff was much loved by Opry audiences for his dramatic renderings of mournful ballads, often breaking into sobs as tears streamed down his face during a performance. When remembering both the love and pain he associated with his father, George Glenn Jones would also reach those resonating registers with his voice. When he began to sing in the honky tonks and then to make records, Roy Acuff's ability to project emotion would stay with him, even though for quite a spell, he explored the emotional terrain of Hank Williams' phrasing.

Young George didn't like school much and often played hooky, stealing away from the education system to play his guitar. Soon, he was busking in Beaumont on a regular basis, pitching for tips and shining shoes. When he turned 16, George ran away from home and stayed away. After that, he was just running from his own shadow, or so it often seemed; there was definitely something that pursued him, no matter where he roamed.

He first found refuge in Jasper, Texas, a few miles north of Beaumont, with the family of a guitar-picking friend, Dalton Henderson, but he woke up each morning aching with the pain that he'd been handed while he'd been growing up. It was a complex hurt saturated with frustrations that had been thoroughly confused during his developing years by the dueling values passed on to him by his mother, Clara, and his father, George Washington Jones.

Now that he was out on his own, George Jones had only his music to help him get by, and a strong intuition that if he followed it, wherever it took him, he might come to a place in the road where the angels that had invaded his existence through his mama's deep Pentecostal convictions would win out over the devils that had also invaded during his daddy's drunken, abusive behavior. Until that blessed time, he would just keep singing.

When George Jones sang was the only time that the whole dueling mess of specters was driven clear out of his mind. He sang a lot. Every chance he got. Folks said he had a gift for it, and George knew that they were ready and willing to pay him for the comfort they received when he did. So, things weren't totally messed up. He just had to get away from it all, now and then, so that he could sort things out. When he wasn't singing, sometimes he would lose it, unable to quell the anger that welled up inside and sought release.

People noticed that, and most forgave him, for they also knew George's other side, his good side. This duel between good and bad, this rupture between the joy of singing and the hurt of living, was the predicament he later sang about in his 1981 recording of the J. Chambers and L. Jenkins song, *Good Ones and Bad Ones.*

It's a fine line between Heaven and Hell
When the good makes you feel like you should
It's a fine line between Heaven and Hell
When the bad makes you feel just as good

— *Good Ones And Bad Ones* (J. Chambers & L. Jenkins)

In his heart, as he struggled to make a go of things in Jasper, young George Jones knew all of these things, but none of it made any sense. It just wasn't fair. Nothing seemed to add up. But he hadn't been blessed with a gift for politics or even writing protest songs. He had been blessed with the gift of singing. It was the way he did it, what he thought about as he sang, and what he projected while his mournful tones came from his lips, that seemed to sooth people. So, he kept on doing it, singing what was then called hillbilly music or folk music, although there was a deep measure of gospel flavor in the way George sang it and just a hint of the blues as well.

With Dalton Henderson, George played honky tonks around Beaumont and the two got themselves on the local KTXJ radio station in Jasper. In addition to playing the guitar, George also played the fiddle at this time. When he returned to Beaumont a few months later, he hooked up with the husband and wife duo, Eddie & Pearl, not only touring and performing with them as a harmony singer and lead guitarist on their radio show on KRIC, but living with them in a trailer.

George had a goal, now, though, firmly fixed in his mind. He wanted to sing on the Opry like his idol, Roy Acuff. Many years later, Acuff would tell an interviewer for *George Jones: Same Ole Me* that "I would give anything, if I could sing like George Jones, the way he drops down into that deep baritone voice. I wish I could do that. I don't know anybody who can do that." That acknowledgment must have seemed like an ultimate triumph, but it was a long time in coming, and the road to the Opry was paved with many obstacles, not the least of which was booze, the vice that had always seemed to turn his daddy from a loving, caring father into a crazy man. And booze would be what got George kicked off the Opry for a while many years later.

❧2☙
Honky Tonkin'

R oy Acuff was George Jones's first hero, but in his 16th year, George dis-covered a new star in the galaxy. Hank Williams & His Drifting Cowboys were setting the airwaves on fire with their records. *Move It On Over*, *Honky Tonkin'*, *I'm A Long Gone Daddy*, and then *Lovesick Blues* in early 1949. Driven by Hank's Opry debut performance, where he received six standing-ova-tion encores to repeat the song, *Lovesick Blues* headed to the top of the charts and stayed there for a remarkable 16 weeks. After that, the hits just kept a-comin'. Hank was something else.

Like Hank, George began singing gospel and both young men had earned money busking and shining shoes. Both began to play roadhouses at a young age and fell prey to the lifestyle of the honky tonk singer. In his autobiography, Jones tells of a time when he had been sober for weeks and a club manager kept badgering him to sit down and share a bottle of whiskey. He wanted to brag to his friends that he had drunk whiskey with George Jones. At the end of the multi-night engagement, Jones finally fell off the wagon, but the convivial man-ager was not prepared for the tempest he soon released as George 'John-Wayned' both the bar and the manager before he could be hauled away.

During the lengthiest interview of his lengthy career — an interview that Jones had only reluctantly agreed to give when tricked into the situation by a label exec and a journalist who had conspired together to create the situation — Jones welcomed Nick Tosches onto his bus for the duration of a tour. He soon found himself pressed to answer questions on the issue of singing drinking songs at a time when he had rehabilitated himself. When Jones seemed disturbed and said, "I don't know why we're even discussing that," Tosches kept pressing Jones' button. "I just think," George told Tosches, "it was the environment that sur-rounded you back in those days. If I'd have never played in those places, I prob-ably would have never started drinking."

Tosches kept at, saying, "You think so, huh?"

"I would imagine," said Jones, showing ultimate patience. "Being around it. Not so much stage fright, but being around people drunk all the time in the bars and clubs and taverns. Sort of being around it, you know, the environment. I'm fairly sure. It's just being around it all the time and other people doing it. Like the old saying, 'Birds of a feather flock together.' "

Many successful recording artists will tell you that they discovered they had to stop singing in bars or their career would never have got off the ground. It's not just the alcohol and the drunks hitting on you to sing their favorite song by some artist you have never even heard of — the cigarette smog in bars is tough on singers who have their mouths open so much when they are singing that they literally choke on the wall of smoke, even if they are smokers themselves. Other singers have often told me that working in bars is a whole lot like working in a liquor store. Alcohol abuse becomes a job hazard.

Several years after George senior's passing, and after George Glenn had moved on from singing in honky tonks to singing in theaters and arenas, his mother, Clara Jones, came to Lakeland, Florida to visit George and Tammy. When George would get into the sauce, Clara would challenge her son's drunken moods. In her biography *Stand by Your Man*, Wynette and her collaborator Joan Dew quote Clara as saying to George, "Glenn, don't do the things to Tammy that your daddy did to me. I don't want her having to run out the back door with a brown bag under one arm and a bunch of young-uns under the other to get away from you like we used to run from your daddy when he was drunk. That's no way to live. When your daddy did finally stop drinking a few years before he died, it was too late because we were too old to enjoy life anymore. Don't let the same thing happen to you and Tammy."

At that point in his life, George wasn't able to deal with such confrontations while he was drinking, but, according to Tammy, a few hours or days later when he'd sobered up he would say, "I hated my father for his drinking and for the miserable life he gave my mother, and yet I do the same thing. It just doesn't make sense."

George's daddy's own mama had been the only one who could sooth George Washington Jones' moods, and Clara had the same affect on George. He might not be able to do much about it when he was half-gowed, but he didn't put her words out of his mind. He just didn't know what to make of it, not even in 1969 in Florida, and by that time he was nearly 40 years old.

Encyclopedias of country music and other text books often refer to George Jones as the quintessential honky tonk singer. But "honky tonk singer" has become a glib phrase, and, today, most people are unaware of just how life-threatening entertaining in those venues could be, especially in the late 1940s and early '50s when George first began. Tennessee Two bassist Marshall Grant remembers that there were often more guns and knives at their gigs than there were fans when he and Luther Perkins backed Johnny Cash during those years. Dick Damron begins a chapter of his autobiography *The Legend and the Legacy* with the following description of the working conditions a touring recording artist endured during those years: "For years and years, I watched the scenes unfold on a nightly basis in the 'Paradise Knife and Gun Clubs' of the world — the tiny little 'hole in the wall' clubs, bad-ass bars, honky tonks, watering holes, skull orchards, piss tanks, beer parlors, taverns, cabarets, and a thousand other names that would take forever to mention. They were all different, so different that they were all the same.

"I was caught in the middle. I loved them and I hated them. There were nights of musical magic when everyone in the establishment was into the music and the band and the songs; there were nights of pure hell that would make the Devil cringe or dance with glee.... I was in a small club in Sandy, Oregon, on June 19, 1979 when a truck driver, big enough to burn diesel, beat a half-dozen Mexican migrant workers almost to death. I was still there, terrorized, when one of the 'walking wounded' returned to the club later that night and drove a shiny blade into the diesel-burner's guts."

These roadhouses were first called honk-a-tonks in east Texas, Louisiana, and Alabama during the early decades of the 20th century. The term honky tonk began appearing in song lyrics in the 1920s, but the honky tonk style that we know today really solidified during the late '40s in the music of singers like Ernest Tubb, the first bandleader to introduce electric guitar to his country music, and Hank Williams, who frequently wrote about going honky tonking in those roadhouses. Where Bob Wills & His Texas Playboys had led a generation of western swing orchestras to popularity in the 1930s and '40s, these five or six piece honky tonk bands came to prominence as George Jones was getting into his music.

For those who were never there, honky tonks are often thought of as the kind of places pictured in Hollywood movies where actors like John Wayne or Burt Reynolds cause a lot of mayhem ... someone throws a wooden chair into the bar and breaks up a lot of glassware and a few mirrors ... but, despite the fisticuffs in those silver screen fight scenes, there is little blood shed. Those scenes are often the comic relief in those films, played to a brisk instrumental

47

track loaded with banjos, fiddles, and flat-picked guitars. When Mickey Gilley made a pact with a club-owner in Houston and created a country music venue that was for all intents and purposes a country music supermarket, complete with mechanical bull rides, the concept was skewed forevermore. And when John Travolta rode those mechanical bulls in *Urban Cowboy*, he set off fashion trends, encouraged Nashville producers to make even schlockier music than they were already making, and took country music one step further away from the back porches and hayride broadcasts — several steps toward the line-dancing blare of today's country disco. Don't get me wrong. John Travolta has proven to be one heck of an actor, especially in recent times, and line-dancing has become a much-needed replacement for the old-time square dancing of the past, but in the process of becoming popularized, country music has lost too much of its tradition, too much of its soul.

For the working musician during the 1940s, '50s, '60s, and '70s, the situation was a whole lot more in your face, and the honky tonk singers and guitar pickers did not always walk away without becoming involved in the action, as a young George Jones did one hot, humid night in the early 1950s at Lola & Shorty's, a "roadside rough house" in Beaumont, Texas. At break time, he stepped out from behind the chicken-wire fence that had been erected to protect the musicians from the flying beer bottles and broken glass erupting from the fights that regularly broke out among the couples who were sweating up a storm dancing to the songs George and his duo partner, Jack Marino, sang. But instead of heading for the bar or the washroom, George confronted a suspicious character whom he felt was there to track him down and repossess his car. When the man wouldn't back down from his determination to seize George's Packard, Jones punched him in the face. During the fight that ensued, Jones was cut by a straight-razor and nearly bled to death in the ambulance before he reached the hospital.

"I had fleeting thoughts that the inside of that battered ambulance would be the last thing I'd ever see," Jones recalls in *I Lived To Tell It All*. "Ninety stitches were required to stop the bleeding from a slash whose scar wraps around my waist to this day. For that night, I had all I ever wanted of fistfights, ambulances, booze, and bleeding. Little did I know I had not nearly gotten it all behind me."

Where most singers and musicians who entertained in the honky tonks felt terrorized by the action going down all around them and usually beat a hasty retreat, grabbing up their instruments as they headed for the hills, George Jones seldom stepped down from a confrontation. He might be a little guy, but when he focused the same will power he put into his singing, he could be surprisingly tenacious.

In *Same Ole Me*, Waylon Jennings tells a related story of a time that George came over to visit but was more hostile than a swarm of angry wasps. "George come to my house one time, and I was higher than a kite, but George was drunker than I was high. And he went crazy. And I tried to get on him, and he'd kick me, and he swung at me, and he threw things at me, and I'm tryin' to settle him down. And I can't do it. So, I took him down and held him down. But you know what ... George isn't very big but his stuff was lastin' better 'n than mine. So, I started getting tired ... We laugh about it now. It's about all you can do. It's nothing we can be proud of, you know, the ones who can be proud are the ones that never fell into that trap."

Waylon had to tie George up that time, and while George was being dragged away by his manager, Waylon recalls in his autobiography that George vowed, "I'll get you, you Conway Twitty-acting son of a bitch!" And that was enough to break Waylon up. Waylon was one of the few people on the planet who could talk any sense into George. A few years later, during the days when George Jones was bottoming out, Waylon came to his aid. At that time, he and Johnny Cash secretly contributed money to save George from losing his cars and bus and house. They hadn't asked if he needed help or if he would even accept it, but they did it anyway, although George found them out through his bank. At first there was some embarrassment on his part. But their helping him out was what friends were all about. And he has said so. He has also said it may have been "the blind leading the blind." After all, Johnny and Waylon were up to their eyeballs in alligators with their own ongoing substance-abuse problems through many of these same years.

"Sometimes guys whose talent you've admired from afar become your close friends," Waylon says in his book. "John Cash was like that, and every once in a while I would stand outside our relationship and be a little in awe of him. The same is true of George Jones."

George Jones went on from that dark night at Lola & Shorty's, when he had contemplated his mortality in an ambulance, to become the most successful honky tonk singer of all time. His early records reflect the ambience of the post-WW2 years in America, where everything seemed to be in flux but opportunities did not always appear on the horizon. Widespread poverty and desperate times drove people into those lawless honky tonks where they could dance, drink, and brawl their frustrations right out of their heads. And singers like Floyd Tillman, Hank Williams, Lefty Frizzell, and George Jones were the medicine men, the balladeers whose mournful, often nasal, yodel-inflected vocalizing healed the poverty-born desperation that invaded their souls.

Restlessness was the prevailing mood in those years, and songs like Hank Snow's *I'm Movin' On*, number one on the C&W charts for a record-setting 21 weeks in 1951, were anthems that became engraved in people's memories, frequently serving as the antidote to the stress and frustration in their personal lives. Hank Williams' *Lovesick Blues* was the malady that just about everybody seemed to have at one time or another.

Hank had been influenced by the gospel music sung in the church he attended as a youngster in Greenville and had received pointers on singing and playing the guitar from an African American bluesman, Rufe Payne, a street musician who went by the name of Tee-Tot. Hank began to entertain at the age of 12, playing with older musicians during his teenage years in smokey barroom settings, and he began to write his own songs. Right from his first Top 10 hit, *Move It On Over*, Hank had begun to meld the 12-bar-blues of what, at that time, was called "race music" (by radio programmers and record distributors) with the traditional music of the Tennessee, Alabama, and Kentucky hills.

Tunes like *Move It On Over* were blues progressions with countrified melodies and lyrics. Where African Americans sang the blues to satisfy their souls, Hank's yodel-inflected vocals echoed the songs that silver screen cowboys on cattle drives sang to sooth their herds on moonlit evenings in Hollywood dusters. The real cowboys never did yodel, and they sang frankly sexual and overtly lewd lyrics. Like those real cowboys, Hank's songs were frankly sexual, too, although not lewd. For these several reasons Hank didn't really fit in with the Opry crowd — he was too real, and his music was, too. No one, not even George Jones, filled his shoes. And a half century after his death, he is still the all-time "King of Country Music." However, many people, including hard-nosed music critic Randall Riese, one of many writers to champion Hank Williams as the all-time King, acknowledge that George Jones is a better singer.

Of all the thousands of descriptions written about Hank Williams, Riese has perhaps best captured his character and impact on his audience. In *Nashville Babylon*, Riese notes, "There had been others before him — Roy Acuff, Eddy Arnold, Ernest Tubb — but Hank Williams was country music's first sex symbol. He was a gaunt 6'2" tall, balding on top and not inordinately attractive, but that wailing moan of a voice of his had a way of crawling up a woman's skirt and caressing her in places that her daddy hadn't seen and her husband hadn't found. And, in performance, when he parted those long legs and buckled those knees — way before Elvis did a variation of the same — there was rarely a dry female crotch in the house. Years after Hank's death, country singer Bobby Bare explained the difference between country and rock by quipping, 'In country music, we want wet eyes, not crotches.' Suffice it to say, Hank Williams wanted — and got — both." If ole Hank hadn't been in so much physical pain and such poor health that he resorted to supplementing his alcohol intake with painkilling injections and pills to ease the hurt that resulted from an early injury — a fall off a horse in his youth that had permanently injured his spine — rock and roll might have happened a whole different way than it did, and Elvis Presley might never have become king of anything. Hank's music transcended genres. George Jones has also transcended his genre. He is simply so good at singing country that he has come to represent it to people both inside and out-side of the country music realm. The two singers who took country over the top in the 1990s, Garth Brooks and Shania Twain, are listened to by a wide audi-ence, too, but for different reasons. Non-country listeners like Garth and Shania because they don't sound *too* country, not because they epitomize it.

Hank Williams wasn't the first white singer to work rhythm & blues into his country music, but his recordings were the first real white man's blues to get a whole lot of exposure on the radio. On cuts like *I'm So Lonesome I Could Cry*, Hank knew his 'lonesome' better than anybody. Juxtaposed with his more upbeat numbers like *Hey, Good Lookin'*, *Jambalaya (On The Bayou)*, and *Honky Tonkin'* in his stage shows, the combination of plumbing the depths of despair and soaring to the heights of happy-go-lucky good-timing proved an irresistible combination. His songwriting genius would be resurrected time and time again by artists like Ray Charles, Charley Pride, Charlie Rich, and Ray Price, and eventually by female vocalists like Emmylou Harris, too. When Emmylou sang, "Son of a gun we're gonna have big fun on the bayou," Hank's genius energized the country rock movement, even though some of the newest country fans didn't realize they were listening to one of ole Hank's original creations.

Coming out of Montgomery, Alabama and launching himself from the *Louisiana Hayride* radio broadcast into people's living rooms, Hank played the Opry, too, but mostly he just went down that *Lost Highway* in the back seat of a big old Cadillac and added to the legend every time he stepped out to play another honky tonk. The road life took its toll on his health. But if you wanted to get your music out there, it was the only route to take. Hank Williams inspired both the fans who heard his records on the radio and the jukes and a whole generation of young singers who came after him. And when he died in his sleep in the back of his Cadillac at age 29 on December 31, 1952, he passed on a double-edged legacy to those singers.

"You'd hear all these stories," Waylon Jennings explains in his autobiography, "how he pulled a jukebox that didn't have any of his records on it out to the street and shot it full of holes, or ran around all night dead drunk and pilled out and still gave the greatest show you ever saw. We thought that was the way to do it . . . Did Hank miss concerts? We could, too. Did Hank write great songs and read 'funny books' and take pills and swarm? . . . I wanted to be like him. We all did. Even his contemporaries held him in awe." Dick Damron concurs: "Some of us may have felt that we had to live up to the legend that Hank left behind."

After Hank's death, the media built him into a legend that was taller than life. Music Row adopted him as if he'd never done what he done and had very nearly been a saint. But the younger singers bought into a slightly different myth. It was no longer good enough to simply go out on the road and sing your songs and sow a few wild oats along the way. Suddenly, being a truly great singer meant pushing the envelope to the limit and living on the edge 24-hours-a-day. Many of the recording artists who followed in Hank's footsteps may just have believed that they owed all of their success to their hurtin' and to the lifestyle that hurt them. The truth of the matter has been plain enough to see, but it was Jessi Colter who perhaps most clearly voiced the thought aloud to a writer for *The Tennessean* in 1984. "In some ways, Hank Williams unfortunately did a great injustice. A lot of little boys were out there watching him when he was on top, and they've tried to grow up just like him."

While working with Eddie & Pearl on KRIC Beaumont, George Jones met his idol, Hank Williams. Strangely, George was dumbfounded beyond words and unable to play along on his guitar when Hank sang his current radio hit, *Wedding Bells*. Afterwards, the two spoke briefly.

As George told a Chicago *Sun-Times* reporter in 1988, "Hank sat and talked with us like he knew us his whole life. I worshiped him. His style was all in the feeling. He could sing anything and it would make you sad, but an up-tempo thing could make you happy." For many fans of country music, Hank Williams was a god, fans who hung on every lonesome phrase of every one of Luke the Drifter's lovesick songs and eerie recitations, and seemed to draw life and hope from his music every time they heard one of his tunes on the radio or on a jukebox. In Nashville, Roy Acuff had first called himself the "King of country music" in the 1940s, but by the early 1950s folks everywhere else knew that it was Hank Williams who rightfully held that. When a new "King" was crowned, he would come out of Memphis and he would claim a whole new kingdom, that of rock & roll.

In *Same Ole Me*, George recalls that Hank advised him, "Don't try to be someone else when you sing." During an interview with Alanna Nash in *Behind Closed Doors*, George recalls more of that conversation. "He said Roy Acuff was his favorite back then, and he could imitate him pretty good. When he found out that I loved him and was singin' his songs . . . he said, 'I'll tell you, I was a pretty good imitator of Roy Acuff, because he was my favorite, but I soon found out they already had a Roy Acuff, so I just started singin' like myself.' " This was advice that was easier said than done as George painfully learned when he first began to record for the new label Starday in Jack Starnes' house in Beaumont.

An early marriage to Dorothy Bonvillion, a girl whose parents insisted the couple live with them in the family home, and a brief stint as a house painter assistant to his father-in-law, convinced George that he was not cut out to earn a living laboring. Nor was he cut out for marriage. He and Dorothy were divorced before their daughter Susan was born, and George found himself thrown in jail because he couldn't keep up with the child support payments. The situation quickly became a catch-22 scenario where he couldn't continue to pay half his wages to his wife and child and exist himself, let alone keep himself out of the local hoosegow. To escape from this insoluble state of affairs, he joined the U.S. Marine Corp in 1950. He was 18 years old and he was freed from worrying about payments to his dependents because they were deducted from his salary.

In the marines, once he got past the trials of boot camp in San Diego, George took to the camaraderie of his new-found pals. Naturally, he had taken his guitar along when he joined up, and soon found himself with a Saturday night job singing with Cottonseed Clark, a musician and deejay, near the base in San Jose, California where he was stationed. It paid him $25 per night. It would have been a monthly total of at least a hundred dollars, an amount that was a few dollars more than Uncle Sam was putting in his wallet, but, most of the time, he was only able to play every second Saturday night when he was scheduled for official leave from the base. In California, he performed in his khaki military uniform and was billed as "Little Georgie Jones, the Forrester Hill Flash." He also sang a few times on the radio on Cliffie Jones' *Hometown*

Jamboree on KXLA, a show that sometimes featured the up-and-coming Bakersfield country singer Buck Owens.

While he was in the marines, George learned that Hank Williams had died. On that fateful early morning of January 1, 1953, George hadn't heard the radio announcers' pronouncements that told of the tragedy and declared that news of Hank Williams death was "a bleak beginning for the new year." When he returned to his barracks from a local gig, George was shown a daily newspaper account by a fellow soldier. "I lay there the rest of the morning and just bawled," he recalls. "You know it just broke my heart, cause, Lord, he was, he was just *everything* as far as I was concerned."

Over the years several people have asked George what Hank meant to him. His standard answer is, "Hank Williams came along and, oh, oh my goodness, I couldn't think or eat, nothin', unless it was Hank Williams, and I couldn't wait till his next record came out." However often George has repeated this observation — and it changes a bit each time — a twinkle comes into his eyes as he adds, "He was, really, the greatest!"

George was released from the marines in November 1953 and returned to Texas that month. His second marriage came in 1954 when he met Shirley Corley, an attractive young woman who was working as a carhop at the local Princess Drive-In burger joint. Shirley wasn't exactly rushed off her feet by dating George, who already had a bit of a local reputation as a honky tonk singer, but he persisted. He was difficult to put off once he got something fixed in his mind, and he had fixed on marrying Shirley. Shirley hated the fact that George drank so much. She didn't particularly care for the way that George made his money, either, and told more than one person that she felt embarrassed by his performances. Despite these obvious incompatibilities, when George popped the question, Shirley said, "Yes."

To many of their friends they were mismatched, but they were hitched together for better or worse. When things became less than smooth between the couple, George Jones sought company elsewhere and, according to one observer, sometimes right there in that same town where they lived. Shirley put up with this situation for quite a few years and bore George two children, Jeffrey, in 1955, and Bryan, in 1958.

Having chosen a wife who disapproved of his behavior proved to be one of the factors that would eventually turn George from a happy drinker to a bitter one. Before George met Shirley, he was still very much the carefree minstrel boy who had once roamed the streets of Beaumont with his guitar and his music. Just how serious this crippling relationship grew to be would not come to light until after the couple parted ways many years later.

Back in civilian clothes and back on the street in Beaumont, George found that the music scene had heated up some in his absence. Soon after he was playing Jack Starnes' club and recording for Starday.

—3—
No Money in This Deal

Starday Records was founded in June 1953 by Beaumont booker and club owner Jack Starnes, who had at one time managed Lefty Frizzell, and Houston coin machine magnate and record distributor Pappy Daily. The label derived its moniker from a compendium of their surnames. Daily had dabbled in the record-making process, recording singers like Webb Pierce and Hank Locklin, who played his KNUZ *Houston Jamboree* show, and shipping the masters to Bill McCall at 4 Star Records in California who put them out on his label. Daily would then purchase a thousand or so copies for his jukebox outlets. But he wasn't getting in on any of the royalties operating that way, and forming Starday was his way of eliminating McCall from the equation. McCall's reputation as a ruthless operator was almost legendary. He was not known to do anybody any favors.

In September 1953, Starnes and Daily brought former 4 Star Records exec Don Pierce into the partnership. The three men each put up $333 to kick things off. Pierce and Daily shared a fear and loathing of "4 Star Bill McCall," so, the two had a common ground. And, right off the bat, they had a hot record on their hands with Arlie Duff's *You All Come*, a Top 10 national hit on the Starday label in late 1953 and early 1954.

The relationship with Starnes soon became strained. Starnes was said to have been diverting money from Lefty Frizzell's earnings into his own investments and was being sued by Lefty. And Starnes' interests lay in plugging the artists he booked, not in building a record label. As Don Pierce later told music historian Colin Escott, Starnes "grew to dislike me a lot because I was interested in making a success out of the record company, but he didn't give a damn about it. He was only interested in what the record company could do for him. He was coming from a different direction."

The conflict that had been building came to a boil when Starnes went ahead against Pierce's wishes and began pressing records on the label that were not part of company strategy or policy merely to sell product on the road with his touring acts. Starnes hated Pierce for opposing him and sold his interest in Starday to Daily for $6,000, a handsome profit. Out of spite, he refused to sell any portion of those interests to Pierce. However, Daily re-cut his deal with Pierce, allowing Pierce to make a further investment and the company became a 50-50 partnership. Even though the label was no more than a struggling entity, both Starnes and Daily made considerable mileage out of their original $333 investment, largely because of the potential shown by one young artist they signed before Jack Starnes made his exit. By 1956 Starnes was out of the picture at Starday, and by early 1957 Daily and Pierce had cut a merger deal with Mercury Records in Nashville that would see George Jones signed to the major label. When the merger fell apart, Pierce would continue to work the Starday label and Starday Studios in Nashville, while Daily and Jones would eventually migrate from Mercury to United Artists, then to the Musicor label before they parted ways.

Starnes had proved that he had an ear for talent when he introduced Daily and Pierce to George Jones. The 22-year-old singer was fresh out of a three-year stint in the marines and was hanging around Beaumont playing Starnes' club and generally raising hell.

At Starnes' home in Beaumont in an improvised studio where the rudimentary sound baffling was accomplished by tacking egg cartons onto the walls and ceiling of the living room, and where a Magnecord home recorder tape machine and a single microphone were set up, George Jones and some local musicians recorded two songs that he had written. It was this primitive session that would yield George's first record, but the sides were not cut without a good deal of frustration. At first, Jones sang like his heroes. He simply couldn't imagine that anyone would want to buy a record by someone who sounded like George Jones. Daily, invited along by Starnes to produce the session, became frustrated, and said to Jones, "George, we've heard you sing like Hank Williams, Roy Acuff and Lefty Frizzell, but can you sing like George Jones?"

In the years that followed, Daily told and re-told that story and each time he told it, the dialog evolved. For the liner notes to the 1969 Musicor album, I'LL SHARE MY WORLD WITH YOU, he put it this way: "I said to George, 'Kid, can you just stand there and sing like George Jones?' 'Yes sir, I can,' (George said) 'But I don't think people would care too much about hearing it.' " Daily, not one to shy away from taking credit for discovering George Jones, adds, "Sometimes I wonder how the course of events would have turned out if I hadn't been so darned insistent with a nervous kid hanging on to a guitar for courage."

George himself later recognized Lefty's enduring influence in his art of singing when he commented in his authorized video biography, "Lefty would make five syllables out of one, and that's where I got my slurring, you know, my phrasing." According to Colin Escott, at least one cut of a Lefty impersonation by George that no one could bear to tape over has survived to this day. George was good at singing like Lefty and Hank, but it was a stretch for him to grasp what Daily was telling him. After a bit more persuasion, it became clear to George that if he was going to appeal to folks who bought records and plugged nickels into juke boxes, he would have to stop singing like Hank Williams and a whole lot of other guys. So, he played Starnes and Daily a song that he had just written. *No Money In This Deal* did the trick, and, in February 1954, it became the A-side of his first record, a song that proved to be more prophetic than George could possibly have known at that time. Why had he written those words? It's a good question considering that money problems would loom large in the years to come. Probably, George was just goofing around when he came up with it. As he has said himself, it wasn't much of a song:

> *We can sit in the park*
> *And do some lovin' in the dark*
> *But the radio don't appeal*
> *Because there's no money in this deal*
>
> — No Money In This Deal (George Jones)

Apparently, though, Daily liked what he heard and more sides were cut at an improvised studio that had been set up in Bill Quinn's house in Houston where the engineer *was* in a separate room, but he could not see the pickers or his singer, and would utilize a single light bulb to signal that they were to begin to play. There was no "talk back" set-up. Later, *Why Baby Why* was recorded in the brand-new "Gold Star Studio" where Bill Quinn had moved the portable equipment and where conditions were considerably better than those under which *No Money In This Deal* had been recorded.

In an interview with Nick Tosches, George describes the recording conditions at Starday. "There was no such thing as production at Starday. We'd go in with the band, we'd go over the song, I'd look over and tell the steel player to take a break or kick it off, and I'd get the fiddle to play a turnaround in the middle. I'd just let them know if we were going to tag it or not. We'd just go through it. We didn't take any pains of making several takes. Back then, over three or four takes, they'd say, 'My God, this is costing us money.' So, we'd just get it down as good as we could. If we went a little flat or a little sharp in a place or two, they'd say, 'The public isn't going to notice that, so put it out.' So, we did, and it wasn't too successful, so I think maybe the public did notice."

On his early Starday cuts — *Why Baby Why* included — George does, in fact, sound a lot more like Hank Williams than he does the artist we have come to know as George Jones. As Gabe Tucker remembers, "We all told him and kept on and kept on and it took a while to get it across that you've got to be original. You've got to be yourself and come out with something original or you're not a-goin' to make it."

Of course, some of the similarity of the overall sound on George's early Starday releases and Hank's records comes from the fact that they have the same curious tonal quality because the pedal steel guitar playing featured prominently on both of their recordings sounds slightly out of tune. Invented in the early '50s, early Hawaiian steel guitars were not the versatile precision electrified string instruments that pedal steel guitars were to become for artists recording in the late '50s and early '60s. The invention and continuing development of newer models of the pedal steel guitar were crucial to the modernizing of hill-billy music and country & western music. As Nick Tosches describes the development of the early pedal steel, "It stood on four legs, like an insect, and had up to four eight-string necks. A complex system of cables, pulleys, and rods connected to the foot pedals (and later, knee pedals) enabled the guitarist to 'weirdize' the pitch of the individual strings and to make chords and voicings that no one had heard before. The pedal steel was the invention of John Moore, a machinist and amateur musician who lived in Winsted, Connecticut. Moore worked with the Gibson company to develop the Gibson Electraharp, the first pedal steel. The Bigsby company and other companies began to manufacture pedal steels, also." When Bud Isaacs played his Bigsby pedal steel guitar on a Webb Pierce session in 1954, Isaacs' notes were mixed more prominently than pedal steel had been before this time and people heard the potential right away on the intro of Pierce's Decca release *Slowly* that same year. They liked the new sound so much that the record went right to number one on the survey and stayed there for a remarkable 17 weeks. It was in the Top 40 for a total of 36 weeks.

This technological innovation was merely one of many that took place around the same time that Les Paul built the first solid-body electric guitar, for which, ironically, the Gibson guitar company was not willing to put their brand name on the line, giving this guitar the now legendary name "Les Paul." Due to several features, including the pickups, which were soon modified to "hum-bucking" pickups that increased the "sustain" that a player could achieve, the Les Paul guitar became a favorite with blues players as well as country pickers.

The potential for electrified guitars seemed unlimited and was at least as much a part of the rock & roll revolution as the Hank Williams' inspired gyra-tions of singers like Elvis Presley, Buddy Holly, Eddie Cochran, and Gene Vincent. When Johnny Horton put out *Honky Tonk Man* in 1956, the lower register electric guitar twang created by session guitarist Grady Martin also became identified with the honky tonk country sound. Duane Eddy favored Guild hollow-body electric guitars that had a Bigsby tailpiece with a handle so that the guitarist could bend notes manually. Duane founded a whole career on his twangy guitar instrumental recordings beginning with *Rebel Rouser*, which was huge on the pop charts, and rose to number 17 on the *Billboard* C&W chart in 1958.

The California-based Fender Guitar company came up with the ultimate country electric lead guitar when they developed the maple-neck single cut-away Telecaster model. Rockers preferred the double cutaway Stratocaster model with its sway bar, three pickups, and three position selector switch. Soon, the bass fiddle (or standup bass) would be replaced by solid body electric bass guitars. The Fender Precision Bass was the standard for many country artists. Improved tape recording machines with more than a single mono track added increasing numbers of options to the recording process. Better mixing boards opened up new possibilities for improved dynamics on country recordings. Each of these adaptations changed the sound of country music.

Where many Hank Williams' recordings feature Don Helms' strident Hawaiian-flavored steel guitar licks and Jerry Rivers' matching fiddle style, Herbie Remington played a Hawaiian steel guitar on the original 1955 record-ing of *Why Baby Why* and the steel and fiddle are used together on the fills that answer the vocal. The house band that Jones recorded with for Starday in Houston usually featured guitar, bass, drums, fiddle, and Hawaiian steel guitar. Sometimes there were twin fiddles. Some of the pickers on the Gulf Coast scene at that time, like electric guitarist Hal Harris and steel player Remington, were very good. On Billy Sherrill's production of *Why Baby Why* for a 1970s greatest hits package on the Epic label, a pedal steel is used. Sherrill has the pedal steel play the pick up phrase leading into the choruses which was played on an acoustic guitar on the original, and uses the pedal steel to enrich the entire track with ambience, whereas on the original the Hawaiian sound was used to fill and answer. The 1964 recording of *The Race Is On* is an example of early stereo mixing similar to Beatles' recordings with the drums and bass on one side and the lead guitar and twangy six-string bass guitar on the other. Jones' vocal and the harmony vocals are mixed evenly on both sides. Sherrill's '70s version adopts the current convention of "centering" the drums, bass, and vocals. No doubt, if Hank Williams had lived on into the 1960s, these technological advances would have changed his music as much as they did the music of George Jones, Buck Owens, and Johnny Horton.

The first news to reach the world outside of the Houston-Beaumont area announcing the arrival of George Jones had come in 1954 when *Billboard* printed this two-line entry in their "Who's Who in Country & Western" section: "January 23 . . . Starday Records signed new artists to recording contracts, with releases by George Jones of Beaumont, Texas." At first, promoting George Jones from their Houston office was a challenge for Pappy Daily and Gabe Tucker. Jones wasn't exactly a tall, dark, and handsome matinee idol sort of performer. In fact, he was short, still wore his hair cropped and flat in the military crew-cut that he'd adopted while in the marines, and he had a piercing intensity that was emphasized by close-set eyes and a turned up nose. But he could sing. And he could write, too. Few of the other artists on the Starday label were selling much at all. So, even before *Why Baby Why* hit with impact, Pappy Daily had begun to concentrate on getting George Jones better known. George's reputation for drinking and partying were not exactly what Daily and Tucker had in mind for their national image-making.

For his part, George was happy just to be singing, although he continued to get into quite a few scrapes. And, where he rightly should have been paying a whole lot of attention to the business end of things, he was too busy partying. Daily knew he had a gold mine in George Jones and he mined it for all he could get. Pappy ruled with a firm hand. George was a mere puppy dog, wagging his tail, and eager to make it in the music business. Pappy was a big old cigar-smoking dog whose bottom line was making money not music. And, although he'd begun to rake in plenty of cash with his jukeboxes, coin machines, and record outlets, Daily was quietly cleaning up in the still somewhat mysterious realm of song publishing. He was the kind of music industry player who prompted Willie Nelson to leave Texas, the kind of businessman who would buy up songs for 25 or 50 dollars and grin all the way to the bank when the song came out recorded by one or another of the current-day stars. The starving songwriter could only look back and kick himself for being so poor and desperate to have caved in and sold that song. John Morthland, author of *The Best of Country Music (A Critical Guide To the 750 Greatest Albums)*, comments on the Daily-Jones relationship: "Their relationship was always fraught with ambivalence; though George has always given Daily credit for recognizing his talent when others were passing on him, he has also noted ruefully that Pappy wound up with virtually all the singer's earnings." Nevertheless, Daily was the anchor, along with George's wife Shirley and their children back in Texas, that kept Jones from flying off totally into outer space.

At first, George toured alone and sang with house bands when they were provided. For a while, he hooked up with label-mate Sonny Burns, but the relationship was crazed and competitive, eventually souring when George made it big and Sonny sank into obscurity, turning bitter when Burns later painted unflattering portraits of George's father for biographer Bob Allen. When he finally made it to Nashville, Jones teamed up with George Riddle, the first 'Jones Boy', who played guitar, sang harmony, and provided not only companionship on those long all-night drives between shows but also a steadying influence.

4
Why Baby Why

The lyrics to George's first national radio hit on Starday Records, *Why Baby Why*, contain seeds for songs that the singer would cultivate through his long career, sketches that outline the human situation because, more than anyone who sang country music, George Jones was a people person, a recording artist who seemed to climb inside your heart and uncoil your hopes, fears, and dreams in his distinctively phrased warble. George wrote the song with his pal, Darrell Edwards, a poet of sorts who came to Houston — where Starday Records had set up shop — but remembered, as well as George remembered, the simple way of life left behind in the Big Thicket region where they had been born and raised. Darrell had overheard a couple quarreling, and what they had said to each other had stayed with him. He and George put the flavor of that couple's frustrations into song and onto a 45 rpm record.

Well I caught you honky tonkin' with my best friend
The thing to do was leave you but I should'a left then
Now I'm too old to leave you but I still get sore
When you come home a-feelin' for the knob on the door

Tell me why baby, why baby, why baby why
You make me cry baby, cry baby, cry baby cry
Lord I can't help but love you till the day that I die
So tell me why baby, why baby, why baby why . . .

—*Why Baby Why* (Darrell Edwards and George Jones)

George Jones might pose more questions than he gave answers, but he sang from the truth of himself, from his heart, and people felt his swooping croon in their souls.

Well I don't know but I've heard say
That every little dog's gonna have his day
You better pay attention don't you dare forget
'Cause I'm just a little bitty puppy yet . . .

This reworking of Hank Williams' classic *Move It On Over* canine imagery —
where a husband is consigned to living in the dog house by an irate wife, and a
little dog is told to "move it on over" to make way for the big ole bad dog who
is moving in — became a particularly effective metaphor in 1955 for a rookie
singer. And it has continued to be effective for Jones and others ever since.
George Jones may have been "just a little puppy" when he and Darrell Edwards
wrote the tune, but he certainly would "have his day."

Why Baby Why was the first George Jones record that was widely heard by
a national audience when Starday Records released it in the fall of 1955.
Although written by Jones and Edwards, the recording artist on Starday 45: 202
was listed as George Jones. While George was by now a bit of a local celebrity
with several previous releases on the label, he was mostly unknown outside of
east Texas where label impresario Pappy Daily operated a modest jukebox
empire. Archer Fullingame, editor of the Kountze newspaper, claimed to Dolly
Carlisle that he was "the first person that sponsored him a concert. I liked him
because he was singing his own sadness. He was singing his own love, he was
singing his own sorrow. He was singing right out of his own emotions, good or
bad, and still does it." But it was Pappy Daily who lifted George on to the
national country music scene.

Daily had hired KIKK Houston program director Gabe Tucker to promote
George Jones because his records were the most promising the label had to offer.
Tucker used his position at the radio station to advantage when he sent out
notices to other country stations that informed them that *Why Baby Why* was
play-listed in Houston at KIKK as their number one record. Programmers were
impressed, for Houston was a sizeable market. This strategy paid off, and, on
October 29, 1955, *Why Baby Why* entered the *Billboard* magazine national surveys. The record continued to rise until it peaked at number 4 on the Juke Box,
Best Seller and Jockey charts, remaining in the Top 40 for a total of 18 weeks,
well into the early months of 1956.

Starday followed up with three more George Jones' releases that year. *What
Am I Worth, You Gotta Be My Baby,* and *Just One More* all hit into the Top 10
on the national charts. It was a period of achievement for the fledgling independent label and a breakout year for George Jones.

In June 1956, *Country Song Roundup* magazine ran the feature article "The Stars Paid Off for George Jones," which reported that "in 1954, and the early part of 1955, if you were to have asked anyone to name the outstanding Folk music artist in the Gulf Coast area, George Jones would be among the first to be mentioned. Now, since the latter part of 1955, due to his hit Starday recording of *Why Baby Why* b/w *Seasons Of My Heart*, George has been — and still is — gaining national recognition in the country & western field."

This was big time press coverage, another coup de grace engineered by Gabe Tucker. As the 1950s quickly passed by, George was already easing into his own style with chart hits like *What Am I Worth* and *You Gotta Be My Baby* (both number 7 hits in 1956) and *Just One More* (number 3 later in the same year). And through the lyrics to his songs, he was already becoming identified with a reputation for excessive drinking:

Put the bottle on the table
Let it stay there till I'm not able
To see your face in every place that I go

I've been trying to forget
But I haven't stopped as yet
Well, one more drink of wine
And if you're still on my mind
One drink, just one more
And then another . . .

— *Just One More* (George Jones)

In some ways, Pappy Daily was George's Colonel Tom Parker, his Daddy Warbucks, his General Bullmoose, but in others Daily fell far short of the man who managed Elvis Presley's career from 1956 until his death and beyond the grave. Where Daily and Gabe Tucker were stonewalled for a while at getting their star singer onto the *Grand Ole Opry*, Colonel Tom was masterminding a career that would sell millions of records like *Heartbreak Hotel, Don't Be Cruel, All Shook Up,* and *(Let Me Be Your) Teddy Bear,* cutting deals that would see his star singer appearing on prime time national TV shows like *The Ed Sullivan Show* where Elvis was viewed by audiences numbering in the tens of millions. When 33 and 1/3 rpm long-playing albums became the rage, Presley would sell millions of nearly every LP he put out.

Starday sales for Jones were far more modest, some 50,000 for *Why Baby Why*, although the public would be told the figure was closer to half a million in order to keep George in the same league as Presley in the fans' minds. Pappy steered the label as best as he could with his Texan experience. Pierce, on the road to sell records and secure copyrights, did the bull work. After a while, the two cooked up the idea of linking up with a Nashville-based major label. They were encouraged by Art Talmadge at Mercury Nashville. Talmadge had lost some key personnel and was restructuring his Nashville operation. On January 1, 1957, Starday merged with Mercury Nashville to form Mercury-Starday, the parent label's country division. Pierce was delighted to be located in Music City. However, he chose not to locate the new Starday facility on Music Row because he felt that he was in competition with the establishment song brokers who had their offices there and believed it would be easier to remain independent if he located out on Dickerson Pike. Mercury had already set aside an address on 7th Avenue not far from WSM. When Pierce remained firm on his decision and told Mercury's Murray Nash that "I'm interested in recording *my* songs, not your songs," his stance became the first in a series of conflicts that led to the failure of the merger.

Daily, sensing a need to remain independent, had already formed his own label, Big D Records, and he and Pierce had a falling out. Mercury wanted out of the deal, too. The major label had thought that Starday would bring some hot rockabilly acts to Mercury. Instead, they had brought George Jones and other honky tonk singers like Sonny Burns. Most of the records that they were issuing were recordings of their own songs published by Starrite Publishing. There was little money for Mercury in this sort of deal. Still at odds, Daily and Pierce split up the copyrights that they had accumulated during a deal brokered by a neutral party in a Chicago hotel room where the two men simply laid out all of the published songs and took turns choosing the ones they most cherished. George Jones benefitted the most of all because he ended up on the Mercury label. Pierce continued on with Starday, running the rural Nashville Starday studio with producer Tommy Hill and concentrating on niche markets like bluegrass and older artists who had been cut loose by the majors.

Pappy Daily is the man credited with producing George Jones' records right up until George left the Musicor label in 1971 and signed with Epic Records where he was produced by Billy Sherrill. But Pappy was usually an executive producer and one of the session players (or Jones himself) was the actual producer. Daily steered Jones' career for nearly 20 years, but he was never exactly a manager for George Jones, either. In fact, in the early days of their associa-tion, Daily was happier when George merely played the local barndance radio show that Pappy had organized. The KNUZ *Houston Jamboree* never really caught fire like the *Louisiana Hayride*, the *Grand Ole Opry*, or the *National Barndance*, but it did a whole lot to publicize Pappy's singer.

For a while, George also worked as a disc jockey at KTRM in Beaumont spinning 45s and 78s and making use of the opportunity to mention his own shows, now and then. He lost that job when he mispronounced the word "antique" as an-ti-quew while delivering a commercial announcement. But the days he spent at KTRM were fun ones. George developed his passion for pulling pranks and practical jokes. He met J.P. Richardson, the Big Bopper, there. And he was given his nick-name there, as Gord Baxter, who worked at the station at that time, later told music historian Nick Tosches: "One of the better deejays there, Slim Watts, took to calling him George P. Willicher Picklepuss Possum Jones. For one thing he cut his hair short like a possum. He had a possum's nose and had stupid eyes like a possum." Pappy Daily must have shaken his head in dumbfounded amazement at that one. His kid singer certainly was a handful. Shortened to "the Possum," the name stuck.

Daily and his PR man Gabe Tucker quickly came to realize that George Jones was unmanageable. Don Pierce tells a story of a time when George came to Pappy and said he needed some money. Daily set up a date for a show where George made $2500 in one night. The next day, George was back in Daily's office asking for money because he was broke. As Don Pierce remembers it, "He got out in west Texas and he got into a scrape out there and they threw him in the cooler for overnight. Pappy Daily had to get him out and brought him over to Houston. George was needing some work and needing some money. So, Pappy got him a gig for about 2500 bucks. So, George did the gig and then got on a party and then came in the next day needin' some money. Pappy says, 'Well, George you just made $2500. But I talked to some of the guys you were partying with and they said you flushed it down the toilet.' And he said, 'Pappy, that's a damn lie, it wasn't but 1200 bucks.' What Don Pierce doesn't speak about in this anecdote was that Pappy Daily rarely paid George Jones his fair share of the royalties, not that those royalties were making many of the honky tonk singers and songwriters rich in those days.

Columbia Records, for example, probably the most successful and generous of the major labels, was paying a five percent royalty to artists like Marty Robbins, Carl Smith, and Ray Price. At 75 to 85 cents a copy, five percent of the 20,000 or so records, which a best-selling single might achieve, is somewhere around $1,000. When the costs of recording and paying session musicians had been deducted, there wasn't a whole lot left even if you went number one on the survey. It is not known just what percentage Jones' contract with Daily was set at. There were some stinkers signed in those days, though, like the time 4 Star Records' Bill McCall locked Patsy Cline into a totally compromising contract that dictated she record only songs from McCall's publishing catalog, even when Decca became her distributor, and for a paltry 2.34 percent royalty. During more than half a decade with McCall, Cline had only one Top 10 hit, *Walkin' After Midnight* in 1957. When she finally got away from McCall, her first release, Harlan Howard and Hank Cochran's *I Fall To Pieces*, went right to the top of the C&W charts. Of course, by that time Patsy had herself a manager. There was also the example of Jack Starnes who had mismanaged Lefty Frizzell's career to the point where Frizzell had sued Starnes. In fact, Starnes had appropriated and invested Frizzell's money in various enterprises, including Starday Records, and Lefty would not recover any significant amount of what had been misspent.

Daily once told Dolly Carlisle that he did what he did with Jones because he saw talent there, but he never took a dime for his services. Perhaps his tongue was in his cheek when he made that statement to Jones' biographer because Daily indeed made a whole lot of money from George's songs, if not from his performances, because he held the publishing rights. By June 1955, Daily had already seen George's *Let Him Know* recorded as *Forgive Me Dear* by Faron Young on Capitol; *Play It Cool, Man* recorded by Tibby Edwards on Mercury; *Why Baby Why* first recorded by Red Sovine and Webb Pierce on Decca, then Hank Locklin on Starday, and a pop version recorded by Frankie Castro on Wing; *Seasons Of My Heart* recorded by Spade Cooley on Decca and Jimmy Newman on Dot; and *What Am I Worth* by Terry Fell (RCA) and Roy Drusky on Columbia. Pappy cleaned up when the Red Sovine and Webb Pierce cover of *Why Baby Why* went number one. The durability of *Why Baby Why* was further demonstrated when Pat Boone recorded the song and scored a number 5 hit on the pop charts in 1957. (In 1983, Charley Pride recorded it and the song went number one on the *Billboard* Hot 100, again, 28 years after George Jones first recorded it.) In 1960, Johnny Cash would have a Top 10 hit when he recorded *Seasons Of My Heart*. As Don Pierce notes, Daily "took him to Mercury and he became 'the' artist for their country division. And he took him to United Artists and he *was* the country division at United Artists. And he took him to Musicor and he *was* the country division at Musicor. So, a lot of people have been riding on ole George."

These were the kinds of management deals George Jones knew. George was so grateful that Daily was interested enough to record him that he endured his one-sided deals. Together, they did record some remarkable hits for the radio. However, it is supremely ironic just how prophetic the lyrics to his first song, *No Money In This Deal*, recorded back in Jack Starnes' home, would turn out to be, not just with Pappy Daily, but with several of the managers, publishers, and record labels that George Jones signed deals with over the years.

There wasn't exactly no money at all in the deal that George Jones had with Pappy Daily and Starday. But it was close to none. Mostly, how it worked was that singers in those days made their loot off their tour dates and the record labels hoarded the revenues that resulted from publishing royalties and record sales. The gray area was always the number of records that actually sold. These were huge when record company representatives were bragging to journalists and tiny when they were speaking with their singers. The music business simply was not accountable to the artists who created the music. Not in pop, not in rock and roll, and certainly not in country music. Still, Jones survived it all remarkably unscathed. It was almost as if the title for his early Starday 45 rpm record *Play It Cool, Man, Play It Cool* had become a silent mantra, even when Starday put out rockabilly sides like *Rock It* and *(Dadgummit) How Come It* that Daily convinced him to record and release under the "Thumper Jones" banner.

In 1955 when they nailed a take of *Why Baby Why* both Pappy and George knew they had something more unique than *No Money In This Deal* or *Play It Cool, Man, Play It Cool*, or even *Seasons Of The Heart*. Recognizing what you had and running with your best shot was what Sam Phillips at Sun and Pappy Daily at Starday were both good at. While Pappy knew that George Jones felt more comfortable cutting country records, he saw the potential for rocking things up now and then, so, he experimented. *Unwanted Babies*, a folk-rock effort written by Earl Peanut Montgomery, was a real dog, an avenue that might have been better off not explored. Fortunately for Jones, he had sagely come up with the clever pseudonym Glen Patterson by combining his given name and his mother's maiden name, and successfully buried his association with that record so that few of his fans knew that he had ever done it. Nick Tosches mentions a further transgression into bad taste, *The Poor Chinee*, which would today be labeled racist, but was so bad that it barely saw the light of day at the time of its release.

George has always claimed that he stopped short of recording rockabilly numbers, balking at putting his own name on *Rock It* and inventing his Thumper Jones, but what else can you call *White Lightning* with its rockabilly boogie guitar riff juxtaposed with Pig Robbins' eight-to-the-bar hammer-on piano pounding and Buddy Killen a-slappin' away on his big bass fiddle?

What Jones was doing was not the same as Elvis, that was for sure. Elvis had attitude and the looks to go with his sneer and pelvic gyrations. While Johnny Cash and Carl Perkins stood in awe of Presley's act at the Hayride shows, Elvis's moves brought out the prankster in George Jones. One night George chose to upstage Elvis rockin' it up with Little Richard's *Long Tall Sally* and his own Thumper Jones version of *Heartbreak Hotel*. As Johnny Cash has commented, "George Jones would have been a really hot rockabilly if he had approached it that way. He *was*, really."

There were other speculative recordings during this period of time like George Jones' cover of *Heartbreak Hotel* that was first put out as a Thumper Jones release on Starday and then on the Tops Records imprint where it was attributed to Hank Smith & the Nashville Playboys. But George doesn't speak of those outings much these days at all, though he did give Nick Tosches in 1977 an account of the "Thumper Jones" recordings. "I don't guess that I'm ever gonna live that down. I was actually getting started in the business about 1954 or so when all this rock and roll really started movin' in, and of course, you know, you didn't have stations back then that played all that much country to start with. So especially with rock and roll getting as strong as it was at that time, it seemed like country music was really a losin' battle except for the three or four major artists that had it made at the time, like Lefty Frizzell, Ernest Tubb, Roy Acuff, some of those people. So we decided to try one, sorta rockabilly like. I was sorta ashamed to even do it at the time 'cause I was so country, so I just used a different name, went under the name of Thumper Jones." Jones told Alanna Nash in a 1980 interview that he *may* have contributed to the scarceness of those records by using just a few of them as frisbees, now and then. There had been other releases, though, under other names, when Pappy Daily leased some of George's cover versions of pop and rock hits of the day to labels like Tops Records . . . names like Johnny Williams and Hank Davis. These same pseudonyms were also attributed, at other times, to recordings made by other closet rockabilly singers. This practice totally clouds the issue for present-day archivists but served the purpose of keeping the purity of George Jones' country identity intact. As George has pointed out, it was tough to make a living just singing country and putting out country records, and a fella did what a fella did, just to get by.

At first, George's Starday releases consistently did better on the Juke Box chart than on the Bestsellers or Jockies charts. George was still mostly a local hero and largely unknown to the national audience. Pappy Daily and Gabe Tucker tried out several tactics in their efforts to publicize their artist to bigger audiences. Gabe would call in favors from promoters who wanted exposure on KIKK. One of those favor-swapping deals involved a big show that A.V. Bamford wanted to put on in the Houston area. Bamford was a veteran promoter. He'd been the person who had promoted that fateful show that Hank Williams never gave on New Year's Day in 1953. And Tucker was able to wangle George Jones onto the big Houston show and lever on Bamford to get George lined up to headline a second package show in San Antonio a few days later.

These maneuvers increased George's profile in Texas and no doubt helped to sell him in the record stores and on the jukeboxes there, but Pappy Daily and Gabe Tucker knew they had to get George on to the *Grand Ole Opry* if he was going to get the national exposure that would lead to selling significantly more records. When Daily and Tucker returned to the Houston area with the disparaging news that some of the good ole boys who ran the Opry might not be above taking a bribe now and then from a newcomer who wanted to get on the Opry, George wanted to have none of that. If they didn't want his singing, then fine, but he and Pappy and Gabe weren't going to buy their way into the inner circle, not into the institution that was already being called the "Mother Church of Country Music."

Yearning, a duet that George recorded with Jeanette Hicks, was his last Starday single to chart when it was released in January of 1957, while *Don't Stop The Music* was his first Mercury release, charting at number 10 on the Billboard survey on the strength of its showing on the Juke Box chart. It would be a while before George Jones would no longer depend upon the juke box empire Pappy Daily had built in the Lonestar state. For the next five years, until 1962, Jones would be with Daily at Mercury, five critical years during which the music truly never stopped.

5
Class of '55

As a stepping stone to the Opry, Gabe managed to book George Jones on the *Louisiana Hayride*. His next mention in *Billboard* magazine's "Who's Who" section read, "February 18 . . . George Jones is now a regular on *Louisiana Hayride*." George was on his way out of Texas. He was more than ready to take on the world. And it was at the Hayride that he met many of the people he really related to. His first experience at the Opry, however, turned out to be a different barrel of apples altogether.

When he got to the Ryman, at first the Opry management weren't going to let him play his guitar because he wasn't a member of the local musicians union. In his authorized video biography, George recalls that night as one of his most nerve-wracking experiences. "I was so nervous. This was the biggest thing that could happen to anybody in the whole world. And I was shaking. I mean just truly shaking all over. And they wasn't going to let me play my guitar because I wasn't a member of the local here . . . and (Jimmy) Dickens and (George) Morgan were tryin' to calm me down. One of them put their guitar right in my hands and said, 'Here, we'll take responsibility for it.' " George performed *You Gotta Be My Baby* and he got some applause, alright, but he didn't get six standing ovation encores as Hank Williams had done on his celebrated Opry debut.

The *Louisiana Hayride*, often referred to as the "grooming ground for the Opry," was, in retrospect, a classier show with a looser attitude and a sense of democracy, which eventually spawned a generation of rockabilly artists who eclipsed anything that the conservative Opry managers hoped to accomplish with their exclusivity. It had been Hank Williams who had put the Shreveport radio show on the map back in the late 1940s, and, after he had difficulties with the Opry management, Williams returned to performing on the Hayride before his death.

"I became a Hayride regular," Jones would tell reporters, "and the company was mighty good. Elvis Presley, Johnny Cash, Johnny Horton, and Jimmy C. Newman were all there." If the Topps bubblegum company had been of a mind to put out cards of country music singers, like they did for baseball players and hockey players beginning in the early '50s, what a harvest of collector's items the 1955 edition would have made! Rookie cards from the early '50s of baseball players like Mickey Mantle, Willie Mays, and Hank Aaron are worth tens of thousands of dollars today. Later on, in the 1960s, there would be cards made of Elvis and The Beatles, but nothing was issued that approximated a "rookie card." As it is, record collectors who can boast of having vintage pressings of Starday and Sun Records 78 and 45 rpm records in their collections cherish both the high dollar value of their collectibles and the pleasure of listening to the early music made in the original mono format. Among the Class of '55 were George Jones, Johnny Cash, and Elvis Presley who had Top 40 hits that year, as well as Carl Perkins, Roy Orbison, Jerry Lee Lewis, Faron Young, Johnny Horton, and more.

Elvis hit the national country & western chart first with *Baby Let's Play House* (number 5), and in September 1955 Sun released *I Forgot To Remember To Forget*, his first number one. *Mystery Train* followed, and early in 1956 his first RCA release, *Heartbreak Hotel*, went number one and stayed there for 17 weeks. It also crossed over and spent eight weeks at number one on the pop chart. George Jones was next with the Top 10 hit *Why Baby Why*. Johnny Cash followed with *Cry, Cry, Cry* in late November. Cash hit into the Top 10 with *So Doggone Lonesome* and *Folsom Prison Blues*, then hit the top of the country & western charts with *I Walk The Line*, also a Top 10 pop hit for him on the Sun Records label in 1956. Sun Records label mate Carl Perkins hit in early 1956 with *Blue Suede Shoes*, a number one country & western hit that also peaked at number 2 on the *Billboard* pop chart. Johnny Horton followed Perkins with *Honky Tonk Man* that same year. There were other country singers making their debuts around this same time, artists like Red Sovine, Ferlin Husky, and Porter Wagoner. All of these singers cashed in on the association they shared with Elvis when they appeared with Presley on the *Louisiana Hayride* or on early tours when Presley was still billed as the "Hillbilly Cat." When Nick Tosches asked George Jones if he'd liked Elvis during those days, George replied, "Oh, yes, quite a bit. I liked quite a bit of the things that came out then."

Jerry Lee Lewis didn't actually hit the charts until 1957, but he hit with impact on *Whole Lotta Shakin' Goin' On* and *Great Balls Of Fire*, the same year that the Everly Brothers put out their first chart-busting soft-rockabilly hit, *Bye*

Bye Love. Later that year Buddy Holly hit on the pop charts with his churning rockabilly version of *That'll Be The Day*, though Holly was never play-listed in the country radio Top 40, even though there was a lot of similarity between his Lubbock, Texas brand of rockabilly and the music being made in Memphis and Houston. Holly had come to Nashville to record a country record for Decca in 1956, but *Blue Days, Black Nights* b/w *Love Me* failed to light any fires at country radio. The label kept after it with Buddy Holly & The Two Tunes for a few more sides but finally dropped the act when presented with an early version of *That'll Be The Day*. Back in Texas, Holly added Jerry Allison to his band, who then started calling themselves The Crickets, and when the new lineup opened for Elvis, they were inspired to rock it up on their recordings. Holly later said, "We owe it all to Elvis." When the Crickets recorded *That'll Be The Day* at Norman Petty's Clovis, New Mexico studio in February 1957, the New York-based Coral/Brunswick label released it, and by September of that year, it was number one on the pop chart.

There was a fine line in those days between country and rockabilly, and when rockabilly evolved into rock & roll, the pure country artist was faced with the financial temptation to go rockabilly. Thus Starday put out George Jones' Thumper Jones record *Rock It* to test the rockabilly waters. As Jones later remembered, "you could have an artist go number one on the country charts with a hit that sold only 20,000 records in those days."

Whether your records were rockabilly or country, the challenge of celebrity for the country boys from the sticks who made these auspicious debuts quickly proved to be a whole lot more than most of them could handle. The road life ate them up as they tried to live up to the life-on-the-road legacy of Jimmie Rodgers and Hank Williams. Whiskey drinking and one-night-stands were part of the legend. So was cutting loose after those long road miles and nerve-wracking stage shows. From this association, George hooked up with singers like Cash and Horton on package tours based out of the Hayride. He signed up for torturous stretches of 15 and 20, up to 40 days and 40 nights, traveling five or six men to a car, driving down the primitive strips of two-lane pavement that existed before construction was begun on the Interstate highway system as part of a late-1950's military initiative, unable to stretch out to get relaxed while they slept during the sometimes 400 and 500 miles between shows. As George Jones recalls, "We traveled many, many miles cramped up together like that. And almost every date was a drive-on that night. When you are on the road you don't eat right, you don't sleep right, and this keeps your body dragged out."

No wonder that they raised a little hell when they climbed out of those vehicles at truck stops and gas stations. Left to their own devices in the hotel rooms on days and nights when they were in one town long enough to book into a hotel, boredom often became their biggest enemy. Boredom, Johnny Cash recalls in his biography, instigated the break-up-your-hotel-room exploits which still mar the reputation of touring young bucks.

In the days when the Class of '55 went out on package tours, country singers traveled together, drank together, fought together, and wrote together, as Johnny Cash also recalls. Country music truly was one big extended family. Cash first met George Jones one night when the two singers were booked onto the *Louisiana Hayride* and the two became instant friends. The next time they met, Jones invited Cash back to his home. "We became friends the first night we worked together," Cash recalled during the taping of *Same Ole Me*. "He was that kind of man. I felt like I'd known him all my life. About the second time that I saw him there, he invited me to come home with him and spend the weekend with him in Beaumont. So, we left Shreveport and went to Beaumont after the Hayride that night. And I remember the songs we sang and the things that George was into. George had an attitude about life, and about things like that, that was awfully unburdening. Be depressed or down about the night we had just passed together, and he would come up with something, and make a joke about it, and laugh about how bad he felt. I guess George was one of the first people that I ever learned from to laugh through my pain. Especially if that pain is self-inflicted — don't take yourself serious."

Cash remembers some of those early tours with fondness. "We had some great times together. I toured with George as much as I did anybody else in the early days. We toured together from Washington State to Nova Scotia and south Texas." In the same video, June Carter Cash recalls with a smile that in those days Cash and Jones were their own roadies. "We were in Sioux Falls, South Dakota. Thirty-four degrees below zero and that place was sold out. And then they were trying to put all the instruments in the car and they all got frost-bitten noses and ears. I sure do remember it. When they woke up the next morning, I don't know if they remembered it or not." George Riddle, who graduated from backing up George Jones to a recording career of his own, laments, "Those tours like that are over. They were a lot of fun."

While touring, George Jones was getting exposure, entertaining on shows with people who were going somewhere in their careers, and he had money in his pockets, money to bring home to his wife and sons. It wasn't the big money that some people thought that recording stars should be making, but it was enough that he would eventually be able to move Shirley and the kids from an apartment in Beaumont to a new home in Vidor, Texas, a nearby bedroom community comfortably distant from the industrial mess and hardscrabble existence of the fast-growing city itself.

But being the wife of a touring country singer was not easy. Once following a show when George had hooked up with his idol Lefty Frizzell, Lefty invited Jones back to *his* home in Hendersonville, Tennessee. Some 72 hours after their arrival, the two were still down in the basement den yelling, singing, and carrying on, as Daniel Cooper tells the story in his book *Lefty Frizzell: The Honky Tonk Life of Country Music's Greatest Singer*, recreating those days from the memories of Frizzell's duo partner, Abe Mulkey. Cooper also reports that down in the Frizzell den in Hendersonville the two singers "roared and laughed, argued and howled. From time to time Alice would pound on the kitchen floor with a broom and yell: 'Hold it down, Sonny!' Cringing, Lefty would put his fingers to his lips: 'George, Shhhh!' Then the two would step lightly around the room, whispering, a conspiratorial glint in their eyes." It was too much for Lefty's wife, Alice, and she ordered her husband to evict his guest. Lefty had sent his underage daughter Lois to make a run or two to the liquor store, and she eventually drove her father and George Jones into Nashville, the duo riding in the back seat of Frizzell's Cadillac. Lois recalls that both men had open liquor bottles in their hands as she made the drive. Jones was dropped off in front of Tootsie's Orchid Lounge; Frizzell's wife had him checked into Madison Hospital to dry out. Jones' behavior during this period, while being at least as outrageous as Johnny Cash and Lefty Frizzell, seldom went as far over the line as Jerry Lee Lewis, who thought nothing of breaking a whiskey bottle over a barroom table and thrusting the jagged edge into the face of an overly curious journalist.

For many of these Class of '55 singers, the specter of Hank Williams seemed to be lurking in the wings when they came off stage. And, although at first no one actually seemed to be actively haunted by Hank's restless spirit, the music surely was. Before Thomas Edison's inventions had made it possible to capture a singer's performance on magnetic tape and press records that preserved that performance forever, ghosts had to depend on haunting the locality of their death scene. In the 1950s, Hank Williams' records were played so often on radios and jukeboxes that his voice was 'everywhere' on the airwaves.

The life and death of Hank Williams surely shaped the careers of the Class of '55 in truly occult ways, as Randall Riese in *Nashville Babylon* suggests. "Hank

Williams was not the first or last country star to be ravaged by drugs and alcohol," Riese observes. "But he was the one who romanticized the pathos of its devastation and lured a legion of awe-inspired desperados to scavenge for a place in his twisted shadow." Ole Hank may have had a more active role than even Randall Riese hints at, that is, if you believe in ghosts, spirits haunting the sites that they once roamed when they had still had bodies, or haunting the folks they had been close to before they died. As Billie Jean Williams, Hank's wife, told Nancy Jones, George's wife, Hank had "haunted" her life during the time she was married to Johnny Horton. Billie Jean survived those years, but Horton did not.

In Horton's case, he was stone cold sober when a drunk driver smacked head-on into the singer's white limousine. Horton, his manager, Tillman Franks, and a band member, guitar picker Tommy Tomlinson, packed up after a show in Austin, Texas and headed out on the highway toward Shreveport. Just like the night that had brought Carl Perkins' career to a screeching halt when his car crashed, killing his brother and injuring him critically, Johnny Horton was sittin' on top of the world. After years spent laboring as a fisherman in Alaska and more years forging a career on the radio in Los Angeles, he had secured his place as a big time country star with the chart-busting number one hits *The Battle Of New Orleans* and *North To Alaska*. At 1:30 a.m. on November 5, 1960, a 1958-model Ford Ranchero, driven by a student who was certifiably drunk, brought about Johnny Horton's Waterloo.

Colin Escott in *Tattooed on Their Tongues: A Journey Through the Backrooms of American Music* picks up on this occult connection between the lives of Johnny Horton and Hank Williams. Overriding the physical locations of their deaths was an incident at the Hayride where ole Hank introduced Horton to his young bride, Billie Jean, and said, "One of these days, you're gonna marry him." As Escott recounts, "Hank Williams' last gig was at the Skyline Club in Austin, Texas — the site of Horton's last gig, almost eight years later. There is an apocryphal story that Horton and his band heard the news of Williams death while they were driving through Milano, Texas — later the site of Horton's death. Hank became one of Johnny Horton's fixations. The window would rattle; Horton would say, 'That's Hank trying to get in touch.'" Horton's fascination with the afterlife was fed by his association with preacher Bernard Ricks. Ricks channeled voices from the beyond and saw a blue haze highlighted with a dollar sign and five zeroes when he first heard a test-pressing of *The Battle Of New Orleans*.

Even more strange was Horton's fascination with seances and hypnotism.

As Escott explains, "the darker side to Horton was his spiritualism. He became a devotee of Edgar Cayce and later built himself a little meditation shed on the back of his property. His preoccupation divided those close to him. His mother saw it as devil worship. Billie Jean had no use for it, and the always practical Tillman Franks (Horton's co-writer and standup bass player) saw it as meddling in an area best left alone." Johnny Cash was not so easily put off by this spiritualism. For example, when Cash couldn't complete a song that had come to him in a dream, he was hypnotized by Horton and taken back to a time when he had dreamed he heard Webb Pierce singing that song. Horton then handed Cash a pencil and a piece of paper, and Cash was successful in recovering the rest of the lyrics to *I'd Still Be There*. Another time, Cash was said to be taken forward in time but that experience gave the man in black the screaming heebies.

The striking thing that emerged from Horton's occult practices was his growing conviction that he was going to die soon. He had most of it right, including the image of being hit head-on by a drunken driver. Horton is said to have prepared himself to steer his car toward the ditch. When the fatal moment arrived, there was no ditch there to steer toward, as Colin Escott reports. "The irony was that Horton had prepared for a head-on collision: 'You don't have to worry about bein' in a wreck with ol' John,' he had told Claude King, ''cause ol' John's gonna take the ditch. Ain't nobody gonna hit me head-on.' He'd trained his mind, probably spent hundreds of hours mentally preparing to take to the ditch — and he did it a time or two. Then he got hit on the overpass with nowhere to go."

Before Horton died, he left Merle Kilgore a code that he would use if he was able to communicate from the "other side." Ten years after his death, a group of spiritualists kept getting messages from a ghostly figure they could not identify. When one of the spiritualists heard a deejay making reference to Johnny Horton and Merle Kilgore, he got in touch with Merle and told him that their group had been getting these messages but they made no sense. The code that Horton had given his friend was pretty good: "The drummer is a rummer and he can't hold the beat." When this spiritualist spoke those same words over the telephone to Kilgore, there was no mistaking that Johnny Horton had "been in touch." Of course, some people get roped into these things with no direct involvement at all, like that spiritualist who didn't know what "the drummer is a rummer" was all about.

There is a Canadian singer, Peter Hodgson, known professionally as Sneezy Waters, who spent nearly a full decade of his career performing a one-man show he called "The Show He Never Gave," a Hank Williams' tribute that imagined what might have taken place had Charles Carr and Hank Williams stopped off at a roadhouse on the way to Canton, Ohio on New Years' Eve in 1952, and sang a few songs for the locals. Hodgson also put out an album of his own material (*You've Got) Sawdust On The Floor Of Your Heart*, but was known from coast to coast in Canada as "the guy who does that Hank Williams show." In essence, for most of his adult life at that time, Peter Hodgson had performed an imaginary show that Hank never gave. His preoccupation became documented as a feature film before he moved on to other pursuits.

Far more spectacular was a display of this connection between Hank Williams and Johnny Horton that took place in 1964 when George Jones and the Jones Boys featuring Johnny Paycheck played a show for the fire department in Fairfax, Virginia. That night, a drunk George was reluctant to come out on stage. Coaxed by Johnny Paycheck, George finally relented, but only if Johnny would introduce him as Hank Williams. So, according to Tom Carter and George Jones, Paycheck went out and said, "Ladies and gentlemen, I'm sorry about the delay, but here to sing for you-all is Hank Williams."

George balked again and said, "I ain't comin' out unless you introduce me as Johnny Horton." Paycheck yelled, "Alright you son-of-a-bitch, I'm whipping your ass right here. If you go out there, it will be with a bloody nose." A scuffle broke out between Jones and Paycheck. George did come on, but just long enough to sing one or two lines from *White Lightning* before he made a hasty exit. A riot ensued. Three hours later the band and the Fairfax police tracked George Jones down. He was the picture of innocence seated in a nearby bar. He had ducked out and left Paycheck and the band to face the music.

At first, the way George Jones dealt with Hank's legacy was to record tribute albums to his hero. He might be chasing ole Hank's shadow when he lived much of his life in the fast lane, but he was young and robust and in those days he didn't mess up all that badly. In 1960, Mercury Records released GEORGE JONES SALUTES HANK WILLIAMS, George's first tribute to his mentor. In 1962, George recorded his second tribute album to Hank Williams, MY FAVORITES OF HANK WILLIAMS, which was released on the Liberty label. In 1984 Polydor re-released GEORGE JONES SALUTES HANK WILLIAMS for the U.S. market. British fans could buy the 1986 Liberty re-release GEORGE JONES SALUTES BOB WILLS & HANK WILLIAMS. These tribute albums are a labor of love, showing George's devotion to Hank's music. None of the cuts became Top 40 hits, but to George Jones' fans, they are a treasure.

While George had begun to sound less and less like his idol since first meeting him and taking his advice to heart, he began to exhibit other behavior eerily close to Hank's, missing shows due to one reason or another, often drunkenness, and developing quite an 'attitude'. As Mark Rose once noted in *The Village Voice*, "The similarities between George Jones and Hank Williams are haunting. Hank was a frail man with a taut, contained smile, an erratic temper, and a propensity for the bottle. He sang the blues, his fate dictated by the perceived hurt of the world around him, as he sponged it up and dripped it out in his songs. He was idolized for those songs and criticized for living out the words that brought him fame. He was kicked off the Opry for his attitude, thought unreliable by promoters for his drinking. 'Live fast, die young and leave a beautiful memory.' That's the way Hank done it. Hank is the model. The big difference between Hank Williams and George Jones is that Hank died when he was 29. . . ." Among the many people who have seen similarities between Jones and Williams, Hank's widow Billie Jean saw a striking similarity in the fierce spirit of independence that both singers displayed toward people who attempted to manipulate their lives and careers. In 1998, Billie Jean told Nancy Jones and Tom Carter for their book *Nashville Wives*, "Hank was where he was at the time, just like George Jones was. You'd hear rumors that Hank was going back to Nashville because he was contracted there, and then you'd hear rumors that said he couldn't go back to Nashville because he was contracted somewhere else. Hank didn't care about no damn contract. Hank would be where he wanted to be."

Weirdly, but true to the overall synchronicity, Billie Jean quit a job working for the telephone company when Hank asked her to accompany him on the road. Nearly 30 years later, Nancy Sepulvado would quit her job assembling telephones to accompany George Jones on his tours when George made the same request.

But why was Hank's spirit so restless? Billie Jean offers one explanation in *Nashville Wives*, which opens another can of worms. From the moment her daddy (a local police official) told her the tragic news, Billie Jean had suspected that Hank's mother, Lillian Stone, had killed her own son. "I think she would have rather seen him dead than married to me. . . . Hank's mother gave him shots the whole time during Christmas. . . . I never trusted any of those shots. I told her at the time . . . 'I don't know what the hell you're giving him but it makes him goofy,' and I didn't know why, but I know Hank — when she popped him with those shots, he didn't like it, but there was nothing you could say to her. I know she gave him those shots and also she paid for the prescription. She called Toby Marshall who was not a doctor." The facts bear out Billie Jean's suspicions of Toby Marshall, who had a criminal record and was later charged and convicted for practicing medicine without a license. The night Hank died, another doctor had injected him with morphine, however.

Hank's mother had been able to keep the mention of morphine out of the official report that declared that the legend had died of a heart attack. However — similar to what Richard Ben Cramer would later reveal in his *Rolling Stone* magazine article on the death of one of Jerry Lee Lewis' wives — an original police report written out by Tennessee Highway Patrol officer Swann Kitts on the events that took place the night Hank Williams died had mysteriously gone missing. Then, just as mysteriously, a few years later, Kitts' report appeared in print in the *Knoxville Banner*.

That report notes that Charles Carr had been apprehended on the highway near Blaine, Tennessee by officer Kitts. The pale-blue Cadillac had nearly hit Kitts' police vehicle head-on. Officer Kitts had Carr drive the Williams vehicle into nearby Rutledge, where Carr was ticketed for dangerous driving, appeared before a Justice of the Peace, and paid a $25 fine. Kitts notes in his report the details of the visit from Dr Cardwell and the injections of morphine and vitamin B-12. He also writes that he thought it odd that Carr and Williams had stayed only three and a half hours in the Andrew Johnson Hotel in Knoxville when Carr had told the desk clerk that the two men were checking in for the night. They had stayed there until Carr had received a phone call from an unidentified caller. Then, despite the lateness of the hour and the poor condition that the star singer was in, Carr had headed out into the darkness of night down the highway. Kitts also mentioned in his report that Carr was not alone at the time he was ticketed: "Carr had a soldier with him at that time."

Kitts had first become suspicious when he noticed that Hank Williams appeared "blue." At that time, he asked Carr if the singer could be dead. The chauffeur told Kitts the story of the injections, capsules, and the six beers that the singer had consumed and said that Williams was "asleep." However, Kitts suspected that Williams had died in the hotel and not later on out on the road in West Virginia: "After investigating this matter, I think that Williams was dead when he was dressed and carried out of the hotel. Since he was drunk and was given the injections and could have taken some capsules earlier, with all of this he couldn't have lasted over an hour and a half or two hours. A man drunk or doped will make some movement if you move them. A dead man will make a coughing sound if they are lifted around. Taking all of this into account, he must have died in Knoxville."

Because this report was 'lost', it did not figure in the case until after the matter had been officially put to bed. And it has since been discredited by spin doctors. Carr, himself, subsequently accused Kitts of being an "overzealous cop with a poor memory, who was eager to jump on the Hank Williams post-death bandwagon."

These conflicting reports raise a number of questions about Hank's death which have never been resolved and which might make the spirit of Hank restless. They raise questions of foul play. To my knowledge, the unknown soldier in the Cadillac when Carr was pulled over by officer Kitts has not been identified. There is an earlier picture of Hank and his mom and an unidentified soldier published in Nick Tosches' 1976 book *Country: Living Legends and Dying Metaphors*, the caption beneath the photo identifying the four figures as "Miss Audrey, Hank, Hank's mom, unknown soldier." The four are posing for the camera, arm in arm. The photo is said to have been taken in Montgomery in 1945, and it appears to be of two couples. After Hank's father went into a veteran's hospital, Hank's mother had operated a boardinghouse in Montgomery. She had ruled his life with an iron grip. During his marriage to Audrey, both women had continued to nurse him when he was ill and pushed him to make a success out of himself. He was their meal ticket. When he separated from Audrey and took up with Billie Jean, his mother and his ex could see it all slipping away. A dead Hank would redirect the flow of revenue back into their bank accounts, although Audrey had previously been awarded 50 percent of his future songwriting royalties, which seems extravagant.

Billie Jean did have other suspicions, based on the fact that Hank's mother was already at the death scene when Billie Jean arrived. Billie Jean also recalled that by the time of the funeral, there had been no embalming done. There is suspicion that no credible autopsy was performed. From studying reports of other questionable deaths involving famous entertainers in the South, I learned that private autopsies performed by partisan coroners were not uncommon, the most celebrated case being the death of Jerry Lee Lewis' fifth wife, Shawn Michelle, scrupulously chronicled by Richard Ben Cramer in a 1984 article in *Rolling Stone*. A Pulitzer Prize winning author, Cramer had cut his teeth in the newspaper business covering the Middle East conflict, but was not prepared for what he learned in the South. "All of a sudden I was in Hernando, Mississippi," he wrote, "where no restaurant order was complete until the waitress asked, 'You wan' gravy?' Where the leading candidate for sheriff was known as Big Dog Riley. Where Jerry Lee Lewis was a legend, and a power, not to mention the spendingest man in the county, which spending had bought for almost a decade, the quiet cooperation of local authorities, who would perform all kinds of 'community service,' like towing the Killer's car out of a ditch without checking his blood for alcohol, or bargaining his drug charge down to a simple fine, or shipping off the bruised body of his dead fifth wife for a private autopsy, with no coroner's jury and little public inquiry into the cause of her death." Cramer got his story — and got out of town alive — but not before Lewis' manager, J.W. Whitten, offered this parting shot: "Listen, they'll never bust him in DeSoto County, it would be like bustin' Elvis in Memphis." Neither J.W. Whitten nor Jerry Lee Lewis were amused by what they read in *Rolling Stone* in the 10-page feature entitled "The Mysterious Death of Mrs. Jerry Lee Lewis," but they were not unduly concerned either. Their letter to the magazine stated that Jerry Lee "was just surprised . . . that *Rolling Stone* would run that kind of thing on us."

Such suspicions had not been raised at the time of Hank's death by any of the Class of '55 or any of those who came after them. But Hank's death was felt by all of them, and by all of those close to Hank, no matter who might be guilty or not guilty of negligence or even foul play. His troubled spirit may have even become angered by the plethora of do-gooders who attended his funeral, the same bunch who had recently treated him badly in Nashville. Ole Hank's spirit may have been agitated by Roy Acuff who sang *I Saw The Light* over his coffin or Red Foley who sang *Peace In The Valley*. Surely these worthy gentlemen were there to pay their respects, not to serve more devious purposes. Hank made a better dead legend than a live drunk who had recently been thrown off the Opry, fired from the WSM radio because he'd missed too many shows, forgetting his words in concerts, and, once up in Canada, falling right off the stage during one performance. Fell so hard that he'd re-injured his back and begun to take heavy duty painkillers. Fell again and cracked his skull. There weren't too many good old boys to be found anywhere in the South who wanted further investigation. The Nashville notables who came to weep and sing over Hank Williams coffin in Montgomery were some of the same senior Opry members who earlier had decided to fire the misfit.

In the years following the tragedy, the official Nashville line was that 'ole Hank never took no drugs, no time'. Rather, he drank himself into an early grave, which these self-righteous types somehow saw as more fitting than the truth. They would later rewrite history and deny they had "fired" Hank, preferring to say it wasn't that they fired him — they couldn't find him. The truth of the matter is that Hank had so much pain from his deteriorating condition of Spina bifida that his drug use was necessary, not a recreational option. His spinal chord was herniating though the discs in his spine, a defect he had suffered from since he was born, aggravated by several spectacular tumbles. His physical condition due to the pain that he constantly experienced was very poor. He was skin and bones thin, and whiskey was often his only nourishment. If he had not planned to come off the road and rehabilitate himself for a lengthy period of time, his continued existence was already a huge question mark — regardless of the drugs, booze, and suspicious behavior that night. Billie Jean says that he intended to do just that, to quit touring and get his health back. He had but one or two more contractual obligations to fulfill.

After the death of Hank and the battles with his mother and Audrey, Billie Jean received pretty poor treatment from the folks in Nashville, and for a while after Johnny Horton died, she had been branded as some kind of "black widow" pariah by the people who hoarded Hank's estate monies. Some of these people really did reduce love to dollars and cents when an obituary became an opportunity for lawyers to fill their pockets during the many post-mortem lawsuits. When Billie Jean's own father died in a motor vehicle accident, she withdrew to live a solitary life within her house where she was tracked down by Nancy Jones and Tom Carter.

Hank Williams' troubled spirit did not go straight to Heaven, of that I am convinced. Ole Hank was tied to all of this earthly bullshit just as he had been tied to some deeper tragedy in his own past that no one ever knew the sense of. Not either of his wives. Perhaps not even his own mother. And certainly not any of the millions of fans who had been so drawn to his mystique, his charm, his overpowering sex-appeal, his amazingly graceful and gifted way of singing.

Before he died, Williams penned two final prophetic songs: *I'll Never Get Out Of This World Alive* and *A Picture From Life's Other Side*. In 1989, George Jones recorded a gospel-style recitation of "From Life's Other Side."

> Now the last scene is that by the river
> Of a heartbroken mother and babe
> As the harbor lights shine and they shiver
> On an outcast whom no one will save.
> And yet she was once a true woman;
> She was somebody's darling and pride.
> God helps her, she leaps, but there's no one to weep,
> It's just a picture from life's other side.

A *Picture From Life's Other Side* (Hank Williams)

⟶⟶6⟵⟵
Phantoms of the Opry

Johnny Horton was not the only country singer of his era to die on the road like Hank under mysterious circumstances. And he was not the only country singer to explore "life's other side." For a while following Hank Williams' death, these tragedies happened with alarming frequency. During the 1950s, '60s, and '70s, some people came to believe that country music itself was cursed. Many country performers began looking for answers in the occult realm.

Carl Perkins was on a roll in 1956 when Sun Records put out a song he called *Blue Suede Shoes*, written on the inspiration he'd been handed when Johnny Cash told him a story of a time when he had been an enlisted man and someone had used the phrase, "Don't step on my blue suede shoes." Perkins sat right down and wrote the tune. Later on, Carl came up with the hook for the song when he was playing a club in Jackson, Tennessee, and overheard a man say to his date, "Uh-uh, don't step on my blue suede shoes." He finished the song at home that night when he got the idea to take a children's verse, "One for the money, two for the show, three to get ready . . ." as the kickoff line. Later, he would call his autobiography *Go, Cat Go*.

Although first recorded by Carl, *Blue Suede Shoes* became a hit for Elvis Presley, his label-mate at Sun Records. The song was the perfect vehicle for Elvis who exuded attitude like no other Sun Records artist did. But it took fate intervening in the form of a tragic car accident before Presley would record the song and eclipse Perkins' own record on the charts. On March 22, 1956, Carl Perkins and his family band were headed for New York City to appear on the *Perry Como Show* when their car crashed. Alcohol was not involved in the Perkins' accident; fatigue was the factor when the driver of that car fell asleep at the wheel and was killed instantly upon impact with a parked vehicle. In *Nashville Babylon*, Randall Riese offers this vivid description of the accident: "At 6:40 a.m. four miles outside of Dover, Delaware, the limousine driven by Carl's manager, David Stewart, 30, smashed into a stalled pickup truck, pulverizing it into scraps of so much metal and burning flesh. The driver of the pickup, Tom Phillips, 44, was killed. Upon impact, the limo went out of control, hit a guard-rail, and careened down an embankment. Carl's brother, Jay, 25, broke his neck. Carl, submerged in a sewer of water and mud, was discovered only when one of the survivors accidentally stumbled over him. He went into the hospital unconscious, with a fractured skull, fractured vertebrae, and multiple other injuries." After a nine-month hospitalization, Carl Perkins healed and survived, but Jay B. Perkins died two years later from brain damage due to injuries he had sustained at the time of the accident. Carl was at his dying brother's side and Jay B.'s death began a cycle of boozing that Carl did not pick himself up from until the early 1970s.

At the time Carl was sittin' on top of the world with his first number one hit, but now he wasn't available to tour the hit. Elvis covered the song and, a few months later, performed it on *The Jackie Gleason Show*, and both the song and the attitude it provided the person who performed it became identified with Elvis. It was one of 11 gold singles on the pop charts for Presley in 1956. The fact that Cash had recollected the serviceman story while he and Perkins were backstage watching Elvis perform, and that Perkins had written the original idea out on a brown paper bag before that performance ended, was part of the synchronicity the Sun singers all felt at that time.

When Steve Sholes, the RCA exec who had signed Elvis, heard Carl Perkins' record, he thought he'd signed the wrong artist. Of course, Colonel Tom knew better, and when Perkins was out of the picture in the hospital, it was these two men who leapt at the opportunity to have Elvis record the song. All in all, spring-boarding Elvis onto the international scene as a superstar was a group effort. The music was a shared common wealth, and they must have felt subconsciously that if they followed the music, it would take them places they had never been. The singers often fed off each other's energy and often helped each other out. One time Cash was recording at the Sun studio and Elvis sat in to play *Blueberry Hill* on the piano. After a while, they got into singing some gospel songs together and were soon joined by Perkins and Jerry Lee, who they were meeting for the first time. Jack Clement began running a tape during this jam session; years later, this remarkable moment in history was released as a record album by the "Million Dollar Quartet." On a Canadian tour it was Carl Perkins who suggested that Jerry Lee should stand up at the piano during his finale. Ralph Emery relates that when Jerry Lee tried that out, he "accidentally knocked over the piano stool. 'Well, that made him mad,' said Carl, 'and he kicked it. And when he swung around to finish the piece, part of his hair fell in

PHANTOMS OF THE OPRY

his face. The crowd went wild and gave him two encores.' " It was the finishing touch on a stage act that put the Killer over the top.

Tragic injury and early death were certainly there to be had when you lived life in the fast lane, there for some singers even if they merely made the mistake of getting on a small plane to avoid the bouncing, bumping boredom of the band bus. On February 3, 1959, a light plane crash took the lives of Buddy Holly, Richie Valens, and J.P. Richardson. Years later, in his autobiography, Waylon Jennings, who had given up his seat on that airplane to J.P. Richardson, would reveal that he had felt a whole lot of guilt along with his grief for many years until he finally forgave himself for still being alive. Four years later, a similar accident swept away Patsy Cline, her manager Randy Hughes, Cowboy Copas, and Hawkshaw Hawkins. A few days later, on his way to Patsy Cline's funeral, Jack Anglin, Johnny Wright's singing partner, was killed in an automobile accident. Cline had survived an automobile accident herself, a head-on collision in 1961 that had claimed another's life. Shortly after Patsy's death, Texas Ruby perished in a fire that ravished her house trailer.

Then in 1964 Jim Reeves and his piano player Dean Manuel were victims of another light plane accident. Ironically, Reeves' career had begun one night in 1952 when he'd been a last minute replacement for a no show Hank Williams on the *Louisiana Hayride*. If Ole Hank hadn't have been out swarming, Reeves, a local disc jockey and amateur singer, would not have been discovered by a record label scout seated in the Hayride audience that night and likely not have gone on to record more than 40 Top 10 hits, including his signature tune *He'll Have To Go*. By 1964 he had ascended to the throne that had been left vacant when Hank passed over to the other side. Gentleman Jim Reeves was at the controls of his single engine plane that rainy afternoon in July 1964, but failed to negotiate his final approach to Beery Field near Nashville. Marty Robbins heard the crash and took part in the search for survivors; however, none were discovered among the wreckage. Ira Louvin was the last to die in an automobile accident during this period of time. Two weeks after Louvin's fatal accident, Roy Acuff was critically but not fatally injured when he and two members of his Smoky Mountain Boys band were smashed up in a road accident near Sparta, Tennessee.

While some fellow performers were haunted by the ghosts of these stars, others found comfort in their angelic presence. Loretta Lynn still believes that Patsy Cline watches over her, a belief that began while Patsy was still alive and took Loretta along to a meeting of busy-body interfering people who were getting together to form a strategy to shut Loretta out of the star system in Nashville. After Patsy's tragic death, Loretta became convinced that Patsy still present in her life. Loretta made no secret of her own seances, and during a songwriting session with duet partner Conway Twitty, he asked her to take him along sometime when she was "getting in touch." Not one to put off until tomorrow what could be done today, Loretta sat Conway down right then and there. He and another man both heard the unmistakably loud knocking that answered Loretta's request that if there were any spirits there in the room with them to knock in acknowledgment. For Loretta all this was doubly eerie because she'd been set up to be paired with both Horton and Reeves before their deaths. Later, she would attribute Patsy's presence for saving her life when she and her husband Doolittle were in a canoe on a rugged stretch of the Buffalo River and their vessel was capsized by unexpectedly rough rapids.

The loss of all of these beloved performers was felt personally by everyone in the country music family. George Jones knew them all. In fact, George was one of the last people to speak to Patsy Cline after the benefit show for deejay Cactus Jack Call in Kansas City. "I remember us working together," he told the producers of *The Real Patsy Cline*, a feature-length video. "I just fell in love with her singing, like everybody did. We were all kind of built up, real high, in our heads that night. As usual, she did a great show, just tore the people up." Her death along with the other passengers seemed even more tragic because Patsy Cline was sitting on the top of the world at that moment in time, a newly crowned Queen of Country, and riding into the Top 10 with her latest Decca release, *Leaving On Your Mind*.

Studio musician Don Helms later suggested that Patsy and Hank Williams were similar in more ways than merely having died before their time: "When I was working with Hank Williams, it seemed like everybody would just stand back and watch Hank with awe. They did the same thing with Patsy Cline. When she sang, all the other girl singers would gather around and watch her. I would say that she and Hank had a lot in common."

When Elvis died, similar weird phenomenon began to happen, only now it was the King who was 'trying to get in touch'. One of the best examples of this was the time when Carl Perkins went into the studio with Elvis's producer, Felton Jarvis, to record *Mama*, a song that he'd written for Elvis just before Presley died. They cut that song but never could figure out where a certain intro chord came from. None of the session players had played it. It was an open G on an acoustic guitar, the kind of chord that Elvis used all the time, but Elvis was gone. They tried isolating the separate tracks and listening to see who had played the chord, but it wasn't there on the tracks. When they turned on the whole mix, there it was, back again. It was, truly, a ghost track. Elvis had liked *Mama* when Felton Jarvis played Perkins' demo of it for Elvis mere weeks before he died. The King is gone but he still manages to influence us, now and then, especially those who were close to him like Carl Perkins and Felton Jarvis and the session players Jarvis called that day for that *Mama* song, most of whom had played with Elvis themselves on more than one occasion.

For hard core materialists, who do not buy into this proposition, there are hundreds of Elvis impersonators who collectively keep the King's memory alive. They also help add fuel to rumors of Elvis showing up, now and then, in laundromats and other exotic locations — rumors that Elvis is not dead. Presley had his own weird liaisons with men like Howard Hughes whose life near the end became spookier than any ghost story ever written. The two men would speak on the phone, sharing secrets that only they could, sequestered away in the penthouses of Las Vegas hotels far from the rest of humanity.

Echoey soaked-in-reverb versions of Presley's hits sung by Elvis impersonators permeate the soundtrack of the feature film *Honeymoon In Vegas*, haunting a distraught Nicolas Cage who has bet his fiance and lost her in a poker game to a smooth operator played by James Caan. At the end of the film, Cage parachutes to her rescue along with the "Flying Elvises."

The country music curse and these various hauntings preoccupied several of the leading stars in the business. A principal practitioner of the seances, consultations, and hypnotism sessions was Merle Kilgore, a singer and songwriter who had followed ole Hank around as a sort of unofficial roadie, carrying his guitars and drinking in the ambience, before playing with Johnny Cash and eventually Hank Jr., who, like George Jones, sometimes became suicidal when he communed with Hank Sr.'s spirit. As Hank Jr. once told Alanna Nash, "I used to cry all the time. But takin' a bottle of Darvon and tryin' to kill yourself and gettin' pump out is not fun . . . Back then, there's no doubt that I was haunted by Daddy . . . I'd sit in front of a record player, play Daddy's records, get the biggest bottle of Jim Beam I could find, and try to communicate with him . . . like about my divorce, I'd say, 'Why do we have to go through this Daddy? Why is it?" Marijohn Wilkins, a publisher and songwriter who penned such spine-tingling lyrics as *Long Black Veil*, a Top 10 hit in 1959 for Lefty Frizzell, and *Waterloo*, a career-making number one smash for Stonewall Jackson that same year, was another well-known Nashville medium.

Johnny Cash had dabbled in spiritualism early in his career and often wrestled with ghosts like the "White Witch of Rose Hall" he encountered in 1971 living next to his newly-purchased villa in Jamaica, but none of these supernatural events was as meaningful as the death of his Tennessee Three band-mate Luther Perkins. Cash had lived through a terrifying series of fires that inspired *Ring Of Fire*, a song written by his soon-to-be wife June Carter and Merle Kilgore. The disasters began soon after Cash and his first wife moved to California and the singer suffered first degree burns to his face when a propane truck traveling in front of his convertible exploded. Soon after that, when he was clearing land, his tractor unearthed a nest of rattlesnakes and Cash set that fire himself, lighting the brush ablaze to kill the snakes which ran out of control and nearly burned down his home. Another propane accident, this time from a camper stove on a fishing trip, burned more than 500 acres of brush before the hundreds of firefighters summoned to the scene were able to put it out. Cash sustained burns to his own hands from his early efforts to put out the flames and was sued for more than $100,000 damages by the California state authorities. But the death of Luther Perkins during a fire that started when Perkins fell asleep with a lit cigarette in his hand led to Cash's rehabilitation from a life of self-abuse and to a rediscovered faith in God that also discouraged further hypnotic regression sessions with Merle Kilgore. Cash's mother has been quoted as speculating that if God had been inspired to reach into this world and help her son become a famous entertainer, then some other presences might be able to reach in and oppose the original gift of intervention just to mess things up.

While not every famous performer took as many astral jaunts as Cash, who regularly experimented with the 'other side' while touring with Merle Kilgore in the early 1960s, many did. "Only a few years ago," Cliff Lindecker wrote in his 1979 book *Country Music Stars and the Supernatural*, "such songwriters and stars as Faron Young, Webb Pierce, Bonnie Guitar, Roger Miller, Harlan Howard, and John D. Loudermilk were regularly journeying to Marijohn's rustic farm ten miles out of Nashville to attend seances." Harlan Howard, the dean of Nashville songwriters and the author of such memorable ditties as *Mommy For A Day* and *Pick Me Up On Your Way Down*, was bent on finding out if spirits really existed. "Not only did he prove to himself that there were such things," Linedecker writes, "he also concluded that it is dangerous and wrong to communicate with them." Howard himself said, "As human beings, we're not capable of handling the truth about the universe. If we really knew the truth of the universe, we might go instantly insane. Human beings just aren't equipped to handle the truth."

Harlan offers one explanation for the curiosity that thrived in Nashville for the occult. "Creative people seem to have more interest in the supernatural than the average person," he told Linedecker. "Maybe it's because our minds are more open, or more questioning." Despite his reluctance to pursue these matters, Harlan confided, "I'm not a psychic person at all, but even I was aware beyond a shadow of a doubt that there are spirits. They're out there, and they're around us. There is a spirit world, which means there is life after death. And that means there is a creator of the universe."

While George Jones was not as adventuresome as Harlan Howard when it came to formal rituals like seances, he held his own meetings with the spirit beings who were both "out there" and "all around us." George viewed them through his experiential world as devils or angels. He has said that he was victimized by demons of his own making. A devil lived inside him, Nancy Sepulvado told him when they met. Up until he met Nancy, his method of dealing with his demons had been to mask them temporarily with booze. While he didn't seem to be intrigued by all the phantoms of the Opry, Hank's ghost wouldn't leave him alone. "He drove me crazy," George once told a reporter. As he tried to fill Hank's shoes, that specter would drive him even crazier during the 1960s and '70s as George came to know the hurt of loving and losing Tammy Wynette.

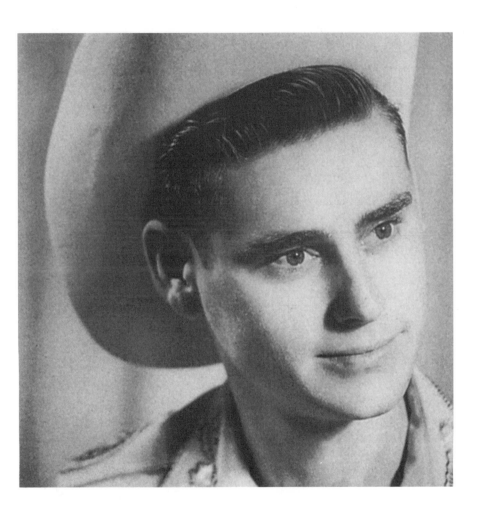

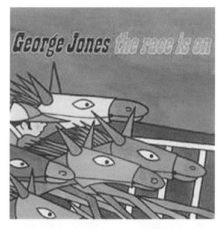

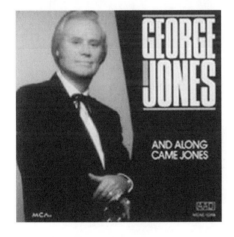

Part Three

If Drinkin' Don't Kill Me Kill Me (Her Memory Will)

White Lightning

eorge Jones was not the first artist approached by Mercury Records in
1958 to record *White Lightning*, a song written by J.P. Richardson, The
Big Bopper. At the time, Sonny Burns was the artist of choice at
Mercury. George and Sonny had done some duets together, and Burns was the
singer Pappy Daily originally had in mind to sing duet with Jones on *Why Baby
Why* for Starday back in 1955, but when Sonny hadn't shown up for that
recording session, George got the nod to record his own song solo which he
overdubbed with his own harmony vocal. In 1958, Burns turned down what
were figured to be the top songs available at Mercury, and Pappy Daily then
offered these tunes to George, including *White Lightning*. Right away, George
said he wanted to record that one. This decision and the hit record that followed led Pappy Daily and Gabe Tucker to regard Jones with more respect.
"George Jones," as Gabe put it, "could smell a hit plumb across town!" *White
Lightning* became George Jones' first number one hit.

Buddy Killen, the bass player scheduled to back Hank Williams on the
'show he never gave' that fateful January 1, 1953, in Canton, Ohio, was hired
to lead the session for *White Lightning* at Owen Bradley's Quonset Hut studio in
Nashville. George was once again connected with the career of his deceased
idol. In his autobiography, *Flying by the Seat of My Pants* (written with Tom
Carter), Buddy offers further insight into George Jones' early Nashville recording sessions. "I was hired to play bass on these sessions and occasionally played
on the road with him as well. For a number of years, I gained valuable studio
experience acting as the leader of those sessions. To a great degree, I served the
role of producer, although his official producer was Pappy Daily. On occasion,
when Pappy couldn't make it up to Nashville, he would have me produce the
records for him."

Put in charge of producing the session by Daily, Killen, a bass player, decided, not surprisingly, to use a bass intro, but that decision backfired on Buddy

because it took George Jones quite a few takes to get the song down on tape the way Killen wanted it. As Killen recalls, "I arranged the song and came up with an unusual kick-off that I played by double slapping the strings of my upright bass. I had Hargus 'Pig' Robbins playing straight-eighths on the piano. I gave Floyd Robinson, who was playing guitar and singing harmony, a counter melody to add on the guitar. . . . I don't recall exactly how many takes of the song we recorded that day, but George tells me it was 84. I only remember that, even though my fore and middle fingers were heavily callused from years of playing, blisters still formed. During take after take, I continued the rapid action, tearing the blistered skin from my fingers. I wrapped them with adhesive tape, and, before too long, the incessant playing even wore through the tape. It was an uncommonly long session, but finally we got a great take." Prolonging the session was the fact that Jones kept slurring his words. And every time he had a nip from his flask, things got worse. On the final recording, though, there is just one slur on the word "slug," and if you listen intently, you can hear it there. Of course, fans thought it was part of the act. And it merely made the song more believable. In a studio today that colorful detail would be digitally edited from the mix; in 1958 musicians had to learn to live with what went down without any after-the-fact airbrushing.

> Well, in North Carolina 'way back in the hills
> Lived my old pappy and he had him a still
> He brewed white lightnin' till the sun went down
> Then he filled him a jug and he'd pass it around
> Mighty, mighty pleasin', pappy's corn squeasin'
> Phew, white lightnin'
>
> — White Lightning (J.P. Richardson)

By the time of this recording, Buddy Killen had already founded Tree Publishing, a decision that would later make him a multi-millionaire when he sold that company to the Japanese investors that were buying up as many Nashville interests as they could lay their hands on in the late 1980s and early 1990s, a corporate climate that explains much of what is wrong with Nashville today. Buddy was a smart businessman, but what he did was sell the songs that the songwriters had spent their collective lifetime supply of creative energy writing — to a foreign company, a company that owed its allegiance to a foreign power that could one day, again, even be at war with the United States. This is not likely to come about, but it had happened in the past, and country singers and songwriters remember that war. When questioned about the loss of American control of the country music business by Jennifer Ember Pierce in *Breakin' Into Nashville*, Buddy noted that "Warner Brothers and Mike Curb" are the only large American firms left on Music Row. "When I sold Tree International, I sold it to the Japanese because they offered me about twice the amount that anybody in America would give me. . . . The bottom line is money. I worked for many years to build the company, why would I be stupid enough to give it away? I wasn't pleased that I would sell it to someone outside this country, but why would I want to give it away? That wouldn't have been good business. I've always been bothered that more American business people, especially here in Nashville, don't get involved in the music business." Buddy Killen wasn't the only person who made the "good business decision" and sold to foreign investors, but he is one of the few willing to even discuss the subject.

As the years passed and corporate music publishers bought up all of the songs they could lay their hands on, the independent publishing companies run by colorful individuals like Buddy Killen no longer controlled very many of the copyrights. This shift in ownership changed country music forever. Changed the creative emphasis from looking for a great song to recording anything that would make money. Anything, regardless of long-established traditions and allegiances. Motives that had at one time to do with entertaining the fans gave way to exploiting them. Fans became consumers to be tabulated in surveys. Statistics. Numbers on test-marketing analysis sheets. By the 1990s, critics were saying that new country stars all came from the same cookie-cutter mold shaped at corporate strategy meetings. George Jones and the Class of '55 didn't fit this mold.

White Lightning had been written by J.P. Richardson, the Big Bopper, a Beaumont deejay and singer who hit big with *Chantilly Lace* on the pop charts, the flip side of his "D" Records release *The Purple People Eater Meets The Witch Doctor*. A little known fact about these two artists is that Richardson penned Johnny Preston's 1959 number one hit, *Running Bear*, and together Richardson and Jones contributed the background vocals. According to the Virgin *Encyclopedia of Country Music*, they laid down the harmonies and oom-pah-pah background chants for Preston's record mere months before the Big Bopper took that fateful plane ride with Richie Valens and Buddy Holly. Jones would record *Running Bear* himself in years to come but would not release it as a single.

Other novelty tunes were huge at that time with Sheb Wooley's *Purple*

People Eater, David Seville's *Witch Doctor,* Betty Johnson's *Little Blue Man,* and Brian Hyland's *Itsy Bitsy Teenie Weenie Yellow Polkadot Bikini* often becoming gold records for relatively unknown artists. With the immediate success of *White Lightning,* Pappy Daily knew he was on a roll with novelty songs. He'd support-ed the Big Bopper and put out *Chantilly Lace* on his own indie label, Big "D" Records, before shopping the cut to Mercury when it hit big on the charts. With J.P. Richardson suddenly and tragically removed from the scene in February 1959, Pappy had to turn elsewhere for more novelty numbers for George Jones. It was George himself, along with Darrell Edwards, who came up with *Who Shot Sam,* which peaked at number 7 on the *Billboard* C&W chart. These records had an irresistible rockabilly boogie feel, but as long as no one reminded George that he was rocking, he was okay performing them.

Pappy next had George record *Money To Burn.* For a publicity stunt, Daily would burn fake dollar bills during a press conference in Nashville. This zany side of things provided his singer with an identity. To Daily *The Race Is On* was just more of the same. Pappy had that P.T. Barnum instinct Colonel Tom Parker knew so well. Parker had the handsomest singer on the planet to promote, but he would make sure that Elvis would be mobbed everywhere he went by inform-ing local radio stations that a "mob" of teenage girls were already there at the scene. Pappy didn't have the same resources but he knew that country fans were willing to pay good money to visit the sideshow tents and view the freakier side of life. Hence, *Love Bug,* the Curtis Wayne-Wayne Kemp novelty tune in 1965, which owed quite a bit of its appeal to Buck Owens' *I've Got A Tiger By The Tail* and Roger Miller's *Dang Me.* Of course, Jones had been an influence on both Owens and Miller, so it was payback time. Dallas Frazier created *I'm A People* for George Jones, and in return for the favor George recorded a whole album of Frazier's material, covering Frazier's previous hits like *Mohair Sam* or *Alley Oop* for his single releases.

For George Jones, though, *White Lightning* was more than a novelty tune — it was a chapter from the book of his life, recounting the 'big hurt' his family and the South had endured over the past 100 years. In 1976, George told *Country Song Roundup* writer Rick Bolsom, "It took us years to live down the word 'hillbillies'. We haven't really lived it down. I really get stirred up and mad about it when somebody calls me a hillbilly now. Not because I get mad about the word, it's the idea that takes shape in their mind when they use it.... A lot of your sophisticated people that don't like country music, they look down on us as peasants."

In this context, *White Lightning* reads like a New World peasants' revolt or the revenge of the Southern hillbillies on Yankee revenuers. Thus, while some radio listeners heard *White Lightning* as a "novelty" song, others heard the deeply-rooted truth of the lyrics. George Jones didn't write *White Lightning*, but when George sang the lyrics in the studio, he was drinking as he sang, and the words ring true down through the decades. There is a defiance in Jones' delivery. George knew full-well the injustice of the situation and he responded emotionally:

> *Well a g-man, t-man, revenuers, too*
> *Searchin' for the place where he made his booze*
> *They were lookin' tryin' to book him*
> *But my pappy kept on cookin'*
> *Phew, white lightnin'*

The strength and purity of the freshly distilled whiskey becomes a metaphor in these lyrics for the strength of the mountainfolk and the purity of their intentions, their hearts and souls.

> *Well, I asked my old pappy why he called his brew*
> *White lightnin' instead of mountain dew*
> *I took a little sip and right away I knew*
> *As my eyes bugged out and my face turned blue*
> *Mighty, mighty pleasin', my pappy's corn squeasin'*
> *Phew, White Lightnin'*

Drinking this untaxed elixir "way back in the hills" where it was distilled represented a rebellion against the injustices that were enforced, now, in the 20th century, not by a red-coated British officer or a Yankee carpetbagger, but by men in suits from the cities. The whiskey was so strong that it made you cry out a rebel yell. Johnny Horton tapped the same well of emotion with his 1959 number one *The Battle Of New Orleans*, followed by *Johnny Reb*, though Horton had first expressed this defiance in in 1956 with *Honky Tonk Man*.

George Jones *was* a honky tonk man and *White Lightning* was the song that put him over the top, the song that made it easier for Pappy Daily to get him booked on Opry tours with Patsy Cline, Johnny Cash, and Ernest Tubb. George lived the life 24-hours-a-day. He didn't play the role of honky tonk man as if he were merely buttoning up a rhinestone suit. Hard-drinking had become identified with rebellion, with being a man who made his own way in life, rather than someone who stayed at home, had a wife, raised kids, went to work on Monday mornings to open a shop, punch a time clock in a factory, or slave over columns of figures counting other people's money. When a country star stepped off the stage, he usually already had hundreds of dollars of cash in his pockets because he sure as hell wasn't going to take a check and he sure as hell wasn't going to go on before he was paid. Those dollars were sure to burn a hole in his pocket if he didn't spend some of them right away. And when he drove off into the distance in a big old Cadillac or a beat-up Greyhound bus, he was a rambling, gambling, traveling man living out the legend that ole Hank had begun.

The promoters, managers, agents and other music business types Jones met along the way were often bullies, liars, and cheats. Sometimes, he would be late going on simply because he was holding out until he was paid. Veteran country singers knew better than to go on before that. When you came off the stage to pack your guitar into its case, the promoter could well be long gone — leaving his lackeys hanging around to concoct stories of woe. It wasn't just the g-men and the t-men and the revenuers that made life miserable for folks. Promoters could be pretty nasty characters, too. All of this resentment toward those in authority comes out in *White Lightning*, directed at the suits who represented the taxation system.

Well a cityslicker came and he said I'm tough
I think I want to taste that powerful stuff
He took one slug and drank it down
And I heard him a-moanin' as he hit the ground
Mighty, mighty pleasin', pappy's corn squeasin'
Phew, White Lightnin'

Real country men could hold their *White Lightning*, cityslickers couldn't, a myth perhaps, but one that has become an article of faith in country music. For quite a few years, until his periodic bingeing went completely out of control, George was a drinker who could hold his own with any man in any drinking contest. It would take a further trauma, a severe blow to the heart, before he would merely become a drunk. In the late 1960s when he met a girl singer named Virginia Wynette Pugh Byrd Chapel, he had just about faced up to the fact that his own marriage to Shirley Corley Jones was on the rocks. But for the singer of *She Thinks I Still Care*, breaking up was just as hard to do as for most people who didn't sing country music at all.

2
The Race Is On

During the Mercury years the relationship between Pappy Daily and George Jones worked fairly well. Pappy had a sense of what his singer could do; George had a sense of what he would and wouldn't do. Both Daily and Jones would follow Art Talmadge when he moved to United Artists in 1962 and then to Musicor a few years later.

George Jones' second Mercury release was *Too Much Water*, a song that he had written with Sonny James. In 1958, George hit into the Top 10 with *Color Of The Blues*, a whiskey-soaked vocal outing that was as much his own as anybody else's. He had adapted Roy Acuff's phrasing and his gut-wrenching approach to ballads. And he'd absorbed a lot of what Lefty Frizzell and Hank Williams did best. This influence showed especially on up-tempo tracks like *White Lightning*, but by the late 1950s, George had synthesized all of his heroes into his own distinctive style.

The 1960s would be good years for George Jones. While Ray Price, who had recorded the ultimate honky tonk song in Harlan Howard's *Heartaches By The Number* in 1959, would succumb to the temptations offered by the smooth urbanity of the Nashville Sound of the 1960s, Jones would keep his edge. Somewhat smoother on numbers like his own composition *The Window Up Above* and Darrell Edwards' *Tender Years*, he was not saccharin. He continued to record with a fiddle and steel in the band, and his vocal style remained unique. He was known as a honky tonk singer, a rough and ready character, but he had a tender side in him, as well, a vocal style John Morthland describes in *The Best of Country Music: A Critical and Historical Guide to the 750 Greatest Albums*. "His biggest trick was to drop from his normal tenor into a bass register when he wanted to admonish or tease, as on *Uh, Uh, No*. On *One Is A Lonely Number*, his voice pines like the Hawaiian-based steel licks, and there seems to be a frustrated sigh at the end of each line. The rise and fall of his voice on *Don't Do This To Me* echoes the waltz meter. On *Color Of The Blues*, his voice is deeper, more resonant, and he's breaking it (as on the word "blues" in the title phrase) with new sureness. On *What Am I Worth* he injects a glimmer of hope into a most pessimistic song. His brand of honky tonk heartbreak rang true at a time when the rest of country music had gone limp. Most important, it was during this period that Jones truly freed himself from most of the conventions of the honky tonk genre and originated the intensely personal style he's been refining ever since." For George's authorized video biography, Emmylou Harris put it this way: "He has a remarkable voice that flows out of him effortlessly and quietly, but with an edge that comes from the stormy part of the heart. In the South, we call it high lonesome. I think it's popularly called, Soul."

With *Tender Years* in 1961 and *She Thinks I Still Care* the following year, George Jones scored his second and third number one hits. *Cashbox* and *Billboard* were calling him country music's top male vocalist while handing him awards. Jones' ballads, where he called upon everything he'd learned listening to Roy Acuff, Lefty Frizzell, and Hank Williams, distilling their phrasing into incredibly complex swooping vocals that broke apart syllables into more than just the usual you-all dualities, sweeping up to hit high notes and dropping down into surprising baritone-range notes, put his personal imprint on country music. When it came to living the song he was singing and projecting the desolation of the folks he was singing about, there was no one who could equal him.

"If you're gonna sing a sad song, or ballad, you've got to have lived it your-self," George has explained. "You can think back to anything that made you sad — anything. Maybe your little dog died, and you think about that while you're singing, and pretty soon, it makes you sad. You become lost in the song and, before long, you're just like the people in the song."

However you choose to describe George Jones' singing style, all of the above would be abundantly clear on the remarkable *She Thinks I Still Care*, George's first release for United Artists in April 1962, which held the number one spot on the survey for six weeks. It had been nearly a full decade since Pappy Daily first told him that he'd have to stop singing like Hank Williams and Lefty Frizzell and sing like George Jones; in 1962, people recognized the Possum when they heard him on the radio. His voice had become as familiar as Hank's to country fans from coast to coast.

Cowboy Jack Clement first thought *She Thinks I Still Care* had potential as a George Jones' cut. Clement had been a recording engineer at Sun Records studio in Memphis during the glory days where he had also produced records for Jerry Lee Lewis and Johnny Cash. He had written *Guess Things Happen That*

Way and *Ballad Of A Teenage Queen* for Cash. And Jack would return to Tennessee in the late 1960s and 1970s where he formed a publishing company, operated a recording studio, and produced several hit albums for Waylon Jennings. But in the early '60s, Jack was working out of a little studio in Beaumont, where songwriters would demo their material. Nineteen-year-old Dickie Lee Lipscomb brought Clement *She Thinks I Still Care*. Jack thought the song was very nearly a gem; it just needed a minor adjustment in the melody. Rather than playing him the demo, Jack sang it to George Jones the way he *thought* it should be. At first, George wasn't sure he wanted to be singing "Just because . . ." so many times.

> *Just because I asked a friend about her*
> *Just because I spoke her name somewhere*
> *Just because I rang her number by mistake today*
> *She thinks I still care*
>
> *Just because I haunt the same old places*
> *Where the memory of her lingers everywhere*
> *Just because I'm not the happy guy I used to be*
> *She thinks I still care . . .*
>
> *Just because I ask a friend about her*
> *And just because I spoke her name somewhere*
> *Just because I saw her then went all to pieces*
> *She thinks I still care*
> *She thinks I still care. . .*

She Thinks I Still Care (D.L. Lipscomb)

After Jack persisted, George decided he liked it a lot. He was home in Vidor at the time to spend Christmas with his family, and when he returned to Nashville, he told his singing partner, George Riddle, that he had a hit in his pocket. Pappy Daily thought so, too. *She Thinks I Still Care* gained respect for George everywhere he went, especially when he ventured into unfamiliar territory, like the time he appeared on Jimmy Dean's network TV show in New York City, where the producers asked him to perform *She Thinks I Still Care*. George Jones might still be billed as "Mr White Lightning," but the song everyone wanted to hear now was *She Thinks I Still Care*. The song would become Jones' most covered single, and when Anne Murray recorded it as *He Thinks I Still Care* in the 1970s, it again went number one for her.

The record's success also made it possible for George Jones to hire his first band. Jones put George Riddle in charge of the hiring. The initial 'Jones Boys' included Riddle on harmony vocals and rhythm guitar, Billy Wayne on pedal steel, ex-Wanda Jackson band-member Jerry Star on lead guitar, Garry Prawl on bass, and Glen Davis on drums. Hal Rugg replaced Wayne soon afterwards, the first of many personnel changes that would number nearly 200 by the 1990s. The first Jones Boys appeared in a set of band outfits popular in those days, and at first, all six men traveled in one car, though it was not too long after that George Jones bought his first touring bus. It wasn't too luxurious, just a battered, rusted, old hull with bunks that weren't fastened down and folding chairs. But it was a bus, a status symbol for traveling artists in those days, and a whole lot more comfortable.

While on the road, George had already been in one serious car accident, suffering a broken arm, which he re-broke in a tussle with Mel Tillis while it was still in a cast not long after. (Broken bones were something he could get over. He'd been doing it since the day he was born. When he first entered this world, a 12-pound infant emerging from his mother's womb, Jones had slipped through the delivering person's hands, dropped onto the floor, and sustained a broken arm for the first time.) The incident had even been reported in *Billboard* magazine's "Who's Who." In the band bus, there would be more accidents.

One time, George and the Jones Boys were on their way from a show in California to Salem, Oregon when the bus plunged off a mountain highway and skidded down the mountainside. George sustained broken ribs and missed the Salem show as he flew home to Texas to recuperate. Another time a groupie hijacked the bus and took the boys for a wild ride before they could get her reined in. Yet another time, a local fan-club president, who had boarded their bus for only a few minutes after a show, was found brutally murdered later that same night. Even though they had had nothing to do with that foul deed, George and the Jones Boys had to answer a whole lot of questions from the investigating officers. Like many of the scrapes they got themselves into, this one was splashed in newspaper headlines across the country and Jones was indicted by the press. The police later arrested a man in Dallas, who had confessed committing the crime to a friend; he was charged with the woman's murder and convicted. But the damage done to George by the media stuck. He was their bad boy of country.

With George Jones for a husband, Shirley could depend on a cyclone hitting her home whenever he came off the road. Once George hit the Hayride and Opry tour circuits, Shirley seldom saw him. Although he had bought that house in Vidor for her, he was not home much, and even when he came home, he was not always welcomed back with open, loving arms. He could count on facing a different kind of music, so to speak. Some of George's marital problems were of his own making, as he admits in his autobiography, and to give Shirley her due, George was not the understanding, mature person who put that book together in the mid-1990s with Tom Carter, not in 1955, not even in the 1960s. George knew he had to cut loose some or he simply wouldn't make it in the music business. He also fell victim to the temptations that fame brought in the form of young women who literally fell into his arms nearly every night he performed. Looking back on those days, George admits that "I was too often gone, and too often drunk, to fully realize the first signs to my second divorce." Today, that admission sounds like the lyric to a country song. Shirley had to choose between raising her children, who Jones *did* provide for, in a compromised marriage, and the even more unpleasant prospect of life as a single mother. In the 1950s, this was not a route many women chose. Not many men honored their support payments. In those days, George was that kind of guy.

Melba Montgomery was a girl singer who showed up in George Jones' life about this time with a song in her pocket and a healthy sense of self-worth not susceptible to his charms. She was not about to become just another one-night stand. Melba was a straight-shooter, whom Jones quickly came to respect. Together, they made some of the best country duets of all time. The first one they recorded was the song that Montgomery brought to her first meeting with George and Pappy Daily, a song that she called We Must Have Been Out Of Our Minds. After George helped her put the finishing touches to this song, their recording went to number 3 on the *Billboard* Hot 100 and stayed in the Top 40 for 28 weeks. From that encouraging beginning, George and Melba went on to record several more charting singles. In 1964, they followed up their radio success on We Must Have Been Out Of Our Minds with their first two full-length duet LPs: GEORGE JONES AND MELBA MONTGOMERY SINGING WHAT'S IN OUR HEARTS and BLUEGRASS HOOTENANNY. George had found a new outlet for his singing talents, and Melba Montgomery's career had been kick-started in fine fashion. An added plus was that George also met Peanut Montgomery, Melba's brother, who became a friend and a valuable songwriter.

George and Melba survived the rigorous touring schedule they maintained, but she soon found that she was forced to multi-task. In addition to fending off George's suggestions that his marriage was through and that she should marry him, Melba was often the only person around who could coax the reticent singer on stage when he'd flown off the handle over one thing or another and locked himself in his bus or in a washroom somewhere backstage. The Jones Boys took advantage of this. They'd had their fill of George's antics, which included the time he had pulled out his revolver and vented the floor of the band bus with bullet holes that became the only air conditioning they ever got touring with the Possum in those days. This system worked fine when the bus was in motion, but when it was idling, they breathed the choking exhaust fumes that seeped through those same holes. George was really taken with Melba, sometimes embarrassing her by proposing to her onstage. However, she had eyes for Jack Solomon, the lead guitar player in the Jones Boys, and the two were married and still are to this day.

George Jones and Pappy Daily hit the number one spot on the country charts again in 1964 with *The Race Is On,* but the song stalled at number 3 on the *Billboard* pop chart when covered by Jack Jones. Somewhere around this time, George began to feel dissatisfaction with his association with Pappy Daily, especially in the studio where Daily often rushed the players through the sessions and seldom took much care with any one cut. But George stuck with Pappy because the hits kept coming, and when Daily left United Artists to form the Musicor label with Art Talmadge, Jones also made the move. At Musicor, Pappy adopted the assembly-line approach, pumping out 286 George Jones cuts between 1965 and 1971. Thirty-two of these were issued as singles; 24 of those charted in the Top 40. The race was on.

Well, the race is on and here comes pride
Up the back stretch
Heartache's a-goin' to the inside
My tears are holdin' back
They're tryin' not to fall

My love's out of the runnin'
True love's scratched for another call
The race is on and it looks like heartache
And the winner loses all

The Race Is On (Don Rollins)

With the release of *The Race Is On* in 1964, George had his signature tune, a sure-fire show opener energized by the echoey twang of the six-string bass guitar solo, which had been created in the studio for the hit record by session guitarist Kelso Herston, and was duplicated nightly by the Jones' Boys road guitarist. The song is an up-tempo romp, and Jones just beams as he delivers the lines. For most of those mid-60s years, George bounded along with carefree abandon. His pranks often kept his tour-mates from dying of boredom out on the road. He was adored by his fans and cherished by his peers for his camaraderie.

Melba Montgomery told Dolly Carlisle just how special that camaraderie was in those days. "Most of the country artists were, like George, financially naive and professionally unworldly. It was a much slower pace then. Everybody was real friendly. A lot of times five or six different artists would be on the same show, and everybody'd stay at the same hotel or motel. Everybody would eat breakfast together. Then, they'd usually line up and follow each other going to the next show. That don't happen anymore. Now, it's very impersonal. . . . Back then George would come out in the middle of Buck Owens' show and do something, or one of them would come out in the middle of George's. It was just everybody having a good time and enjoying themselves. It really was a fun thing back then."

For a while during the early 1960s, George Jones and Buck Owens toured together on a regular basis. Buck often hogged the spotlight for himself and regularly closed their shows. One night, George pulled a prank that Buck would never forget. At the time, he was not amused, but over the years he has come to see the humor in it. As Buck recounts in *Same Ole Me*, "George and I heated up pretty good. And we toured a lot together. I remember this one time in Regina, Saskatchewan, there was just the two of us. We was always arguing who was going to open the show and who was going to close it." As Loretta Lynn adds, George would say, " 'You go on last every night. Why can't I go and be the star tonight? Why can't I be on last?' And Buck would say, 'No George, you gotta go on first again tonight.' " George himself remembers that when he had figured out what he was going to do to turn the tables, he said to Buck, "Okay, you come to the curtain and watch my show tonight, Buck. When I get through out there, you ain't a-even-goin' to want to go out there." Loretta nearly falls to pieces when she says, "George got drunk, and walked out on the stage, and done Buck's show!" She gets really tickled about this part. Jones pronounces proudly, "I didn't sing *one* of my songs. I did his *whole* show." Buck remembers this with a chuckle, "George came off the stage and he looked over at me and he said, 'Your turn . . .' "

George would up-stage Buck again in 1964 when they played the first ever country show staged at New York City's Madison Square Garden. Some of the reviews that appeared in articles printed in the *New York Times* and both *Time* and *Life* magazines would stir some resentment in George, but he could live with the description of the country music jamboree that he and nine other artists gave as a "circus" simply because any praise at all in those prestigious New York print media outlets meant so much for the future of country music. In the mid-1960s country music was hugely popular in regional areas serviced by some 250 or so low-power AM stations, though there were a few high-power 50,000 watt stations, too, like WSM Nashville with it's clear channel broadcast and network syndication for the *Grand Ole Opry*. But compared to the pop markets that singers like Frank Sinatra, Harry Belafonte, and Andy Williams sold into, it was a mere cottage industry; and compared to the burgeoning rock and roll industry where Elvis Presley and The Beatles were setting sales records every time they put out a new million-selling record, country music very nearly did not exist at all. Part of the problem here could be put down to lack of national press for country.

In New York City at that time, the mention of country music still evoked images of the under-educated hillbilly families that were depicted in TV shows like the *Beverly Hillbillies*, *The Real McCoys*, and *The Andy Griffith Show*. The music on those TV soundtracks was mostly bluegrass, not the honky tonkin', cheatin', hurtin' country music that country fans were listening to. So, there were prejudices to be overcome, and it was with at least some trepidation that George Jones made his way to the city of high fashion and high finance along with Ernest Tubb, Webb Pierce, Bill Monroe, Bill Anderson, Stonewall Jackson, Skeeter Davis, Leon McAuliffe, Porter Wagoner, and Buck Owens. Ralph Emery was the master of ceremonies.

Jones had some experience playing big shows in other cities, but was not looking forward to what he believed would surely be a hostile audience. When he learned that he and the Jones boys would be limited to performing only two songs on the New York show, he wondered why they had come at all. There were complications, of course, unions and promoter budgets and time limits — the sort of bureaucratic red tape that brought out the worst in George Jones who had already begun to carve out a modest reputation as a rebel and a non-conformist.

When George headed out onto the stage, he was nearly blinded by the spotlights. This was the largest crowd he had faced, the largest room he had played, and when that audience responded with explosive applause to the opening bars of *White Lightning*, George knew that he really had hit the big time. After a similar response to *She Thinks I Still Care*, he wasn't about to leave the building. Not right yet. Ralph Emery was hopping up and down and waving frantically from the orchestra pit. Promoters were losing their cool. But George Jones and the Jones Boys were having the time of their lives out there. 'Round about the fifth song, big Bill Monroe and one of his bandmates took matters into their own hands and hauled George off the stage. The show was in danger of running overtime and costing the promoter every cent he'd made — and Buck Owens had yet to perform. Still, they did finish ahead of the deadline, just barely, as Buck raced through his two numbers to fulfill the contract. But George Jones had stolen the show.

The jamboree show at Madison Square Garden sold out three times over, testimony to the growing popularity of country in the urban world. It would be a while, yet, before Garth Brooks would stage the biggest country show, ever, in Central Park, performing before a crowd said to number more than 250,000, but country music was on its way.

Pappy Daily next paired George with Musicor label-mate and pop star Gene Pitney as a duet partner. This unlikely pairing produced two radio hits — *I've Got Five Dollars And It's Saturday Night* (number 16) and *Louisiana Man* (number 25) in 1965 — and a number 3 album, GEORGE JONES & GENE PITNEY. George and Gene's harmonies sounded a whole lot like the Everly Brothers on helium, but their fans loved them singing together.

1965 was a banner year for George Jones. United Artists issued THE RACE IS ON, a number 3 album, and Musicor put out a compilation titled MR COUNTRY & WESTERN MUSIC. Then came *Love Bug* and *Take Me*, both Top 10 singles that same year from the album NEW COUNTRY HITS, which also hit into the Top 10 on the album chart. In October 1965, a second George & Gene album, IT'S COUNTRY TIME AGAIN, contained their second hit single. George was becoming known for his duets as well as his novelty numbers, his honky tonk songs, and his emotional ballads. He was quickly becoming one of country's major stars.

On the home front, however, things were not as rosy. Shirley had endured the poverty of their early marriage, the years in Beaumont before George was able to provide her and the children with better surroundings in Vidor. George had endured her disapproval of his career and colleagues. Just how damaging Shirley's disapproval of Jones had been did not come out until years later when Dolly Carlisle spoke with George's sister, Helen Scroggins. "Shirley used to get mad," Helen told Carlisle, "and wouldn't go to see George play 'cause he'd dance all over that stage. . . . He really showed his feelings. She told him if he didn't quit doing that and embarrassing her to death, she wasn't going no more. She stayed on him for years about that. She told Pappy Daily, herself. She said it embarrassed her. I never could understand why that would embarrass her. He was happy, then, and he didn't drink that much, but after he quit that, having to be so still and trying to be so precise with everything on the stage, that's what started him drinking so much. I guess he had to have something to calm him down and keep him still 'cause he would just dance all over that stage before." George's brother-in-law, W.T. Scroggins (Uncle Dub), adds, "It was a way of him showing emotion. Then he couldn't get it all out and he had to hold all that in. He had to have something to keep him calmed down and to be able to get out there and face the public." "George was deeply hurt by his wife's criticism," Dolly Carlisle concluded. "His fragile ego needed her endorsement, above all others. And when he didn't get her approval, he suffered."

Once when he had come home to Vidor in 1958, George was moved to write *The Window Up Above*, a song where a man wakes up to discover the bed empty and his wife outside the house speaking to a stranger, telling this man that her marriage is not working. By the mid-1960s, it was an insight that Jones had begun to feel might be coming true in his own life. Shirley would not always be at home when he would come in off the road. He wondered about that, too. In an effort to save the marriage by coming off the road, George tried to bring his audience to him. For a while, Shirley worked with George and, together, they built the world's first country music theme park, complete with RV hookups, a permanent stage, and bleachers. Years later, Conway Twitty with his "Twitty City" and Dolly Parton with "Dollywood" would try the same, with greater success than George, however.

George and Shirley called their new creation the "George Jones Rhythm Ranch" and kicked things off in grand style on Independence Day 1966, with Merle Haggard and Lefty Frizzell as George's guests. They had intended this to be the first of many shows, but it proved to be the one and only. Neither George nor Shirley had counted on just how many "friends and relatives" they had until it came time to pay admission to the show and for hookups at the trailer park. And those friends and relatives brought even more friends and relatives. George couldn't say no to any of them. That July 4th concert proved to be a bang-up one musically, but a disaster financially. The thing that George knew best was the music and that part went off just fine, then George found himself in an unfamiliar role. While he was able to pay off the local opening acts, Merle, Lefty, their bands, and the Jones Boys, there wasn't nearly enough left to have made the effort and investment worth while. Jones spent whatever was left when he dropped out of sight for a month to lick his wounds. Shirley had a posse out looking for him; Pappy Daily was in on it, too. George had acquired too many mouths to feed to allow the luxury of going AWOL.

The Rhythm Ranch was the first of many such dubious enterprises Jones would be associated with over the next 20 years: none of them took for long, though some of the times that were had were good ones. When the good times were done, it was George who got sued for this, that, and everything. He just didn't seem to have the business head required to organize, promote, and operate a music business venue, but he sure kept on tryin'. "I've never been too good with money," George confessed in his autobiography. "I've always been able to earn it better than manage it."

George and Shirley then tried living in Nashville together, but it came as no surprise that Shirley didn't last long in Music City. She packed her bags and returned to Texas. Soon after, George caught Shirley in a compromising situation with their business partner, J.C. Arnold. George suggested Shirley call her lawyer over to dissolve the marriage. His reputation betrayed him, though, and he was credited in the headlines of the newspapers as having shot J.C. in the butt with a shotgun blast of raw salt. Or it had been genuine buckshot that Jones had helped pick out of the man's rear . . . or had Jones been the person to take him to the hospital, paying the doctor to hush it up . . . or . . . In his autobiography, George sets the record straight. He did not fire a gun at J.C. He had Shirley call her lawyer. He told that man to give Shirley what she thought she deserved. Shirley was saying she'd given up her whole life for Jones. He agreed he owed her some. In retrospect, Jones should have called up a lawyer to act on his behalf and let Shirley hire her own representative. But he just didn't have the heart to get into all of that. The result was that Shirley got the 'goldmine', and George got the 'shaft'. Shirley was awarded all the money he had at that time, plus a percentage of his songwriting royalties. Several cars. His tour bus, band equipment, and a home in Florida. You might think it would have been a lesson to learn from . . . but George had loved Shirley. And he hadn't necessarily stopped loving her because things had turned sour. The media reported that in the divorce decree, George was cited for "harsh and cruel treatment."

George Jones moved into the Executive Inn in Nashville, a broken and broke man, but soon recovered to begin living the life of the bachelor he'd never really been. His bachelor pad partner was Billy Wilhite, an old pal who sometimes traveled with the Jones Boys and shared bus driving duties. George wasted no time making up for all of the times he had felt guilty about his one-night stands. He hit the bottle with a vengeance. He was free of the marriage and free of Shirley. He might miss his kids . . . and years later would have to deal with that . . . but there was one more immediate blow that would fall.

Clara and George Washington Jones lived in a small house in Vidor that their son had bought for them. Or so they understood. Then one morning a man from a mortgage company knocked on their door and delivered an eviction notice. They thought George had bought them the house. George thought he had, too. But he'd never paid much heed to money and never checked to make certain that Shirley had paid that mortgage off. She hadn't. In fact, she had purposely thrown away the eviction notices that arrived as each mortgage payment went unpaid. It was her revenge on her ex. George senior took it pretty hard. George junior was nowhere to be found. As the family scrambled to locate George Jones, the wayward singer, old George Washington Jones fell into a coma.

By now the press had fallen into the habit of 'sensationalizing' George's life. Some writers reported that George tore up his father's hospital room in his frustration and anger and pain. George says he didn't. No doubt, he was beside himself with grief. He had meant to be looking after his daddy, and now this had gone down because of his split-up with Shirley. A doctor told George that his father's health had been on the decline, and that George Washington Jones' drinking had finally caught up to him. It had hardened up his arteries. His sisters told him that they hadn't wanted to upset him about his father, so they hadn't told him about the situation. George senior did not regain consciousness. He passed away and was laid to rest in a cemetery in Vidor. All that was left for George to do was to pay the funeral costs. George left his mother with his sisters — Ruth, Helen, and Loyce — and his brother Herman, then headed back out onto the road from which they had tracked him down. He had hoped to spend more time with his father. He really had. The only solace he took was the memory of the time a year earlier when he'd done things up right, hiring Brother Burl and Sister Annie to stage a bang-up celebration for Clara and George Washington Jones' 50th wedding anniversary. And he had the memory of the gospel music sung that day.

Out there on the road, George was popular at truck stops where the drivers often rubbed shoulders with touring bands. *The Race Is On* became one of the first so-called trucking songs, even though there was no reference in the lyrics to truckers or trucks at all. Eight-track and cassette tapes were becoming the rage in those days, and you could slam Jones into your dashboard player and truck on down the highway. Truckers are among the biggest country fans of all and they regularly tune in to all-night country stations. Dave Dudley catered to the truckers with songs tailor-made for their nocturnal excursions, songs like *Six Days On The Road, Truck Drivin' Son Of A Gun, Trucker's Prayer,* and *Keep On Truckin'*. Years later, Kathy Mattea would get good mileage out of *Eighteen Wheels And A Dozen Roses.* Jerry Reed also hit big with the traveling population with that same kind of 'put it in gear and let 'er rip', pedal-to-the-metal energy in his songs as George Jones did. Reed's *When You're Hot You're Hot* was another late-night favorite for long distance drivers, and the former Nashville session guitar picker starred into the movies, too, where he played the part of a trucker as well as that of a musician. Dudley, Reed, and Jones were big favorites late at night out there between nowhere and somewhere as the miles flew by. Jerry Reed would figure into the scenario again a few years later when he would introduce Tammy Wynette to Burt Reynolds. That introduction sealed the Jones-Wynette divorce, if for no other reason than that Tammy was even more infatuated with the Hollywood actor famous for his *Smokey and the Bandit* films than she had been with the Possum when they had eloped.

Truckers and country singers in the 1960s also shared those little white pills that kept them awake, alert, all through the night, but they bit back. Johnny Cash was the first country singer to come clean about just how vicious pill-popping had been for himself and some other country musicians during that era. In his first book, *Man in Black,* he told how on any given night while the band was tearing down the equipment, someone would declare that they were exhausted. One of the veterans on the tour would say, "No problem, take one of these." Some people tried those prescription drugs that were being dispensed with no prescription on for size. Others didn't. A few got seriously hooked. And then the race really *was* on. George Jones never had the same kind of fascination for the uppers and downers that nearly killed Johnny Cash, but he used them — and he kept on drinking. In 1990, Johnny Cash remembered those years with a nostalgic smile. "We drank together. We took pills together. We got in trouble together. But we had what we thought were some great times together." In the 1970s, those times would turn sour as both Cash and Jones would seek treatment for their addictions. But in the 1960s while the race was on, George and Johnny kept at it harder than most of their fellow travelers. Cash's career peaked in 1968 and 1969 when he recorded multiple million-selling live albums in Folsom Prison and San Quentin that led to his own national TV show on the ABC network. In those days, George still had Pappy Daily to reel him in, now and then, and talk some sense into him when he needed an ally.

Together Jones and Daily kept on putting out records that a whole lot of people could relate to. *Love Bug* and *I'm A People* were the toe-tappers. *Walk Through This World With Me* (number one in 1967) and Dallas Frazier's *If My Heart Had Windows* (number 7 that same year) were the ballads that everyone loved. Everyone who loved their country music, that is.

3
I'll Share My World with You

While his relationship with Pappy Daily continued, George had at least one advisor (and protector) who was more or less on his side. When George moved to Epic Records and began to work with Billy Sherrill, his records got better production but he no longer had Daily in his own corner to keep the jackals at bay when his career blew up. George had been going along from show date to show date, recording session to recording session, with no real pretension to being a superstar, no aspiration to being one, really. He still got nervous as all get out when too much fuss was made over him, when his audiences were big or potentially hostile. If that kind of situation came up, George often bailed. But when he put all of his chips on the table, betting everything he had and everything he could offer on a career alongside Tammy Wynette, he stepped beyond the life of a country boy who had never really grown up, into an arena where the press writers were merciless and the woman he'd opened his heart to was far more liberated from the old ways of the South than he could possibly have anticipated.

In order to record with Wynette, George had to sever his ties with Pappy Daily and Musicor and make the move to CBS Records or one of their subsidiaries. When George parted ways with Pappy, the goodbyes were not all that friendly. Daily was merely retiring, going back to count his piles of money in Houston. Piles of money he'd made on records like *Family Bible*, dealing with Paul Buskirk, the man who had bought the song from Willie Nelson for $50. Willie had needed the quick money, but he didn't hang around Houston much after the record came out without even a nod in his direction for creating the song. Pappy Daily had other piles of money to count that he'd taken as more than his rightful share of George Jones' songwriting and recording career. "There's no love lost between Pappy Daily and me," George told one interviewer. At the time, George didn't merely air his dissatisfaction over the "haphazard, uneven production" of the records that Pappy had pumped out, nearly

300 of them during the Musicor years alone. His assessment of his years with Daily was laced with bitterness. "I have been kicked around worse than a damn mule. Nothing ever seemed to matter but the almighty dollar."

It was all just rain off Pappy's back and he would counter with platitudes like, "I like to think I did my best for George," Pappy told Dolly Carlisle. "I was George's advisor. . . . George was more like a son to me than anything else. I treated him like I would have my own boy. If he did things I didn't like, I'd raise hell about it. No, I never was a manager. They might call it manager, but, contractually, no, I never took a dime of George's money." And then the old man would haul out some example of George messing up and cite that as reason to doubt Jones and believe that it had been Pappy who'd helped George out each time he'd screwed up. A whole lot of people have sued George Jones over the years and this is where — if he'd sued Pappy for some of those royalties — he might have received some compensation. But George didn't have the heart to do it. He just chalked it up to the price he'd had to pay to play. That price included a final $300,000 paid to Musicor merely to get out of his contract with Daily and Talmadge. George had divvied that up, too, but it had turned him sour.

The price he would pay for his third bid for a happy marriage would be far stiffer than he could afford to pay. More than any of the money, houses, cars, or liens against his royalties that he would eventually pay in alimony to Tammy Wynette, he would pay a far more crucial price in the form of a broken heart. It hardly seemed fair. All he had wanted to do was share his world with someone who understood him. Someone who loved him for who he was.

I'll share my world with you
Everything that I own
My earthly possessions
They're no good if I'm alone
Let me give you the sunshine
When it's fresh with morning dew
Can't you see that I'm waiting
To share my world with you

I'll Share My World With You (Ben Wilson)

George and Tammy met when they were both married to others. They flew to Mexico City where Tammy got a quickie divorce. They returned home and learned that such things were not recognized in Tennessee. They were both sued by Tammy's husband, Don Chapel, but learned that Wynette's marriage to him was not legal because she hadn't waited the required number of months after divorcing her first husband, Euple Byrd, in Alabama before marrying Chapel. So, Tammy got an annulment, and for a while she and George "lived in sin."

In the fall of 1968, George went number 2 on the *Billboard* chart with *When The Grass Grows Over Me*, a song that Don Chapel had penned and George had recorded. Tammy's *Stand By Your Man*, which she wrote with Billy Sherrill and George Richey, hit number one for three weeks. Like most everything else in George's life, it didn't exactly make sense for her to be singing it. She hadn't stood by Chapel . . . or the first husband she had left behind in the dust before she met Chapel. But she was standing beside Jones nearly every night, up there in the lights, singing her heart out. In late March 1969, Epic released Tammy's *Singing My Song*, while Musicor put out George's *I'll Share My World With You*. Tammy went to number one, George to number 2. There they were at the top of the heap. Love could overcome adversity, it seemed, and, for a few years, it did. Their first record together was *Take Me*, a re-working of George's 1963 hit they'd sung on stage since 1968 and a Top 10 hit again in duet form in the early months of 1972. *Take Me* was hot stuff for country artists, an open invitation to lust.

Of course, the press gobbled up each tasty tidbit and spewed out exponentially larger reams of gossip and rumor. When Wynette sought to divert this unwanted attention in 1968 by telling the fans that she and George were secretly married, the "George & Tammy" soap opera lurched forward into its first full season. Then they *were* secretly married in a small chapel in Ringold, on the Georgia-Tennessee border, where Dolly Parton had also secretly wed her husband, Carl Dean. And they were 'married' again on record amidst the hokey production of an announcer's voice and chiming chapel bells that introduced *The Ceremony*, the second George and Tammy duet to chart, rising to number 6 on the *Billboard* Hot 100. *Old Fashioned Singing* barely took hold on the survey, and their fourth duet to chart, *We're Gonna Hold On*, came in 1973. Songwriter Peanut Montgomery took the phrase from one of their episodic fighting-and-making-up sessions, but by the time the record hit the radio, Wynette had filed for divorce and then made up again. However badly their relationship might be going, their fans took heart. George and Tammy were "holding on." As *We're Gonna Hold On* dropped from the Top 10, Johnny Paycheck's *Once You've Had The Best*, one of George's best recordings, began its climb to number 3 on the national charts and became a favorite at his shows. And early in 1974, George and Tammy were back on the radio with their saucy *We're Not The Jet Set*.

They might not be the jet set, but the longer they lived together, the more garish their lifestyle became. While at first George would exercise some taste when he decorated their home in Florida, by the time they had moved back to Nashville into the exclusive Belle Meade district, they decorated some rooms in their home on Tyne Boulevard with "shag carpeting on the ceiling," Nick Tosches reported in *Texas Monthly*. While living alone in the 12-bedroom mansion on Franklin Avenue Tammy and George purchased only weeks before their divorce, Tammy decorated her boudoir in what has been described as "early Vegas hotel" style. As their relationship disintegrated, was patched back together, and fell apart again, the fans followed each new development with the same fascination that they followed episodes of *Dynasty*, *Dallas*, and *As The World Turns*.

That's the public record of George and Tammy's life, but there was much more going on behind the scenes which fueled the curiosity of fans who had accepted them as 'Mr & Mrs Country Music'. The fans had linked them through their appearances singing together even before they eloped.

Some of their fans had taken George's 1967 recording of *Walk Through This World With Me*, which became his first number one hit in five years, as a declaration of his love, even though he had recorded that song before he met Wynette and before Tammy's first Top 40 record, *A Good Girl's Gonna Go Bad*, was released. Probably even before Billy Sherrill, inspired by the success of the Debbie Reynolds film *Tammy and the Bachelor* and the number one pop hit *Tammy*, convinced her to change her stage name from Wynette Byrd to Tammy Wynette. Yet Tammy's recording of *D-I-V-O-R-C-E* seemed to be encouraging to match-makers among their fans.

While fans speculated that Tammy and George were having an affair before they eloped, this was not so, though George admits that on at least one occasion, he and Tammy had shared a motel room bed when, along with the driver of the car, they had stumbled into that roadside refuge dog-tired and needing immediate sleep. George also claims he never laid a hand on his girl singer at that time, which, if you have ever traveled with a band, will seem entirely believable. Those messing around things do happen, but they don't happen all the time, especially when witnesses are present. And what Tammy and George had going at first was a widening friendship and a mutual admiration for each other's singing abilities. Like Jones, Tammy Wynette could really sing. She was the best to come along since Patsy Cline and she was as country as all get out.

In 1968, George confronted Tammy and her husband Don Chapel. George's own divorce had come through and he had told them so. George had grown fond of Tammy and respected her. But now he felt more than respect, he felt love. This was something that even Don Chapel could see. Everybody but Tammy could see it. At least, this is what she claims in her autobiography. And when jealousy drove Chapel to confront her on the issue, she admitted that she had thought it would be wonderful if it were to be true. The story she tells has a fairy tale quality.

According to Tammy, she worshiped George with the fervor of a fan. He had responded to her damsel-in-distress performances several times. He had helped her out at that David Houston show. He had sold her his old bus for a mere $2,000 to help her and Don Chapel out. And when he began showing up, unexpectedly, at shows like a benefit in Red Bay, Alabama, she felt flattered. Her mother was thrilled to meet George. For the first time, Tammy explained in her autobiography, her mother was impressed that her daughter's career as a country singer amounted to more than a hill of beans.

This attention merely heaped gasoline on the brush fire that was building between Wynette and Chapel. Tammy had fought hard for the respect she was now getting from many of the men in the music business, but she was getting little respect from her husband. When she discovered that Chapel was distributing nude pictures of her to people that he contacted through ads in magazines, she'd had enough. But it took a temper tantrum from George Jones to convince her that it was time to do something about it.

Jones came over during one of Tammy and Don's all too frequent domestic confrontations. Jones was always dropping over. They were friends and he had recorded one of Don Chapel's songs. This particular time in the kitchen the fur was really flying. Wynette had accused Chapel of lying about his whereabouts the night before — when she'd had to rush their children to the hospital because the infants had become victim of food poisoning. Tammy knew her husband was lying, she related, because she'd phoned George's manager looking for Don and the manager and George had come over and helped her with the children at the hospital that same night. Chapel had not been with them. In the kitchen the following afternoon, while Jones sipped on a drink that Chapel had poured for him, Tammy kept up her accusations. Chapel said he'd been with the manager, which Tammy knew to be a lie. And she kept after him. According to Wynette, Chapel said, "Well, you bitch, you're not fit to sleep with anyway . . ." And George exploded.

"He grabbed the end of my huge dining room table," Tammy remembered, "and flipped it over like a matchbox. Money, bills, drinks, and papers went flying everywhere. Don and I just stood there gaping. George is a small-framed man (five-foot-seven-and-a-half, about 150 pounds) and you don't expect such power from a man his size. All of a sudden he was like a tornado."

To George Jones' way of thinking, you didn't talk to your wife like that and he said so. Chapel persisted, saying it was none of George's business. It was then, in the heat of this moment, that George blurted out that he loved Tammy and challenged her to deny that she loved him, too.

As George remembered this scene in his authorized video biography, *Same Ole Me*, "I went over there and had a few drinks and he called her a bad name and I called him down on it and turned his table upside down. It's a wonder that he hadn't a-killed me."

George took Tammy and her children away with him in his Eldorado. Considering that Don Chapel had been humiliated and would certainly seek some sort of revenge, it *could* have turned ugly, but George made one smart move when he installed Tammy and her kids in a nearby hotel and went home alone. Soon after Jones arrived at his own house, Don Chapel and the police showed up with a search warrant. They did not find Tammy or her children there.

The following day George took charge of Wynette's life, taking her and the children home with him and announcing he'd arranged for someone to take care of the kids so that the two could fly to Mexico and Tammy could get herself a quickie divorce. He got no complaints from Wynette. She had waited too long for someone to take charge. Someone to protect her. "I didn't know where George was taking me and I didn't care," she remembered. "I would have gone anywhere with him. My heart was so full of love for this man I'd worshiped since childhood that I felt as though it would burst in my chest. He had rescued me from a husband that I didn't love. . . . I wanted to bask in the safety of his arms forever, and I would have done anything he asked."

As Tammy recalls in her autobiography, that night while she lay beside George as he watched Anthony Quinn in *Requiem for a Heavyweight* on the television in his bedroom, she was comforted by the fact that Jones had designed the Spanish decor himself. She savored the satisfaction of sleeping with her idol and imagined what a famous couple they would become. Life was sweet. The only thing that seemed out of place to her was the bottle of whiskey on the night table. This was the stuff that Hollywood melodramas were made of. She would come to crave the attention she got as a result of her controversial liaison with George Jones as much as George craved whiskey, and when their relationship became more normal she would become restless and George would hit the bottle again.

When the news of their relationship first became official, some reporters painted the picture as if Tammy had left a healthy family life to elope with a brigand, being lured away from her husband by a rich, indifferent superstar. Other journalists reported the story of an opportunistic Tammy Wynette who had schemed, all along, to catch herself a more attractive meal-ticket than Don Chapel. Tammy and George had become something more than singers — they were news and news sold newspapers and magazines, especially tabloid magazines — and a whole mess of records for both singers.

George and Tammy soon become the most documented couple ever to perform country music. More than just the country media and country fans were interested, though, and their grand love affair caught the fancy of America and the world, inadvertently creating a wider audience than ever before for country music. Meanwhile, George and Tammy dealt with the lawsuits that Chapel brought against them. They went about their business touring and making hit records. And when the fires had been put out and the smoke had drifted away, they moved out of the backbiting environs of Nashville to live in Florida. At the Lakeland residence, Tammy could be a regular person with neighbors. She enjoyed having her mother live nearby in a trailer park she and George owned. George completely refurbished the 42-acre estate mansion, adding extra rooms and improving the grounds. It was the best days of their lives, though something was amiss. While on tour, George got drunk and missed the opening show of a Las Vegas engagement, leaving Tammy to face the casino show-room audience alone. He was called "No Show" for the first time.

George Jones' hankering to create a special venue for country music had not been quashed by the failure of the George Jones Rhythm Ranch. In 1967 he opened a nightclub called "Possum Holler" in Nashville where friends like Merle Haggard, Willie Nelson, Faron Young, or even Porter Wagoner could drop in and sing a song. Since there were very few country music clubs in Nashville in those days, he wanted to find a regular gig for the Jones Boys when they weren't out on the road with him. The club was located above Roy Acuff's country music history museum, a 500 seat venue on lower Broadway within walking distance of Ernest Tubb's Record Shop, Tootsie's Orchid Lounge, and a stones throw from the Ryman Auditorium, where the family of country performers willingly brought their learned-on-the-road camaraderie to town. They began to celebrate country music the good old-fashioned way at Possum Holler, jamming together long into the night after their official functions were completed on Music Row and at the Opry. Plenty of good times were had and plenty of good music was played there until the night when one of the club's toilets overflowed and dumped human effluent onto Mr Acuff's exhibits in the museum down below. Mr Acuff was not amused, and Jones was evicted, the very next day.

In Florida, George made a second attempt to establish another country music theme park, The Old Plantation Music Park, and this time he was more successful. A crowd of 20,000 flooded the park on opening day, and thousands more were disappointed at the gate. Conway Twitty and Charlie Pride got into a gospel jam with George and Tammy at the end of the show, and the fans were treated to a lengthy impromptu encore. *Rolling Stone* magazine covered the grand opening, praising George and Tammy for the initiative and publishing photos showing Tammy's influence on her hubby: George no longer had a crew-cut, his hair was growing longer, and he'd shucked his rhinestone outfits for a stylish Western-cut suit. Merle Haggard, Johnny Cash, the Carter Family, Loretta Lynn, the Statler Brothers, Jeannie Seely, and Tom T. Hall were among the featured performers joining George and Tammy for the theme park shows. George's vintage car museum on the site was also a hit.

Despite this success at their Florida home, George and Tammy began to skir-mish. Although George cannot clearly remember the incident, he reportedly smashed the interior of their palatial estate in Florida to smithereens during one argument, and Tammy had him hauled away in a straightjacket and spoon-fed to the point of humiliation in a padded cell at the Watson Clinic in Lakeland. Tammy later alleged that George had pointed a gun at her. Soon after, Tammy announced that she intended to divorce George: she wanted a sober George or no George at all. But after that first taste of a rehab center, George straightened himself out and he and Tammy reconciled and moved back to Nashville.

George remains puzzled by this incident, which became a central scene in *Stand by Your Man*, the made-for-television movie version of their lives. In his autobiography, he tells how he was amazed to discover the damage that had been done to the furnishings, the walls, the drapes, and appliances upon his return from the padded cell at Watson Clinic. In a particularly poignant segment of his book, George describes how he re-plastered the walls and replaced the broken furniture, wondering how in the world he will ever be able to convince anyone in the whole wide world that he was not responsible for this mischief. When the producers of *Stand by Your Man* seized upon this incident for a dramatic finale, it was if it had happened in everybody else's mind. Over the years George has come to suspect that Tammy either broke the furniture herself or hired someone to do it in order to gain public sympathy for his alleged abuse. Tammy had grown to hate the Florida home, feeling exiled from the action to be found in Music City. At the time, George did not realize just how much Tammy wanted to get out of Florida. As Nick Tosches noted in an article in *Texas Monthly*, "Joan Dew, the coauthor of Tammy's autobiography *Stand by Your Man*, believed that Tammy was not only distraught by George's drinking, but jaded by the marriage as well. 'I think she really got bored with him very quick down there (in Florida),' Dew said. 'George is a little fuddy-duddy. He's like a little old lady. He's not exciting. He sits around and watches TV all day and goes fishing. George is only exciting onstage.' " That Jones had bought, renovated, and redecorated a mansion for Tammy apparently was not enough. That Conway Twitty and Charlie Pride and a host of other great country singers appeared on stage with Tammy and George at The Old Plantation Music Park apparently was not.

This turmoil was again reflected in the songs George was recording at the time, like *The Battle*.

Dawn breaks on the battlefield
While the morning mist lays heavy on the ground
And the silence is like thunder
As the enemy prepares another round
In her soft satin armor
Lying on the far side of the bed
Wounded and heartbroken
And scared by the killin' words I said

The Battle (Larry Kimball, Norro Wilson, George Richey)

George was puzzled by Tammy's behavior but penitent, none of which helped him to stop the progress of their break-up. Between Tammy's need to be comforted because she was no longer in the spotlight and George's diminishing ability to deliver that attention, a gap had been widening for some time. George has said that Tammy wouldn't sit down and discuss issues. Tammy has accused George of getting drunk and hitting her. After a while the two singers simply were no longer on the same page at all. The story of the final days of "Mr & Mrs Country Music" is not pretty.

Despite their growing animosity, Billy Sherrill was able to get George and Tammy back into the studio — and there they were on the radio again in 1976 singing *Golden Ring*, their second number one together, and touring the country together again. That December, their duet *Near You* began climbing the charts. Being in the studio and on stage with Tammy but shut out of her affections was not easy for George who still held out hope of reconciliation. George made several gallant attempts to reinsert himself into Tammy's soapy existence, flying thousands of miles to be at her side when she was in poor health or circumstances, but Wynette was not moved to welcome him back into her embrace. Sherrill later remembered that in the studio George "would drive Tammy up the wall. He would never do anything twice the same. So, we would usually have him do his part and, after he leaves, she overdubs her part." Years later George would be able to smile as he sang a light-hearted put down of Wynette on the novelty duet *No Show Jones*, which he first recorded with Merle Haggard. At the time it was all happening, he did not have the same serene objectivity.

In 1976 and 1977, while the irony of his situation was being hammered home, George's career was still on the rise, but his personal life had hit the down elevator. He'd been granted partial custody of their daughter, Tamala Georgette, until Tammy married Nashville realtor J. Michael Tomlin and then eloped with George Richey. Jones found himself shut out from his daughter's life. But even before that, George had begun to stumble and fall. As his grief increased, he began to show the world that if they'd thought he was a drinker before this, they hadn't seen nothin' yet. He began beating himself up so badly that by 1979 he missed more shows than he made.

Wynette herself suffered through a series of mishaps during the break-up of her marriage with George, hospitalized right after the divorce after overdosing on methadone. Then an intruder or intruders repeatedly broke into her house and scrawled graffiti slogans like "Slut," "Bitch," "Whore," "Pig," and "Kill" on doors, TVs, and mirrors. Then a wing of her house burned. Then her tour bus caught on fire. There were so many incidents, each of them investigated by the police, who nevertheless made no arrests, that the rumor mill blamed it on Tammy herself. It sure was a bizarre way to get yourself publicity. The co-author of Tammy's autobiography, Joan Dew, once told Dolly Carlisle, "This is conjecture on my part, but the harassment that went on for so long — the hang up phone calls and little harassments around the house — were all done by her as a way of getting sympathy and attention. Because every time something like that was happening, she was going with somebody who wasn't available to her.

They wouldn't commit themselves. And Tammy wants total commitment and if that's not forthcoming, then she will connive and scheme to do things to get that. One of the ways she feels that she can get that is if a guy thinks that you're a woman in danger, he'll protect you and come and save you."

These were the events that led up to Wynette's infamous 'kidnaping', where she was allegedly abducted in her own car, beaten, nearly strangled to death with her own pantyhose, but mysteriously released and left to stumble down the road with the pantyhose still wrapped around her neck. Police investigators and George Jones believe that it had to be someone Wynette knew, someone she was protecting or someone that she was afraid of.

After her kidnaping episode, Tammy hit the road with a vengeance and made the most of her moment in this somewhat dubious limelight. Her bruises nearly covered by many layers of facial makeup, she also made the most of the fact that her assailant *could* be in her audiences, and spoke about this morbid prospect to her fans. She also worked the media wherever she went. Randall Riese quotes her as telling one reporter, "Since that happened, I find myself looking at people and looking at cars and thinking, you know, 'Is that the one?'" Some folks thought she need only raise her makeup mirror to her own face to see the real cause of her suffering. As the melodrama grew in ferocity, she told yet another reporter that she was going to purchase a gun and hit the "pistol range."

No charges were laid in the alleged kidnaping. And her bruises healed. Even less fun to contemplate was her addiction to methadone and her seemingly endless trips to the hospital for operations to her abdomen and other parts of her body. Either someone was harassing her or Tammy was beating herself up badly. The bruises and slogans were not imaginary, even if the phone calls were.

Wynette had needed psychological treatment for her own addictions at least as much as George Jones had needed treatment. But Wynette had been sheltered from public scrutiny when she'd been out of it on prescription drugs like methadone and dilaudid, sheltered from the press by her husband George Richey, who often gave inquisitive types short shrift when they appeared on his property. Tammy had needed help but she had chosen instead to blow the whistle on her ex, George Jones, in her book. Her loud complaints about Jones' abusive and alcoholic behavior had served her well in deflecting public notice from her own increasing drug dependency. Meanwhile, Wynette was making hay while the sun shone on her. "Directly due to her 1978 kidnapping,"

Randall Riese wrote, "Tammy Wynette received more worldwide publicity than she has ever had in her entire illustrious career." Riese was writing in 1988, ten years before Tammy would eclipse this moment of infamy one last and final time by passing away amid nearly as much controversy.

4
Gorillas

When Tammy and George's marriage faltered in divorce and she quickly moved on to a series of well-publicized romances with the likes of Burt Reynolds and Rudy Gatlin before marrying Michael Tomlin, then George Richey — George just seemed to fall apart. He'd always been a heavy drinker and he had frequently gone AWOL for a few days or weeks to seek out some peace way back in the hills or in a smokey bar or a broken down motel room somewhere. Now, he just couldn't seem to cope.

George had always gotten into mischief, and sometimes gotten himself arrested for his capers. Now that he was front page news, all that he had to do was cough and the world learned about it. After a while, every time he took a drink or two or three, it seemed like he could depend on it to be reported in the media. What got George upset was that journalists would see him sitting at a bar and write up a whole story about how he was drowning his sorrows because he couldn't get over Wynette. George just didn't realize that his life had become part of Tammy's soap opera existence, even if he was now cast as her ex. To his way of thinking it wasn't anybody's business but his own. He simply refused to admit that he had forfeited his privacy a long time before this, the price you paid for fame. He certainly didn't like it. That is for sure.

Promoters soon learned that even if George had canceled a show, they could still reap the benefits and then blame it all on 'No Show Jones'. So, while some of the time Jones had been playing hooky from his show dates, other times he was merely a victim of unscrupulous businessmen. After a while, it didn't matter whether George was drunk and a no show, or actually working in another city altogether. It became more and more difficult to get bookings. "Lots of times it wasn't my fault," George told Alanna Nash during the 1980 interview later published in *Behind Closed Doors*, "and there were a few times it was. But it was based around the people who were involved — people who should have canceled the dates, who were told to. I was bein' booked into two or three different places at the same time, and a lot of the times I didn't even know about either one of 'em."

While some people had to contend with George not showing up, Merle Haggard had the opposite problem. Haggard was seldom surprised when George showed up unexpectedly, out of the blue, so to speak. One time during the 1970s, Merle was on the road and took a phone call from George, who told him he'd be right over, even though he himself was in another city on a tour of his own. George had been babbling on the telephone, saying, "It's all your fault, Merle."

Haggard, puzzled had said, "What's my fault, George?"

Jones, slurring his words, was into the sauce, Haggard was sure of that much. "You wrote that song," George said, "the one about throwin' away the rose."

Haggard thought about this as he formed his answer. "Yeah, George, I know the one, but I didn't know my songs would cause you problems . . ."

George said, "I'm comin' to see you."

The line from *I Threw Away The Roses* that George couldn't get out of his mind was, "Now all my social friends . . . look down . . . their noses . . ."

Haggard, in an excerpt from his autobiography printed in *Honky Tonk* magazine, continues with the story. "I hung up the phone and some of the others in the room said they wouldn't be surprised if he didn't show up. I told them I didn't think so, 'cause, hell, he had concerts all week. The next day, who shows up but the Old Possum himself — and he's still singing my song."

George Jones' entry into Haggard's motel room was a classic one, as Merle recalls. "He didn't knock or nothin', just came right through the door. He actually kicked the damned door down, roared right into the room, and announced that George Jones had, indeed, arrived." As he entered, George was singing that troubling song full voice, and Fuzzy Owen, one of the Strangers, looked up from his napping state on a roll-away bed, Merle explains, to "see what kind of a wild man had come bustin' in the room singin' *I Threw Away The Roses*. 'Now, what's going on here?' he wanted to know."

Haggard watched dumbfounded as George Jones went over to the sideman's bed, folded him into it, and rolled it right out into the hallway with Owen bundled up securely inside. "I didn't like the way things were where I was," Jones said as he sat himself down beside Haggard. Merle was always willing to forgive George his 'indiscretions', though, for Haggard understood his predicament. "Success had been crowding him. He had attacked the problem the only way he knew. Even though George was supposed to be someplace else — where he didn't like the way things were — he spent the next few days touring with us. That was the only time in my life that I got a little tired of hearing George sing. Mostly because he kept singing the same song. . . . Even though he was a lot of laughs on that trip, other times George really made me mad."

In George's authorized video biography, Tom T. Hall recalls an encounter with George that wasn't so friendly. One time, when George and Tom T. Hall were on the road together and had a night off, George suggested they head on over to Vegas. Tom replied, "I can't, I'm on tour. I got a whole band and a whole bus here." George said, "Yeah, well, they'll be here when you get back. Don't sweat it."

Tom thought about that but he remained firm. "I can't go. I'd really like to go but I can't." He later remembered that, "I kinda got the notion that George was gettin' to feel adventurous. You know, he's been calm and quiet for a little too long . . . So, I talked my way out of that. I didn't go to Vegas. I got back to Nashville a few days later and picked up the newspaper and George *had* been to Las Vegas, and for some weird reason or another he ended up in New Orleans kicking the windows out of a hospital. So, I got to read about it in the papers and I said, 'You know, I'm kind of glad I didn't make that trip.' "

By the time that George was known as No Show Jones, he would find himself dealing with bodyguards and babysitters forced upon him by managers like Caruth Byrd. George accepted these guardians at the time, but he preferred it when his keeper was a personal friend. George's first choice was his Florence barber, Jimmie Hills. George soon learned that the big bucks ($250 per day) Jimmie was earning watching over him put their friendship on the shelf for the duration. George delighted in eluding Jimmie. He would slip out of a cab that was being watched by a doorman or a bellman while Hills was checking them into a hotel, and sneak away using that same cab as a cover, then often as not he'd walk up behind a distraught Hills and tap him on the shoulder. George could not have known that his frequent haircuts would later open the door to a country singer's very worst nightmare and let all the scary stuff in . . . George was too busy ducking Jimmie and nipping on his Jim Beam and Jack Daniels bottles.

And then there were people like Peanut Montgomery, Melba's brother and George's friend who wrote songs with him until Peanut turned to religion and began preaching at George. In the heat of an argument, George fired a shot over Peanut's head, not intending to harm him, but Peanut told the police that George had tried to kill him. Taking that stance got Peanut Montgomery the publicity he seemed to need. There was even a candid photo taken of Peanut sticking his head out of his car above a bullet hole printed in newspapers. At that time, not many people believed George when he claimed he had not fired the bullet directly at Peanut, not just below Peanut's head as indicated in the posed photo. There had been a couple of times that he'd come a lot closer to people.

In his autobiography, George claims that he fired the shot well over the top of Peanut's car; if there was a bullet hole in the car door, it had been put there by someone other than himself or the photo that appeared in newspapers and magazines had been doctored. Bill Jarnigan, author of an article called "'See if your God can save you now,' George said as he pulled the trigger . . ." noted that "Montgomery experienced some difficulty in getting the law to react. Several officials, such as Lauderdale County District Attorney Lavern Tate, a friend to both men, considered the incident a family affair." But Montgomery went to the media with his quote. Nick Tosches, in an article entitled "The Devil in George Jones" published in *Texas Monthly*, added a few more words: "All right you son of a bitch, see if your God can save you now . . ." To this day, Jones denies that he said those words. Other reports mentioned that the feud had actually been over money that Montgomery owed to Jones. When Nancy Sepulvado began to weed out the entourage of parasites that hung around George in the 1980s, the born-again Peanut Montgomery was one of the first to go. Yes, old Peanut had been back with his hand in Jones' pocket long after he'd called the cops on his friend. But Nancy caught Montgomery out when he came begging money for air conditioning for his church, which Jones forked over. Nancy and George went to the church that same day and discovered it was already air conditioned.

Another one of George's old colleagues who called the police on him was Pappy Daily, not because George shot at him but because of his reaction to an unsuccessful attempt to collect royalties while he was drinking. Stonewalled by Daily's assistant, Jones began his usual John Wayne routine on the office furniture. One of the things that most depressed George was the way Daily had bilked Lefty Frizzell out of the fortune he'd earned. During the 1970s, George continued to visit Lefty in the basement of his house where Frizzell's wife kept him locked away from the rest of her home. And Lefty kept on drinking, relying on guys like George to bring around the vodka, until he died.

The predicament of the songwriter or singer who could not collect his royalties or fees soon hit the silver screen when Willie Nelson and Kris Kristofferson made the movie *Songwriter*, where they played singer-songwriters who were forced in one scene to have their pal, played by Rip Torn, rob their own box office at gun point because of the skulduggery routinely pulled off by the managers and promoters. What Willie and Kris were acting, George was living day-to-day. Right from start with the Starday label, George had not played this part of his career very well. George might have lashed out against Pappy Daily. And he might have been justified in some of what he said. But what he really *needed*, now that he was on his own, was the protection that Pappy had provided. People didn't screw with Daily or his star singer. Now that the old man was out of the picture, the vultures moved in. They readied themselves for the moment when they would get to pick at the remains of the singer who had never grown out of his naivete, his devil-may-care attitude toward business, and was now so down on his luck that his health and vitality were slowly draining away. The weasels moved in for the kill. They wanted a whole lot more from Jones than Pappy had ever taken. They wanted everything the Possum had and more. George ended up hiring people with whom he never should have associated. Not in a million years.

Tom T. Hall, reminiscing on those times, says, "I think a lot of what us ole country boys have done through the years is basically we were tryin' to have a good time. And then, suddenly, it dawns on you that you're not really having that much fun." By 1979, George Jones seemed to be having the least fun of any of the singers. Conway Twitty later put it in perspective when he said, "All you gotta do is think about how, down through the years, George has abused himself. It was almost as if he was set on self-destruct." Rick Blackburn, Vice President of CBS Records Nashville, is more philosophical in his view of things. "All George wanted to do was sing songs. A very simple lifestyle. He could not understand all the hoopla from the success he was having. It's sort of a love-hate relationship when you go through that, because every time George would get in trouble, all I know is . . . we would sell more product and we were at million albums before we knew it."

George's reputation was one reason he was selling plenty of vinyl. Following a now legendary performance at Willie Nelson's July 4th Picnic in 1976, he reached a new audience and gathered up some much needed respect with *Rolling Stone* naming him their country artist of the year. Rick Bolsom covered this event for *Country Song Roundup*, featuring an interview with George. "Up close," Bolsom wrote, "he doesn't look his age, except for the deep lines that have been burned into his face by the years of hard living, hard drinking and keeping the George Jones legend alive." Then Bolsom asked, " 'George,' I said to him between sips of a short, cold one, 'what's the reason for the amazing success you've continued to have despite all the problems you've run up against along the way?' George took a minute or two to light a cigarette and puff it to a bright glow before answering.

"I think it's being strong in what you believe in and mainly being yourself. There's so many of us that are really like each other. There's so many people in the world that have the problems that we have and write about in our songs ... That's what people want to hear. There's going to be a certain amount of people that want to hear about the guy in the barroom, drinking his problems. We have those people who have a breakup in their marriage or something like that. They wind up down at the closest bar and they'll sit there having drinks to drown their sorrow. People have divorce problems, sweetheart problems, maybe things aren't working out ... you have your love ballads. And, you've got songs that are novelties, that talk about white lightnin' stills. There's people for every song, I think, that's written in the country field. That's also the main reason I think that country's become so popular. Because it's just down to earth, home. It hits the working people. It hits down to home to all of them." Of course, George himself was living the very life he was describing. He knew what he was talking about.

"Like the legends of Hollywood or others in the public eye, George Jones the man has been the object of a sometimes harsh press because he is also George Jones the singer," Bolsom continued. "Writers doing interviews get very sensitive to a person's being afraid or unwilling to open up and talk. Not being shy by nature, I put the question to George: 'Has all that bad press you've gotten had much truth to it?' 'Yeah, I've had some bad stuff wrote about me. Had a thing written not too long ago by a writer here in Nashville; it was in a country music magazine. She told things in there that wasn't even true ... She had me selling a car in Alabama that was mortgaged property; I owed on it and sold it and was in trouble over that. And this is no where even near true. It just shocked me when I read it. One thing she had in there . . . down at Possum Holler . . . that I got so drunk they toted me out to my car. I've never done that in my life down at Possum Holler.

" 'It's not good, of course, but I figure as long as they're talking about you, you're still alive. Anybody hates bad publicity, especially if it's not true. I'm a type of person really that I don't mind; it doesn't bother me at all — anybody writing the truth about me. I don't care. If I was down somewhere and pulled my clothes off in front of a lot of people and streaked, drunker than hell, I wouldn't mind — if it was true, I wouldn't mind them printing it.

" 'But the things they add to make a story sound better to the reading public, I just don't appreciate that at all.

" 'They had me brooding, drowning in stuff over Tammy Wynette over at the Hall of Fame (Motor Inn bar): 'He's there every day drinkin' his life away.' They had so much stuff in there about me doing it because of her. This might have been true. I felt lost and very depressed for quite a while after we divorced. But the way they add and build to a story is what gets me.

" 'This one magazine came to me and said, 'We're very sorry about it, we'll give you a retraction.' I said, "Well, hell, the damage's done.' "

While George said he felt like "the oddball" in this outlaw show with Willie and Waylon and feared the reaction from the crowd, he found "they were the most enthusiastic crowd, about 80,000 of them. . . . After I finished my first song, the reaction just relaxed the devil out of me. We really turned on then!" Other writers noted that this one show crossed Jones over into a bigger market beyond die-hard country fans. Some have said George rocked. Jones, of course, denies that ever happened. "I'm George Jones. I've got my style. I've got my hits that I've been fortunate to have, and I don't think they want to come see me do anything different. The only thing different that I added (to the Willie Nelson Picnic) show, which really isn't that different because I've done it for years, every now and then if I'm in the right mood I'll wind up doing a verse of *Long Tall Sally*, a little rock thing. I add it kind of as a novelty to my show. I always wait to last to do it, because if they're gonna throw anything at me I've got a chance to run."

During the country rock era in the 1970s, Hank Williams became a hero all over again to a new generation of country rockers who were discovering the genius of his songwriting for the first time. These newcomers were first fed a resurrected version of ole Hank's myth by Gram Parsons, a college kid who dropped out to pursue a career singing good old country music the way Hank sang it, but died tragically of a drug overdose in the desert before his time. You see, Hank was also admired at that time for his lifestyle. His independent spirit and attitude toward music business types also appealed to country rock artists who were wrestling with their own record label execs. Tall tales of his pilling and boozing were told and retold. Ole Hank was also the inspiration for several influential albums like Gram Parson's GRIEVOUS ANGEL, which co-starred Emmylou Harris, and Leon Russell's HANK WILSON'S BACK. But mostly, country rockers hung out on the west coast where the living was easy and there were plenty of wide open spaces. In Nashville when country got rockin' it would be called 'outlaw' music.

The outlaw movement was launched with appropriate help from life's other side when Waylon recorded *Are You Sure Hank Done It This Way*, a number one chart-topper late in the fall of 1975. It was a recording so different from what had gone before it that no one could clone it and no country record would even resemble it until the late 1990s when Emmylou would again shake the dice and roll out a whole new alt-country sound with her WRECKING BALL album, a collaboration with Daniel Lanois.

Waylon Jennings and Tompall Glaser had this old building on 19th Avenue South in Nashville called "Hillbilly Central" where increasing numbers of rebels with a cause crossed paths. At one time, Hank Jr. had given Waylon a pair of boots that had belonged to his father. Whenever Waylon wore them, a series of near disasters was triggered, like the time he was recording and lightning struck a tree outside the studio. That tree fell on his Eldorado, but strangely, when the boys rushed outside to see what damage had been done, there was nary a scratch on his Cadillac. Life got scary when you tried to fill ole Hank's shoes.

"Driving to Hillbilly Central one morning during the DREAMING MY DREAMS sessions," Waylon recalls in his autobiography, co-authored with Lenny Kaye, "I was thinking about Hank's influence and the example he'd set for us both good and bad. I grabbed an envelope and started writing, one hand on the wheel, the other balancing pen and paper on my knee."

Waylon's song began, "Lord, it's the same old tune, fiddle and guitar/ Where do we take it from here?" And it was recorded that same morning with Waylon reading the lyrics he had written from the envelope propped up on a music stand. Two weeks later someone called his attention to that envelope. It was still there on that music stand, but he couldn't make heads nor tails out of it. "It was just scribbling." Hank Williams seemed to be speaking through Waylon. And the way it was cut that morning became the inspiration for the outlaw movement. Twenty-two years after Nashville insiders had wept over his grave down in Montgomery and thought they had put the rebel in Hank away in that grave — thought they had snuffed out the confrontational attitude that he had begun to ignite on their turf on the Opry and throughout Nashville — here he was again come back to haunt them in the lyrics of Waylon's song. This song was the match that kindled a fire that would not be put out a second time. Now when something questionable went down, people were saying, "Are you sure Hank done it this way?"

As Waylon would later tell *No Depression* magazine writer Grant Alden, "They tried to destroy what we were doing. . . . There wasn't no way they could destroy it, and they didn't know that. When we came to town you had to use their studios, you had to use their songs. . . . Me singing with the Nashville sound was like putting honey on chocolate cake. It was just syrupy; it just didn't work. And I didn't want to cause no trouble, because when you get there you think they ain't goin' to let you sing. . . . The thing about it, it was people who had gone to college and got four-year-degrees in marketing, and they wanted to tell you they knew more than you did . . ."

With a punch line that was variations on "I don't think Hank done it this way," the recording was a whole different kind of country, a seamless wash of phased guitars where chorus and verse and instrumental break conventions disappeared into something new. "Jack (Clement) mixed the guitars together," Waylon remembers, "so they sounded like one instrument, matching their equalization settings so that you couldn't tell where one blended into the other. . . . It felt like a different music, and Outlaw was as good a description as any."

George Jones was never directly associated with the Outlaw movement, but he became singled out as someone who sympathized with this Texan outlaw attitude. He was, after all, from Texas, and he and Tammy Wynette were directly involved in the formation of ACE, the Association of Country Entertainers that opposed the trend represented by the CMA endorsing Nashville outsiders Olivia Newton-John (CMA Female Vocalist to the Year in 1974) and John Denver (CMA Entertainer of the Year in 1975), pop artists who were perceived to be undermining country music traditions with their crossover number one hits, *Honestly I Love You* and *Thank God I'm A Country Boy*. Tammy hosted ACE meetings in her living room.

George was viewed as being a shit-disturber like Hank Williams had been. But he wasn't the only person opposed to some of the practices going down on Music Row. There was Cowboy Jack Clement who had worked at Sun Records in Memphis when rockabilly got going and who had handed George that marvelous ballad *She Thinks I Still Care* back in 1961. And there was Waylon and Willie and the boys. Tom T. Hall was speaking out about how slick countrypolitan productions were ruining country music. He would write a whole book about it. However, George's political involvement with ACE and the upstart association's attitude toward the pop country music being made on Music Row just might have been one of the reasons so many people came to hate him. It might have been the reason why some journalists went after him so relentlessly, especially if some of the magazines they wrote for were owned or funded by Music Row personalities or corporate advertising. When Jones seemed headed for disaster through his drinking, and then his drugging, some people on the Row seemed to breathe a deep sigh of relief. They were pleased that the potential threat of opposition to the good ole boy system, which George Jones had represented, was melting away with each lurid trumped-up story.

No one on Music Row came to George's rescue when public knowledge of his cocaine use became mythic. Many people stood on the sidelines and made side bets on the action. Few of the execs wanted to speak about the subject anyway because several of the major record label corporations at that time had someone on their payroll dispensing corporate checks to outside promoters who routinely paid bribes to disc jockeys, payments of cocaine and money, in order to control chart action. The corporate offices of record companies preferred to conduct their drug control in secrecy and let the stars who became screwed up by substance abuse bear the assault of public opinion. It was the stars who were messed up, they said. Not the record labels. However, label types were often to blame for the stars' frustrations. Machinations such as these, although not drug or alcohol specific, had bothered Hank Williams when he was in Nashville and this type of controlling influence was first being exerted. And it bothered George Jones who often spoke out about how radio sucked. As it turned out, there was a reason for that.

Another reason George continued to do well musically in the mid-1970s despite his off-stage behavior was that Billy Sherrill kept coming up with key songs for him to sing, songs that worked as well in live shows as they worked on the radio. Songs that continued to provide George with material that seemed frankly autobiographical, in tune with his despair, although by this point in his career they were nearly all written by other songwriters. Some of the writers, like James Taylor, were actually George Jones fans and wrote some of those songs with George very much in mind. Norro Wilson and George Richey were Sherrill's in-house writers — they were more than familiar with the George and Tammy affair. Tammy herself supplied the lyrics for George's 1975 hit *These Days I Barely Get By*, a song she finished up with some help from George.

The songwriting team who perhaps best captured George's state in the late 1970s was H. Sanders & R. Beresford with their composition, *If Drinkin' Don't Kill Me (Her Memory Will)*.

The bars are all closed
It's four in the morning
I must have shut 'em all down
By the shape that I'm in

*I lay my head on the wheel
And the horn begins honkin'
The whole neighborhood knows
That I'm home drunk again*

*If drinking don't kill me
Her memory will
I can't hold out much longer
The way that I feel*

*With the blood from my body
I could start my own still
But if drinking don't kill me
Her memory will*

If Drinkin' Don't Kill Me (Her Memory Will)
(H. Sanders & R. Beresford.)

Another Sherrill produced song composed by Norro Wilson that gave George Jones a contemporary edge was *The Door*, a song which sympathized with the plight of Vietnam war vets. George himself had put three years of his life into serving his country, although he had been stationed in California and he had not enlisted early enough on to see active duty in Korea. Nevertheless, when George sang the lyrics to *The Door*, he could feel the conflict and unrest that was rocking America, feel it all around him. On television he could see and hear the bombs falling, the napalm burning villages. This newest war had invaded people's homes along with earthquakes, plane crashes, and every kind of disaster imaginable. They watched it all on the evening news while they ate their dinner, no longer seated facing each other at the dinner table, but each of them facing the one-eyed monster and the war and the games shows and their favorite primetime soaps, *Bonanza* and *Gunsmoke*. The song did not focus on the war at all. It focused on the sound of a slamming door that a young soldier heard when his girl walked out of his life. But the overall tragedy included all of the chaos that challenged his courage.

*I've heard the sound of my dear old mama cryin'
And the sound of the train that took me off to war
And the awful sound of a thousand bombs exploding
And I wondered if I could take it any more*

There were times when they almost drove me crazy
But I did my best, I took it like a man
But who would think in my lonely room I'd hear it
The one sound in the world my heart can't stand?

To hear that sound and to know that it's really over
Through tear-stained eyes I watched her walk away
And of earthquakes, storms and guns and wars
Lord, nothin' has ever hurt me more
Than that lonely sound of the closing of the door

The Door (Billy Sherrill & Norro Wilson)

Country music continued to appeal because it was rooted in situations that were real to the people who listened to it. Sure, the Nashville Sound got smoother and the rhinestone cowboys and country queens were just a tad melodramatic, but the bottom line was that a few singers like George Jones kept on keeping it country and keeping it real, no matter what the latest fad or trend might be. Jones sang country because he loved it. Because he had to sing it or he just went plumb crazy. He was not ever part of the Music Row mentality that schemed to turn country music into something that wasn't country, more downtown. Even though the fiddles on *The Door* were violins playing a string arrangement, there was the swooping 'gliss' of a pedal steel and there was George's vocal, climbing, reaching out for notes, and plummeting to baritone depths, hitting people where they hurt most, yet healing them at the same time.

Like Billy Sherrill, Rick Blackburn stuck by Jones through thick and thin during the late '70s and early '80s. However, Rick quickly learned that putting pressure on the Possum could lead to disaster. The time he first learned that lesson cost Nashville-based Blackburn some credibility with his New York people. "I was sitting in my office at one o'clock in the afternoon," Blackburn remembered. "We had this huge event planned in New York at The Bottom Line. 'George Jones and country music comes to New York.' That's the way it was billed. It was a really big event in New York. A lot of the top press was going to be there. As I recall, most of the cast of *Saturday Night Live* was going to be there. It was a great media event, certainly an event for country music, in New York. We made our plans, our travel arrangements and so forth, and George excused himself from my office and left — and we didn't see him for three weeks. He just did not show up."

These were the kind of events George hated, and he told Blackburn so. The Possum's way of dealing with people who put him in compromising situations was to bail out. When he did finally perform at The Bottom Line club in 1980, he discovered that his fears of feeling out of place were unfounded. Bonnie Raitt and Linda Ronstadt were among the people he met there, and both were eager to join him on stage for a song or two. By 1980, he had begun to deal with his demons, although he had not yet found a cure for his restlessness. And before that came about, he was often out of control. After a while, he had few friends left, as Rick Blackburn explains. "It's the dangedest project I've ever worked on. We're dealing with all this negative press. Promoters were down on him. Radio was down on him. Everybody hated him except his fans."

One friend who never gave up on George was Waylon Jennings. But Waylon had his worries, too. "I was afraid he was going to die," Waylon remembers. "I thought I was gonna live forever. We both had drug problems." George himself admits that by the late '70s, he just couldn't see the forest for the trees. "I couldn't begin to see that I was out of control because I was so out of control that I couldn't see anything." Others *could* see, and it was Waylon who made the first move.

"So," says Waylon, "I called him over to the house and he came out there. And I said to him, 'George, this is gonna sound awful funny comin' from me but you gotta do something. You gotta straighten up.' " George did not follow Waylon's advice.

George's persistent desire to run a country music club for his friends and fans would get Jones into a whole lot more trouble than even Tammy Wynette could connive. In 1975, while his divorce from Wynette was running its course, George met Shug Baggott, who became the manager of the second Possum Holler Club. Shug was a sly fox of a fellow, though, and soon he was managing every aspect of the Possum's career that George knew about and some that he didn't.

During George's worst of times, he simply fell in with a crowd who had no respect for the music, no respect for their singer, and even less respect for the country music fans who paid everyone's wages by buying records and concert tickets. To those thuggish people, Jones was a high dollar meal-ticket and little else, no matter what pretty things these wily entrepreneurs told the press about how they were looking after George, their crazy man. Having set that craziness into motion, few of those fellows were sincerely interested in seeing George recover. In fact, some of them may have put the bug in the Possum's ear that he was crazy in order to instill a fear of rehab institutions. The tangled relationship between managers Caruth Byrd and Shug Baggott (whose contractual obligations overlapped) and the equally confusing relationship between Baggott and booker Shorty Lavender (who both laid claim to the exclusive right to book George Jones) would result in Jones filing for bankruptcy in December 1978. During this period, there were so many people shuffling in and out of George's business life as managers and road managers that Billy Sherrill came to the point where he said he didn't want to have anything to do with any of them.

From several sources we learn that Shug Baggott was involved with Jones' cocaine abuse in the mid-70s. None of this is conjecture. In his autobiography, *I Lived To Tell It All*, George has confirmed this in his own words. "Shug got me started on it to keep me messed up. Just the way he got me drunk all the time. . . . He's a crook. He robbed me blind." Baggott was later arrested, charged, and convicted for dealing in a sizeable amount of the narcotic. Making cross reference to all that has been written by Bob Allen, Dolly Carlisle, Nancy Jones, and George Jones himself, as well as the dozens of the interviews and newspaper articles that appeared during this time, a rough idea emerges of how George's drug problems may have begun. There is no need to learn every nasty detail. Just the nuts and bolts of it.

Baggott became interested in Jones' career during a period when both men were in the habit of having their hair cut by the same barber. Shug allegedly hated country music, and through his visits to the barbershop, he had inside information about how malleable and susceptible Jones really was. He kind of weaseled his way into becoming George's manager. He began his campaign by telling Jones that he wanted to reopen Possum Holler, an idea that appealed to George. The club opened and was an immediate success. George next found himself asking Shug to manage his career. At first, Baggott played hard to get, declining this initial offer, but he was soon in charge and put his brother, Sandy, in place as George's road manager. When Shug wrestled George's booking contract away from Queenie Acuff and Bill Wilhite, dangling an attractive $25,000 advance in front of the Possum's nose, he had the control he needed to exploit his artist fully.

George didn't realize what he was getting himself into. And during the next seven years he found himself shuffled back and forth between several managers. There were two separate stints with Baggott himself, although Shug seems to have preferred to work indirectly behind the scenes, possibly even from inside the slammer when he took up residence there. There were a lot of intermediaries involved. Even George Richey and Tammy Wynette got into the act for a while, passing off Paul Richey as their candidate as George's manager. In the end it came out that all of these types were in cahoots with each other, at one time or another, along with booking agent Shorty Lavender, cutting each other percentage deals which left George with smaller and smaller pieces of his own pie. Few of them were paying him the money he was due. None of them were paying his debts when they were hired to do so. What these managers were best at was managing to ferret away as much for themselves as possible.

Scott Faragher, author of *Music City Babylon: Inside the World of Country Music,* worked for a while with Shorty Lavender at the Lavender-Blake Agency in Nashville. "One buyer bought a New Year's Eve date for the Possum," Faragher relates. "I told him that I did not think George would show up. He said that he did not care one way or the other. He figured that since it was New Year's Eve and there would be other acts on the show, he would use George Jones' name to help sell tickets." Some promoters didn't bother to make a booking and incur a booking fee, and merely went ahead and advertised Jones, got their audiences drunk, and blamed Jones for not showing up — when neither George or any of his own people knew diddly about these promoter's machinations. On another occasion, Faragher received a call from a promoter at eight o'clock on a Friday night. Where was George? Faragher called Shorty Lavender. Nobody home. He called George Jones who answered the phone. "He dismissed the matter casually," relates Faragher, "saying that he had told Shorty on Wednesday that he was not going to make the date. In other words, Shorty had known about it for three days but had intentionally withheld that information from me so that he would not have to hear me raising hell about it. Shorty had gone fishing and left me holding the bag. I called the buyer back and told her that George was not going to make the date. I did not tell her, however, that the agency had known about the situation and failed to protect her. She was crying on the phone, saying that she had borrowed money on her music store to do the show. There was nothing I could do to help her."

Sometimes George was booked into up to three venues in one night and his managers routinely blamed his non-presence on his drunkenness. His band members were seldom paid, and when they finally mutinied, he was forced to form a new band. George had already lost one band to Wynette with the divorce. When George went AWOL, his managers and promoters sent out posses to find the Possum. The most spectacular of all posses that ever set out to locate Jones was a parade of limousines and 4-wheel-drive vehicles that descended on Florence, Alabama, one fine day, all looking for George who had ducked out of flying to war-torn Ireland or some other undesirable destination and headed for the hills. Shug Baggot was on a Possum hunt and he had brought with him a small army of lackeys and bodyguards. All of their vehicles were equipped with CB radios. At first, all this extra attention tickled the Possum's funny bone no end. Jones was swapping vehicles with friends. First, he was sighted here, then, he was sighted there. He would come on the CB band as if he were a character in one of those *Smokey and the Bandit* movies or an episode of *The Dukes of Hazzard*, his voice taunting his pursuers in a gleeful chortle. Shug didn't sweat it all that much, he just dug in his heels and waited things out. After a few days, the Possum came down from the hills and Baggott put him back to work.

George was not the only person who had his life bullied and threatened by Shug and Sandy Baggott. Ralph Land, the Jones Boys' drummer at that time, had been vocal in stating that the band members needed to be paid regularly, they had mouths to feed, too. For his efforts Ralph was viewed as a shit disturber. When Land received an anonymous threat on his life, he informed the police that if he was murdered he wanted them to know who would have done it. And he named them.

Another time, when Jones was too far gone to take the stage, a shady Memphis doctor was called in to pump George full of get-up-and-go shots. This same physician, who was later indicted for supplying drugs illegally, then taped Jones tightly from his armpits to his thighs so that he could not bend over without toppling and falling. Taped up thusly like a mummy, Jones was forced on stage and propped into position before the microphone, night after night, for a full week engagement. He was kept a prisoner all this time. After the performances, he would endure the agony of someone ripping the tape off so that he could breathe properly. This sort of brutal exploitation might have continued had Shug Baggott not been arrested in August 1979 for selling a quantity of cocaine to undercover federal police agents.

Jones was a miserable wreck half of the time, and the other half of the time, he'd resurrect himself, get straightened out, then someone would show up with more cocaine — just to make sure he didn't get straight enough to notice what was happening in his career. Or straight enough to do anything about it. He has claimed that he was seldom paid in money and often paid only in cocaine. He has also admitted that he was weak and vulnerable to their actions at the time.

Thugs delivered cocaine concealed in guitars. Managers lured Jones to places where gorillas filled his nose. In one sense, George's naivete was what got him through. If it was true that he was at times only being paid in cocaine, it is also true that he didn't make the same mistake that Shug made. George never sold that cocaine to people. Writers have slagged him for his casual generosity in spreading the powder around at parties and the like. What they have never said is that George would have been dead in the water, just like ole Shug, if he'd started *selling* that powder to people. And he never did.

Peanut Montgomery's wife, Charlene Montgomery, who was getting herself into the real estate business in those days, went shopping for a house for George Jones in Florence, Alabama. She also fixed it up a bit and furnished it complete with live-in companion, Linda Welborn, Charlene's recently separated sister. Well, it wasn't done exactly that obviously, but the introduction was made and soon Linda would be described as George Jones' "live-in girlfriend." George liked Linda for her down-home ways but his association with Welborn did little to turn around his sinking career or his self-abuse. Oddly, Peanut Montgomery was the friend who convinced George to seek treatment for his addictions, but when George Jones responded well to treatment, he fell into the orbit of another threesome — George Richey, his wife Tammy Wynette, and his brother Paul Richey. While all of these people said that they were George's friends, it would not be until he had separated himself from his acquaintance with all six of them that he would begin to straighten himself out.

George's bankruptcy proceedings in 1979 brought an accounting of just how sad his financial situation had become, but it was not immediately granted when George's lawyer first filed. Some of the debts were highly exaggerated. While there were a few 'hard' debts for hotel bills and mortgages, most of the debt came from civil court settlements of claims George never contested. Tammy had also sued George at opportune moments for missing child support payments — she knew when his royalty payments would be made. If George had contested these various claims in court, no doubt some would have been dismissed.

"I didn't want to do it," George told Dolly Carlisle, "but Shug talked me into it. He filed bankruptcy at the same time I did to save his ass." The media feeding frenzy that took place when it was announced that George had filed for bankruptcy was not confined to Nashville. National television networks and newspaper chains found the story newsworthy. George Jones was headline news all over the country. Again. Jones' debts were said to be nearly one and a half million dollars, his total assets less than a hundred grand. And there was plenty of juicy gossip to bulk the story out. After a while, facts and figures were abandoned altogether as the writers built up the next story based on their previous stories. Few of them had compassion or insight into Jones' personal situation. As Dolly Carlisle later wrote, "in the cold winter of 1979 only the lurid and sensational details of his disintegrating life seemed to be news. George oftentimes wondered why the reporters didn't tell the public why he was in such bad shape."

While George's sorry financial state was being aired in bankruptcy proceedings, he was coping with the sorrow of losing family and friends. Tammy had been at his side performing in England when he'd learned that his mother was gravely ill, and they'd flown from Wembley to Texas to be with her before she passed away. Without Tammy, and with both his parents gone, there was no one to turn to when people he cared about died. In 1975, Lefty died, victim of a life-ending stroke. That same year Darrell Edwards shot himself. In 1977, Elvis left the building. And a year after that, Mel Street, a Nashville recording artist who had befriended Jones, ended his life with a .38 bullet to the head. By this time, George, not in the best of shape to begin with, was grief-stricken. He was granted a safe zone by the Nashville police on strictly a gentleman's agreement that he come to town, go to Mel Street's funeral where he would sing, and go back to Florence — and they wouldn't pick him up. This period of exile and Mel Street's suicide were merely two more of the facets that were added into George's confused state of mind. As the worst year of his life, 1979, came 'round, there was no relief in sight.

Jones has used the expression "the writers were clobbering me in those days" in reference to the articles being printed about his no shows and his personal life. Heck, that is putting it mildly. And the more lurid the stories on George became, the more peculiar his behavior became. There was that cut-out of Hank Williams which he got from Billy Sherrill and which traveled with him in the back seat of his Lincoln or Cadillac (George bought, sold, and traded cars more regularly than some folks take showers). As Billy's daughter Diane Sherril commented to Dolly Carlisle, "I think he had decided he was going out like Hank Williams. My father had a life-size picture of Hank that was given him by Ernest Tubb. It meant a lot to my dad because Ernest had given it to him. But George came in here to our house one day and asked for it to keep a few days, just to keep in the car with him . . . I heard later that George drove around for days with that picture in his car talking and singing to it. Jones wanted to go out, but it just wasn't his time."

There were people like Rick Blackburn and Billy Sherrill at CBS Records and Waylon Jennings who wanted to see George either commit himself or get committed for treatment. There were people like Helen and W.T. Scroggins back in Texas who wanted nothing more than to see George go in for some treatment. When he finally did, ten friends chipped in $1,000 each to cover the cost. "But George was paranoid," Carlisle observes, "afraid that if he checked himself into a clinic or hospital that he would be declared insane." Jones himself said, "A lot of people would like to see me do that so they could say I was crazy." While this fear was still based on his ignorance of the fact that alcoholism was a disease rather than a moral failure, his fear of being declared insane probably wasn't a totally paranoid one.

With George threatening to sue Shug Baggot and his brother Sandy, Baggot responded by campaigning to discredit George by divulging his "Deedoodle Duck" personality. "He was having periods where he would go insane and didn't know what he was doing," Baggot told Dolly Carlisle. "George could talk like Donald Duck and did so at times to amuse children. But one day when George and I were having a heated discussion, George began to cuss me in the Donald Duck language. I was shocked and asked him, what did he mean talking to me like that? George immediately started warning Donald not to talk to Shug like that. George and Donald became involved in a real argument."

Shug alleged that Jones' friends, Johnny Cash and Waylon Jennings, had come to Jones' aid with big money, with Cash prepared to write a check for as much as a quarter million dollars. Perhaps, in his interviews with Dolly Carlisle, ole Shug had been setting the stage for the times he would be held accountable for all of that money that had gone missing from George Jones' shows. Cash and Jennings have suggested far smaller amounts of aid were provided. Shug even told a story that had Jones driving around with $60,000 in the trunk of his car that had been given to him.

Whatever hidden agendas Baggott may have had in those days, what he did have to say about the duck behavior is revealing. "George began to use Donald to talk anytime he was afraid to say something as George Jones. . . . Around this time, George was beginning to forget the words to his songs. His shows were spotted with forgetting the words, but Donald never forgot any of the words. . . . Donald would take over and finish the line. . . . This went on for months until everyone realized that George had lost control of Donald." Jones himself has always referred to the duck as "Deedoodle."

Things became much darker for George as Donald took over. As Baggott told Carlisle, while performing at the Exit-In club, Jones no longer sang like Jones at all and was carried out in a straightjacket. During his darkest days,

George no longer performed except in an unshaven state on the streets of Nashville, but more often he just hung out in his car. Tourists might recognize him on the street, but they soon decided the bum they were looking at couldn't be George Jones. "I went to about the lowest that you could go on the booze," George admits. "When I was at that point, I knew there was no way out of it . . . so, I went to the other stuff . . . the hard . . . drugs. And then I really got in bad shape. I got down to about 105 pounds, they said. And I looked terrible. I sung terrible. And I *was* terrible."

Here is the crux of Jones' next big hurt hurt. George just couldn't stand it to know that the world believed him to be a nasty, wife-beating son-of-a-bitch. What drove him over the edge was his frustration that everybody believed Wynette and treated him like a mean dog. George was in the dog house for all the world to see, and he could see no way of getting out of there. In the murky atmosphere, he fell prey to all of the ghostly presences that had dogged him throughout his earthly existence. Although not recorded until 1981 on his SAME OLE ME album, the lyrics to *Good Ones And Bad Ones* must have come to mind.

> *Some come from Heaven and some crawl from Hell*
> *And the good fight the bad for your soul*
> *But it's hard to tell a lie from the truth*
> *When you find one that easy to hold*
>
> *There's no way of knowin' which one you've been lovin'*
> *Till you leave her or lose her for good*
> *And by then its too late, you just mark it to fate*
> *Either way you end up a fool . . .*

Good Ones And Bad Ones (J. Chambers & L. Jenkins)

Here we see George Jones' basic philosophy of life laid out in black and white. George recorded this same song again in 1994 as a duet with Mark Chestnutt. On the 1994 recording, it still seems like George is singing about Tammy, about how the absolute worst thing in the whole world that could happen to him is to be made to look like a fool. Sparked by the commanding bark of James Burton's lower register, slow motion, honky tonk boogie guitar riff, Jones and Chestnutt deliver their lines with passion. As they sing, they evoke the essence of the South, where dueling forces not only compete for a man's soul, but also *force* a man to decide between a series of choices dividing his world into good or evil, wife or lover, friend or enemy, cold or hot, left or right, jail or freedom, country or city . . . This is the basic belief system upon which country music has been founded. This was also the root of George Jones' 'problem.' George has lived every song he has sang.

Any such fundamentalist belief system leaves a sincere person wide open to the ravages of shame, remorse, and guilt, as well as the plethora of crippling complexes resulting from these negative emotions, with no clear course to recti-fy things except to abuse oneself or be 'born again'. Left untreated, a self-abuser will often perish before they find the light, and even then, nothing has been fixed. Modern psychological insights and techniques often work hand in glove with kicking substance-dependency and pave the way back to being able to accept redemption — in the Christian world of the South, to accept or Jesus into your heart. Without professional treatment or exceptionally insightful personal help from a friend or loved one, a person's world — once split into two by guilt, trauma, or humiliation — remains divided. That person can no longer see the wholeness of life. The ability to make simple judgements deserts them. They can't see how things can become whole again. See how wife can be your lover, too. Fire and ice together can make water. But you cannot arrive at this decision if you keep looking from one to the other trying to figure out if the woman you are about to hand the key to your heart will cherish yours in return or whether all she really wants is the key to your door, your BMW, and your bank account. The sheer fear of deciding paralyzes you.

Before you can become whole once again, you have to trust trust your judg-ment. See through whatever veils of deceit are being woven before your eyes. If you've been upping the ante with substance abuse, you've got to dry yourself out before you can even hope to become whole.

During the late 1970s, George Jones had lost his faith in himself because he had been made to look like a fool. Several times. When he was accused of violent actions he says he did not commit, George's dualistic view of the world short-circuited. When he saw himself as a bad person, he could no longer also see that he had plenty of good in him, too. He became trapped within this on-off situation and the world disappeared. Jones could only see himself forever hung in public, perhaps even publicly crucified, guilty of crimes he had not committed. His existence had become a battleground. "Some come from Heaven and some come from Hell. And the good fight the bad for your soul."

George Jones loves to drive a car, and drive he did in those days, some-times with Jimmie Hall from Jimmie's barbershop in Florence, up the highway into Tennessee, cruising along until they came to Tammy's house, where they would slow down as they circled the driveway, then speed up again, heading George's Lincoln south for home. More often he traveled alone with Deedoodle and the old man for company, just looping from Florence to Tammy's driveway, over and over.

There was no one to turn to except Luke the Drifter, and at first Jones approached fearfully, ready to accompany ole Hank into the next world — but ashamed all the same to be asking for his help. He was unworthy.

Hank was not amused. He didn't speak for days. Finally, he coughed and said, "Boy, what the hell are you doing to yourself?"

Deedoodle said, "Can't you see, he's messed up in his head. Can't sing. Can't do nothin', 'cept drink from the bottle."

The old man said, "Hee-hee, y'got that right."

Hank said, "Boy, no damn woman is worth that much grief. Take your damn duck and get out of my face. This just ain't your time or your place."

George said, "Won't do no damn good. You won't go away, neither."

"He think's you're watchin' over his shoulder," quacked Deedoodle, "watchin' him all the time."

"Even when he's in the sack!" chuckled the old man.

George said, "Butt out, you guys!"

"So," said Deedoodle, "how will he know when it's his damn time?"

The old man said, "He'll know. Hee-hee."

Hank began to hum. After a few bars George joined in. They began to sing together. "Your cheatin' heart . . ." As they moved on to *I Saw The Light*, a choir of angels joined in, and George was lifted, raised up out of his body. His spirit felt light as a feather. He felt so good that he fell asleep.

When George woke up, he was alone, and it was cold there in the back of the car. He opened the door and stepped out into the alley. It was even colder out there. He reached into the car to get his jacket. The empty bottles rattled around, one of them falling onto the floor between the seats where it rattled around some more with the ones down there. But he got the jacket and put it on. He closed the rear door and opened the drivers' side front door. He got in and sat behind the wheel and turned the key and the motor turned over. After a few minutes, he put the Caddy in gear. He was tired and hungry and it was a long way back to Florence.

George was hauled away from his Florence home by paramedics on December 11, 1979 and taken to the Eliza Coffee Memorial Hospital. A few days later he was transferred to the Hillcrest Hospital in Birmingham. Tammy Wynette sent George Richey down to Alabama with some money to help out, but Jones was admitted with no down payment before Richey even arrived. He was in the treatment center for 21 days, far less than the predicted 90-day period doctors had first thought would be necessary. Upon his release, he appeared to have gained back sufficient health and vitality so that people believed his resolve to reclaim his career. In his authorized video biography, George referred to this treatment episode as "the best thing that ever happened to me. The first couple of weeks was the roughest. I hated everybody. I still didn't see no way back. I was sayin', 'Wait till I get out of here,' that's all. And in the last couple of weeks, you're in there, you got time to think . . . you're gettin' your body back in shape, your mind back to where you can think. And then havin' some fine cards and letters from so many fans — that really gave me that big lift that I needed to get back on track. Then I met Nancy, right after I got out of the hospital." When George and Nancy met on a double date with his road manager, Wayne Oliver, they hit it off right away, staying up all night in a New York hotel room talking the hours away until dawn crept through the curtains.

Not long after that, George Jones' live-in girlfriend, Linda Welborn, found herself displaced by Nancy Sepulvado. Someone who cared. George Jones provided Nancy with hope because, when he was sober and hadn't been woofing his cocaine, he was the nicest person she had ever met. There were still the gorillas to deal with — but George had seen a glimmer of light at the end of the tunnel of fear and loathing.

Preparing for The Bradley Barn Sessions with Marty Stuart, Brian Ahern, and Alan Jackson.

George with Tammy
live one last time
(above) and with
Nancy for all time
(right).

George Jones has lived to tell it all in his autobiography.

Part Four

⋯⟞⟝ ⟞⟝⋯

Who's Gonna
Fill Their Shoes?

1

He Stopped Loving Her Today

B illy Sherrill was one of the reasons that George Jones could step right back into his career as if he'd just taken that 21-day vacation at Hillcrest for a little R&R. After several years of chronic no shows, disappointing performances, and a sorry period of drug and alcohol abuse that nearly put him in the grave, the Possum was back. Within days of his release from the hospital, he was in the recording studio working with Billy on *He Stopped Loving Her Today*, and in early March 1980 he and Wynette were back on the radio together again. Critics called his return to top form a miracle comeback.

Sherrill's job was to keep the records coming, but he was delighted to have his friend walk back into the studio with a smile on his face. During George's worst of times in the fall of 1979, Sherrill and Jones had set about recording *He Stopped Loving Her Today*, written by Bobby Braddock and Curly Putman, but George kept singing the melody to Kris Kristofferson's *Help Me Make It Through The Night*, which was fine if you were singing that song. As George and Billy tell the story in *Same Ole Me*, the authorized video biography, when he got over that hurdle, there was the spoken recitation to be done. Four spoken lines and you're outta there. Piece of cake. While George could *sing* real well when intoxicated, he slurred his words when he tried to enunciate that recitation. Eighteen months went by, George went into the Hillcrest detox center, and when he came out, it *was* a piece of cake.

> *You know she came back today for the last time*
> *Oh, and we all wondered if she would*
> *And it kept runnin' through my mind*
> *Well, this time he's over her for good*

— *He Stopped Loving Her Today* (Bobby Braddock & Curly Putman)

When George began to work with Sherrill in the early 1970s, at first the two were wary of each other, but soon learned that neither one bit. They both were singular characters after all. Sherrill seldom felt at ease in crowded rooms and would often simply walk away. He had little patience for time spent sitting around boardroom tables talking marketing strategy. He was a former musician who had cut his studio teeth as a recording engineer working for Sam Phillips in Sam's Nashville operation in the early 1960s. At CBS, Sherrill had become a legend in his own right before he began to work with George Jones, but he was known for his countrypolitan productions on records by artists like David Houston and Charlie Rich, not for hard country records. Sometimes, Sherrill rolled up his sleeves and did the writing himself, including such standards as *Almost Persuaded, Stand By Your Man,* and *The Most Beautiful Girl.* In September 1999, BMI named him the most successful BMI songwriter of the 20th century; he has won 65 BMI Country Awards.

"We were both scared to death," Sherrill recalled in the authorized video biography. "I was scared of him. He said he was scared of me. I think all I did was to change the instrumentation around him. I don't think he's ever changed at all. I did ask him to sing lower, in lower keys, because in his older recordings he's really, really high, and kind of annoying, to me."

George remembers that their early meetings established a rapport that grew as time went by. "I got to know Billy, and he got to know me," he notes in *Same Ole Me.* "He got to know my feelings that I wanted to do strictly country arrangements, hard core country arrangements. But, soon as he learned me and I learned him a little bit more, and we was able to communicate — it all worked out just fine."

From that point on, Billy Sherrill and George Jones set out to create truly classic recordings. For the first time on Jones' cuts there were real dynamics, skillful arrangements, and, when Jones was not too far gone to keep on laying down tracks until Sherrill was satisfied — ultimate takes. The collaboration between Jones and Sherrill continued on through George's worst personal years, climaxed in 1980 and '81 with the award-winning *He Stopped Loving Her Today,* a two-time winner of the CMA Song of the Year Award (for writers Braddock and Putman) that helped Jones win back-to-back Best Male Vocalist CMAs. In 1992, both *Country America* magazine and *USA Today* asked fans to name their favorite country song of all-time: when the results of the poll were tabulated, *He Stopped Loving Her Today* was number one.

Sherrill had encouraged Curly Putman and Bobby Braddock to return to their song *He Stopped Loving Her Today* to re-write it until it clicked for George Jones. Braddock thought that *He Stopped Loving Her Today* was a "pretty good song, but not spectacular. We were doing tongue-in-cheek things like 'If you think he looks natural now, you should have seen him two weeks ago . . .' " Braddock and Putnam were, after all, fooling with powerful material, a guy who only stops loving a gal when he dies. Curly Putman credits Braddock with the original idea, which started as a "funereal joke." When Sherrill encouraged the two songwriters to go back to it, to make it work, they applied their songwriting 101 skills. "We had to find a way to get around the controversy of the guy being dead," Putnam acknowledged. "You do have to have a little finesse."

When Jones and Sherrill sat down to listen to the final mix, George said, "Nobody will buy that morbid son-of-a-bitch," but Billy wagered a $200 bet that the song would become a hit. Needless to say, Sherrill won the bet. "Billy Sherrill really believed in the song," Braddock says. "George Jones' performance and Billy Sherrill's production have a hell of a lot to do with that record becoming a standard."

He said I'll love you till I die
She told him you'll forget in time
I watched the years went slowly by
She still preyed upon his mind

He kept her picture upon his wall
Went half crazy now and then . . .

He stopped loving her today
They placed a wreath upon his door
Soon they'll carry him away
He stopped loving her today

Sherrill had an uncanny ability to find songwriters who composed lyrics that sounded like George wrote them. Taken autobiographically, this song marked the beginning of George's freedom from the demons his relationship with Tammy Wynette had loosed. He had stopped loving her that way.

To cope with George's downward spiral over the previous few years when he often arrived at the studio in rough shape, Sherrill had simply adopted the practice of going ahead and building tracks in advance so that when Jones did appear ready to sing, he could sometimes cut a song in a single take and be out of there in a few minutes. "I'd rather spend three minutes with George Jones," Sherrill told Dolly Carlisle, "than three hours with most singers." This haphazard way of doing things led to the disappointing 1979 album MY VERY SPECIAL GUESTS, however. Because it took a while to put together, with duets by a lineup of heavyweights that included Elvis Costello, Linda Ronstadt, Johnny Paycheck, Willie and Waylon, Emmylou Harris, and Tammy Wynette, by the time the package was finished and in the record stores, it was a much anticipated release. After the initial hoopla, critics and fans alike responded with less enthusiasm when they heard the music in the grooves. Jones, himself, was disappointed. "I'm proud that I was lucky enough to have such fine beautiful people to agree to do it. But I'm not proud of my work on it . . . I'm not proud of what I did."

George had simply not been around when very many of those duets were recorded, and his voice had been in pretty rough shape when he *was* there. He had not met James Taylor, the author of the title track for the 1978 album BARTENDER'S BLUES, either. In fact, he didn't really know who Taylor was but responded positively to *Bartender's Blues* when Rick Blackburn first played him a demo of the track, complete with Sweet Baby James' harmony vocal. All that was left to be done was for George to record the lead vocal. That recording had been a number 6 hit in 1978. For James Taylor, having George Jones sing his song was a privilege. "So often somebody will take your song and it comes back to you not quite what you had in mind when you wrote it," Taylor comments in *Same Ole Me*. "With a George Jones singing it, it's like having somebody breathe life into your song." Later that year, George had more input during the sessions with his pal Johnny Paycheck and their version of Chuck Berry's *Maybelline* rocked. Their album of duets was called DOUBLE TROUBLE — and I'll bet they were.

Regardless of how poorly George may have performed on this duet album, he came back with a vengeance with *He Stopped Loving Her Today*, and though another four years would pass before he completely put his substance abuse behind him, he regained the respect he had momentarily lost. In fact, he was receiving praise right, left, and center. As Johnny Cash remarks in the authorized video biography, "a rock & roll singer pretty well summed it up. . . . I was with Nick Lowe and Elvis Costello in the recording studio and I was playin' a demo of George Jones. And Elvis Costello and Nick Lowe were sittin' there with tears in their eyes. We were drinkin' a little bit and Elvis Costello held the bottle up and he said, 'The greatest country singer in the history of the world, George Jones!' I said, 'You're right.' "

Recognition from his peers and fans was never a question for George Jones, but like Hank Williams, Elvis Presley, and Johnny Cash, who had all had their troubles with Opry managers at one time or another, George was not immediately recognized by the Nashville establishment and the politically inbred Country Music Association — not until he'd been around for quite some time and a few years after most people on Music Row "thought he was a goner." Then in 1980 Jones was voted the CMA's Male Vocalist of the Year and winner of the Single of the Year award for He Stopped Loving Her Today. This was recognition that was long overdue.

Sure, he'd had that brief period during the early 1960s when the trade magazines recognized his talent for singing She Still Thinks I Still Care and handed him a few of those elusive awards that mostly seemed to go to everybody else. However, during the following decade when George Jones and Tammy Wynette were known as "Mr & Mrs Country Music," he and Wynette were consistently overlooked by association voters who chose combinations like Porter Wagoner & Dolly Parton, Conway Twitty & Loretta Lynn, Waylon Jennings & Willie Nelson, Jim Ed Brown & Helen Cornelius, Kenny Rogers & Dottie West. "We had gobs of hits together," Jones has said, "and big albums. We were nominated every year and we never won one award together."

Despite his complaints, George had never felt comfortable about awards shows. He'd messed up on Tammy the first time they had gone to a CMA Awards show together in the late '60s, power drinking all afternoon before the show. After winning in 1980 for the first time, he was nominated in 1981 for a CMA Male Vocalist award and scheduled to perform on the show at least once, maybe twice, if he agreed to sing his few lines from I Was Country Before Country Was Cool, a vocal collaboration he'd recorded with Barbara Mandrell which was also nominated for an award. George messed up again.

Expecting the worse, Rick Blackburn installed Jones on the day of the show in a room at the Opryland Hotel adjacent to the theater where the awards show was being held. Late in the day, it was nap time for the Possum, and thinking that things were under control, Blackburn left the hotel to go home and get dressed in his tuxedo. He wasn't gone long, but during his absence, one of the Possum's cronies came by with a bottle and the two started nipping. When Rick came back to the room, accompanied by Tom Binkley, George's attorney, he found Jones alone once again but passed out in the bathtub. It was only an hour to show time, and Rick Blackburn — as vice president of CBS Records Nashville — was not about to have his star pull another no show, no matter how drunk he had gotten himself.

Blackburn and Binkley ran a cold shower on George, poured black coffee into him, dressed him, and forcibly walked him into the Opryland Theater. They knew he had to watch the Possum closely — you could see in his eyes he didn't want to be there. Backstage, they pulled George out of his scheduled slot where he was supposed to sing *He Stopped Loving Her Today* for the TV cameras, and they thought they had persuaded Barbara Mandrell to go it alone, too. But while she was singing, Mandrell came down the aisle to where George was seated and held the microphone out to him. He had only a hoarse whisper of a voice. Once again, Jones felt totally humiliated.

A few minutes later, George heard his name announced as winner of the Male Vocalist of the Year Award. Blackburn propelled him toward the stage. When he turned to the audience while accepting his award, he thanked Johnny Wright and Kitty Wells and no one else — they were the only folks he could make out through the bright lights sitting there in the audience. What he actually said was, "Well, I'm one of the Jones' Boys," holding his trophy aloft for all to see, "and I just want to say one thing. I'm very proud and I love . . . Johnny Wright and Kitty Wells. Thank you! We love country music!" Then the show producers faded up the fanfare as George moved to the wings.

The show was not without a light moment or two, though, as Merle Haggard recalls in his autobiography. A few months before the 1981 CMA awards show, Haggard had been asked by George's management to fill in for the Possum on a date he couldn't make because he was messed up, and in return he made George promise to straighten himself out in time to play his next show. George didn't keep his end of the bargain, and Merle was pissed off. But Haggard could not stay mad for very long. When both men attended the awards show, Jones was seated in the row behind Haggard, who initially ignored the Possum. As Haggard recalls, "I could feel his eyes on the back of my head but I wouldn't turn around. Finally, he leaned over my shoulder and said real close to my ear, 'Hag, you still mad at ole George?' " Merle did his best to keep up his stonewall, but the Possum persisted. " 'Hag . . . are you really mad at pore ole George?' What could I do? I broke up laughing. Nobody, not even Tammy Wynette, can stay mad at George very long."

A year earlier, Tammy and George indeed seemed to have made up. In a cover story published in the June 1980 in *Country Music* magazine, Tammy interviewed her ex-husband. At the time Wynette and Jones were reunited on record for *Two Story House* and a tour during which Jones would refer to Wynette's songwriter husband, George Richey, as "my husband-in-law." Some of the repartee was quite funny. For example, when Wynette asks Jones who his favorite girl singer is, Jones replies, "Connie Smith." While this is the truth, Wynette and Jones had fun with the question. Wynette quipped, "I think we're through with the interview." Jones began to speak and they both broke up laughing. "No," says Jones, "you know *you're* my favorite. Of course, Connie has to be second." Wynette *has* to say, "Connie's second, and I'm first. That's a much better way to end the interview." Throughout the nine-page print interview, the two sparred over Wynette's book *Stand by Your Man* which had just been published. Jones maintained that he hadn't read it, yet. No one had given him a copy. Wynette pledged to make sure he received an autographed copy.

While it lasted, some writers had fun with the reunion. An article put together by the combined writing talents of Jim Albrecht, Stacy Harris, and Bob Battle for the June 1980 issue of *Country Style* magazine was whimsically titled: "George & Tammy Du-et Again — A Soap Opry." The extensive subtitle read, "Tammy Wynette is standing by her men — fifth husband George Richey and former husband George Jones. She's now singing with a healthy and sober Jones. The days of her 'nagging' and his 'nipping' are over. It's just another chapter in the soap opry story of George and Tammy."

"I guess we're the Sonny and Cher of country music," Wynette bantered. Her reason for the divorce was short and concise: "my nagging and his nipping."

After the 1975 divorce, Billy Sherrill had kept the two together on record for a few years. He'd chosen provocative songs for George to record, songs like Bobby Braddock's *Her Name Is . . .* where the fans could fill in the blanks with Tammy's name, even though George never mentioned her name specifically as he sang the lyrics. But that, too, ended when Wynette's lawsuits — claiming $80,00 for unpaid child support payment — along with dozens of other debts and legal judgements, all contributed to Jones' bankruptcy. In the interim, George Richey and Wynette had gotten hitched.

Yet somehow in 1980, Sherrill had his duet partners back in the studio to make the TOGETHER AGAIN album. *Two Story House* was a song that Wynette had written specifically for the two of them to sing. Billy Sherrill recorded it, and their fans ate it up. For a while, Wynette and Jones toured together in 1980 — along with George Richey. Richey had previously contributed songs like *A Picture Of Me Without You* (a Richey co-write with Norro Wilson) and *The*

Grand Tour (a co-write with Richey, Carmol Taylor, and Norro Wilson) to Jones' recording career. *The Grand Tour* had been a number one hit on the radio during the faltering final two years of the Wynette-Jones marriage, the period when Jones was on the rise and Wynette was no longer hitting the top of the chart with her releases. The song begins with Jones singing, "Step right up, come on in . . ." and he proceeds like a tour guide to walk the listener through the rooms of this imaginary house, which used to be a happy home, where each detail and nearly every piece of furniture reminds him of the woman who has left him stranded there. His fans, naturally, thought of Wynette as they listened along.

For the tour to promote *Two Story House*, Richey would sometimes play the piano when Jones and Wynette sang. But everything was not peaches and cream. Not all of the time. Jones would later say that he hated being coerced into that odd triangle. Still, Wynette's career had been cooling off, and she needed the help. On the road and in the tabloids together, Tammy and George were news and, once again, they sold a whole lot of product for Epic Records and the parent company, Columbia Records.

Fans turned out in droves to witness the spectacle of the ex-Mr & Mrs Country Music on stage again. Country's newest soapy threesome posed for numerous photos portraying the image that they were happy at least some of the time together. No matter what anyone said later on.

Patrick Carr reviewed the initial reunion concert for *Country Music* magazine. "For many of us, tonight is a great occasion. We're George Jones fans, and for the last few years we've been biting the bullet, showing up for gigs at which George has failed to materialize, hearing about his problems from afar, and beginning to wonder whether we would ever see him perform again in the flesh. Tonight's the night, then; George is here in this hall in New London, Connecticut, and that beautiful, subtle, bitten-back sob of a voice is a tonic. The voice is in trim, too, and so is George. Standing up there in a nice conservative dark brown suit and acting humble, he is obviously in a condition of non-alcoholic competence. The voice is supple and controlled, and George is remembering all the words to his songs. The audience seemed puzzled, as well they should be. Is all this romantic tension real, or is it showbiz? They'll never know. We find out, though, because the second show of the evening features all the same George & Tammy & George jokes, in all the same places, as the first show did."

Jones had made a major miscue when the new George & Tammy act had appeared on the *Tonight Show* to debut the new record. Jones had never performed the duet *Two Story House* in public before that night, and he had been reading his lyrics off cue cards. When the person holding the cards advanced the shuffle too quickly, Jones had been left with his face hanging out on national TV. In *The Village Voice*, Mark Rose described the *Tonight Show* debacle. "After Jones went in the hospital and supposedly got himself straight, a media blitz heralded the return of 'everyone's favorite singer.' One of the first stops was the *Tonight Show* with Tammy Wynette. After Tammy talked with guest host Roy Clark, she brought George out to sing their new song, a duet she wrote called *Two Story House*. Tammy, in a sequined evening gown, looked bright and attractive as usual, but George, well, he didn't look exactly right . . . about six shades short of pale. Kind of like he was prepared by a mortician for the affair. After beginning a few lines of the song, George fell silent, whispered to Tammy, 'I forgot the words,' and stood there awkwardly smiling at her, mouthing who knows what, a marionette with loose strings. Tammy smiled brightly, lovingly prodded George along, and tried to remind him of the words, but he seemed to have other things on his mind, like where the closest exit was." George would later state that he had thought that the show was being taped and was waiting for someone to call out "Cut!" — waiting for them to begin the segment over again. Along with an overly coiffed hair-styling that the TV show crew had slapped onto George, once again, he had been made the fool. To her credit, Wynette in that frivolous, funny interview with Jones had gone out of her way to point out the cause of the forgotten lyrics — the cue cards. Some writers never mentioned them at all.

Not long after this incident the camaraderie between the two broke down and they would not record again together for nearly 14 years. One of the issues had to be what George read in Tammy's autobiography when he finally got his hands on a copy. Another was that while Tammy and George Richey had come to Jones' rescue with money and advice, they had also hooked Jones up with Paul Richey, George Richey's brother, as a manager. At first, that liaison had seemed promising. A deal was cut with the prestigious Jim Halsey booking agency, and for a while the truce between Jones and Wynette seemed to have taken hold. Wynette and George Richey went on record as saying that they were helping Jones. Jones went along with the charade. However, as several commentators have pointed out, both singers needed help. Jones with his health and his drinking problem. Wynette with her sagging popularity.

In her book, Wynette alleged that Jones had beat her. That he had held a gun on her. That he had fired a gun at her. These allegations appearing in cold, hard print for all the world to read stung George. He had that old-fashioned sense that you simply didn't kiss and tell. Who would believe him if he denied these allegations? Who would believe him if he told the world what Tammy was really like? Likely, no one. He had squandered his credibility years ago. George held his tongue for 16 years until 1996 when he came out with his own book, repudiating some of Tammy's claims but also recognizing that his behavior had been at times intimidating. And, even if he never struck Wynette, he was guilty of spousal abuse in the wider sense of that word that has now come to be accepted. Nowadays, he's sorry that any of those things happened. At the time, though, the publication of Tammy's book was merely one last straw that tipped the scales against the continuance of their odd reunion as recording and touring artists.

The CMA, ACM, and Grammy awards had made George an even more inviting target for unscrupulous booking agents and promoters. Almost overnight he went from being an act who was booked for venues seating two or three thousand a night to 10 times that many. Almost as quickly, George began to spiral downward from the lofty heights of his miracle comeback. In many ways, he was the *Same Ole Me*, the title of his 1981 hit where he was joined by the Oakridge Boys on the vocal tracks.

To begin functioning better, George really needed to find someone he could trust. But before George could find that someone, he had to rid himself of some of the bullies who had taken over his life. His one decent chance to work with an honest, capable manager had been when he had approached Neil Reshen, Waylon's New York-based manager, but by the time George got out of his rehab at Hillcrest, Reshen had been admitted to hospital himself where he underwent open-heart surgery. With the Baggott brothers and then with the Richey brothers, George was constantly bullied and pushed around.

George had felt out of place during the taping of the HBO Special *George Jones: With a Little Help from My Friends*, a glitzy production arranged by Paul Richey to garner even higher fees (and percentages) for George's road shows. The production had been inappropriate, to say the least. George's personal musical friends had been scripted to recite a litany of show-writer accolades that made him feel even less comfortable than usual. But there seemed to be no limit to the plans that Paul Richey had for his star singer. He even had begun to execute plans for an album where George would sing duets with Hank Williams' disembodied voice.

Not coincidentally, journalists again began to speculate on George's apparent death wish — his desire to join ole Hank on the other side. In the *Village*

Voice, Mark Rose published a feature entitled "George Jones: Last Exit Off a Dark Highway." Rose began his article reporting accurately Jones' appearance on the 1981 Grammy show. "It was last February, the best of times for George Jones," Rose wrote. "He was in New York to appear on the Grammys and he looked healthy and sober, ready to resume his role as the ordained king of country music, a title he has held for two decades, even in the worst of times, which were not far behind him. He was sorting out his life, trying to come to grips with his past and looking forward to next year, which promised to be even brighter. When he stood on the stage of Radio City to accept the Grammy for best performance, male artist, country category (*He Stopped Loving Her Today*), Jones thanked God, and said, 'This has been the greatest year of my life.' Winning the Grammy capped what some have called a comeback, but it was actually closer to a raising from the grave." While noting that George's born-again manager, Paul Richey, was in the habit of reading the Bible to Jones during their touring schedule, Rose feared that Jones was getting closer to the early grave Hank and Jimmie had dug for themselves. For a while in the early '80s George once again barely had one foot still here in the world of the living.

As more and more writers were predicting George's death, there were people in the industry who were taking bets on whether Jones would show up for one show date or another, leading the public to believe that it was now time to lay odds on the day that No Show would show up in a coffin. In his autobiography, George alleges that he feared for his life when he heard a rumor that someone had taken a life insurance policy out on his name. If he were to die from an overdose . . . or in an automobile accident . . . or . . . To give him his due, George Jones certainly worked diligently at fulfilling their prophesies. Ironically, he had at one time during the 1960s done just that, shown up in a coffin, playing possum, as part of one of his pranks. Stonewall Jackson and some of the other artists on that tour had carried George in and set him down in that casket before a promoter who began to worry that, with Jones dead, he had no one to headline his show and would have to refund the ticket money he had already collected. The performers all got a kick out of the expression on that gullible promoter's face when George sprang from the coffin.

While George was playing with destiny, Paul Richey was allegedly robbing him blind. He could have even been using the holy book in vain to distract the singer from noticing that he was being swindled. But there was more than "swindling" going on. Jones reported being severely beaten by one of the gorillas trying to collect from Richey. "I'm not going to be bluffed and beat up on while they're stealing my money. They came to my house twice and beat up on me. They took me, George, my husband-in-law as I used to call him, and Paul, my manager, over to his house and beat up on me again. Nobody knows this, but it's the truth." From Jones' garbled statements reported here and there in the press, it wasn't exactly clear who was doing the strong-arm work.

Jones soon after tried to dismiss Richey, claiming that even though he was earning between $6,000 and $15,000 per show and performing constantly, he had only $250 in his pocket. "I have nothing to my name," George complained. "They won't let me have my clothes. They won't let me have anything. For a man who has supposedly won all these awards I'm supposed to have something."

When Paul Richey was not readily agreeable to tearing up the five-year contract George Jones had signed, George enlisted the aid of a long, tall Texan by the name of Billy Bob Barnett, a six-foot-seven former Dallas Cowboy football player and the proprietor of Billy Bob's nightclub in Fort Worth Texas. Barnett came on like gangbusters, but as far as acting in George's best interests went, Barnett turned out to be a disappointment, for he was soon sitting down with Paul Richey making deals. At that time, George Jones finally showed good instinct when he used the situation to free himself from both men.

George could remember the days when a performer walked away from a show with cash in his pocket and never looked back. The situation had complicated itself, however, and in the early 1980s, with the increasing number of agents and promoters — each with a percentage of each deal — a performer seldom saw any money at all. There were simply too many cooks. In an attempt to simplify the situation, George decided to go it on his own and hired a road manager, Wayne Oliver, to handle the day-to-day logistics. When this move coincided with the long-stalled bankruptcy finally being granted, Tom Binkley, George's legal counsel, could begin to sort things out. While they were able to convince CBS Records to divert some of the royalties the bankruptcy decree had directed to George's creditors and to offer another record deal, George's No Show reputation made it tough to secure bookings.

To deal with this, Wayne Oliver convinced George that he had to do some make-up dates for the promoters he'd wronged. One of the more sensational transgressions on his plate was a contentious multi-million dollar lawsuit launched by festival promoter Jim Ryan. As George explains in his autobiography, Ryan had opened several 'Possum Holler Music Park' festival venues that, without paying Jones a permission fee or a percentage, made use of his Possum nickname, then he sued George and two other defendants, Paul Richey and Jim Halsey, in a breach of contract suit for $10.2 million dollars for not appearing at one of the grand opening shows. That no show had sparked a full-scale riot which left the Jones Boy fearing for their lives as their bus was attacked by a mob of angry fans. Tom Binkley and Wayne Oliver worked out a make-up date, but when George and the band arrived by helicopter for the show, they could see that Jim Ryan had a far larger crowd than had been there for the missed date. Ryan cleaned up that day, George suspects, making hundreds of thousands of dollars, while he was paid nothing at all. In order to appease show promoters who had sued him, this approach — playing make-up shows — became routine procedure for a while.

Soon after George ended his relationship with the Richey brothers and Wynette, he told Dolly Carlisle, "They got me to work with them to show people they were concerned about me, that they were trying to help me . . . . You know why they did that, don't you? So the fans and people will believe the lies she's told about me and forgive her because . . . all that must be true, the fans will say. They'll say, 'Look how she's still trying to do something to help him.' I don't need no more of this help."

While George was freeing himself from the gorillas, his friends were trying to convince him to return to a rehabilitation center to finish the work begun at Hillcrest in the late 1970s. There George first learned that he had an illness — that he was not morally weak. He was an alcoholic. He learned that many substance abusers hated themselves. He also faced, for the first time in his life, the fact that many boys who were abused by their fathers developed serious problems with their self-esteem. One doctor even went as far as to tell Jones that he had a problem with prosperity. He was afraid of it. Merle Haggard, in his 1981 book *Sing Me Back Home*, first recognized George's problem with success. The Hag had visited Elvis and come away from his hotel suite experience with the King, Priscilla, and the Memphis Mafia disheartened. After that experience, Haggard went out of his way to attend one of Presley's shows just to reconfirm that Elvis was still the King. Merle was not disappointed. He loved to see Elvis perform because he *was* a great entertainer. Shortly after the night of that show, Presley's death was announced. In response to this Haggard wrote, "Success, with all its promise and glitter, had demanded the ultimate payment from Elvis Presley . . . I guess we all handle success in different ways. George Jones ignores it when he can. When he can't he tries to drink it away. When he can't do either of those, he just walks out on it."

The press was less than sympathetic towards George's problem, as Ralph

Emery remarked in his book *Memories*. "When George Jones was unsuccessfully fighting alcoholism," Emery noted, "the press wouldn't get off his back." They were not above creating a George Jones story themselves from time to time. For example, one television crew followed Jones around in their van, just waiting for a story to happen. When they saw the Possum weaving on the highway leading out of downtown Nashville, they called the police who came and arrested Jones. That TV crew filmed the whole incident and that footage became an oft-used example of his drunken behavior. "The tape showed up as news footage and images were lifted for photographs that hit the newswire services," Emery recalls. "Jones was fighting a life-threatening problem and the press showed him no mercy."

On March 31, 1982, the Nashville *Tennessean* ran the headline, "George Jones Totals Auto; Hit with DUI." The story emanated from Aberdeen, Mississippi. "A day after being arrested on cocaine possession charges, country music star George Jones was charged with drunken driving yesterday after totaling his 1981 Lincoln on a rural North Mississippi road.

"Jones, 50, suffered minor facial lacerations when his car flipped over several times along a 300-foot stretch of gravel road five miles east of Hamilton, Miss., authorities said.

" 'He was conscious the entire time,' said Don Ray, Monroe County Hospital administrator. 'There were no apparent serious injuries.' "

United Press International quoted Monroe County Sheriff Frank Patterson as saying, "Jones lost control of his car about 2:30 p.m. on a county road, about 10 miles from the Mississippi-Alabama line. He had just turned off a paved road when the wreck occurred. He lost control making the turn and flipped several times down the road for about 300 feet." A few days later, a story was published labeling George Jones a "loser beyond help" and a "Godless immoral pauper."

As Rick Blackburn told Dolly Carlisle, "I kept having this fear that George would get too drunk or under the influence of drugs and that he would actually kill himself in a car. George loves to drive a car, and I had bad dreams that he would either kill himself in one or somebody else. That was my biggest fear. I knew that, if he hurt somebody else, he wouldn't be able to live with himself."

But that did not happen. It would be a few more miles down that lost highway before he would successfully seek treatment for his dueling addictions. And there would be some bumpy rides before George finally gave up his obsessions, but, when he did, he began to address the rabble of critics who had followed his downward spiral and fed like vampires off his waning vital energy.

Finally, at one more treatment center, when everyone, including Jones, had pretty well given up, some of those things he'd learned about his behavior started to click in, as he explains in his autobiography. When he came home from a rehab session one time in 1982, he went straight to the refrigerator, located his cocaine stash, and snorted. He stood there for a moment and then he poured the rest of that bottle of coke down the kitchen sink drain. Once he had licked that habit, he still had to deal with his drinking. Before that took place, he ended up in an emergency ward only two ounces of alcohol short of fatal alcohol poisoning. On his death bed, he relented.

During the years that Nancy Jones describes as her "courtship" with George Jones, Nancy tells of the desperate state George was in at the time she met him. As she recalls in her book *Nashville Wives*, George had become a victim of manipulators who bullied him around as if he were *their* employee. While on the road Nancy and George were fine, but their existence in Florence soon became a nightmare. Thugs delivered cocaine concealed in guitars. Managers lured Jones to places where gorillas filled his nose. Nancy soon became a threat to these thugs. She discovered that these shadowy characters had the Florence-Muscle Shoals-area police in their pocket, so she approached the perpetrators directly and found herself in a car chase scene right out of *The Rockford Files* — with someone smashing their vehicle into hers and doing their best to make her veer into oncoming traffic or hit a bridge abutment. She survived that ordeal, then they kidnaped her daughter, Adina. That time, Jones capitulated and signed a series of concert contracts where he barely made any money at all, just to protect Nancy and Adina.

Someone warned Nancy that, if she wanted to survive, she had to get her family out of the deep South where police officers made so little money that there was no chance they were all honest cops. More than once, she and George got in their car and attempted to leave. They were stopped for running red lights they never ran. Jones was arrested for cocaine possession when only a minuscule amount of residual powder was discovered by a narcotic-sniffing dog. Nancy and her daughter were thrown in jail, Jones, into a separate cell. Then they were released. All charges were mysteriously dropped.

George's sister, Ruth, had cottoned onto what was going on with her brother. But she was ignored by the police, and, by the time she went to federal authorities she had become infected with the frantic conspiracy theory paranoia fueled by George's cocaine addiction. And she wasn't believed. No one would help them. The one man who did, a club owner known as Big Daddy, ended up losing his head over the matter, literally. It was severed from his body and the culprit was never arrested. The gorillas had no faces.

Things began to turn around when George and Nancy and Adina left Alabama and lived for a while in Louisiana. Then they headed for the Big Thicket, settling in a trailer home near Colmesneil, Texas. George had come home. There, he began to feel whole, once again. And he again built a theme park. This time, due to his limited budget, he built it stage by stage, adding components as he could afford them. His sense of self worth came back to him as he busied himself working on his land.

"I think he was needing someone that he could trust. And someone he felt close to," Nancy commented in the authorized video biography. "And it took quite a while to get him to that route, you know, because of all the bad times that George had been through."

Dub Scroggins had been sorely concerned for his brother-in-law, but when he saw George reach his higher ground, Dub relaxed. While the race had been on, George had nearly become the winner who loses all. "I think if George had not moved back to Texas," he said in the authorized video biography, "I don't think that he would have lived this long."

"We got him interested in a piece of land out here," Helen Scroggins confided. "My husband went out there and found it for him. So, we got his mind on something else instead of his problem."

"I always figured that someday we'd help him," Dub added. "I guess it just took a long time to do it."

"It took a lot of years to get him to understand that you can cope with life without pickin' up and drinkin' and tryin' to settle it with that," Nancy observes. "So, I think that he's come to the conclusion that you're not gettin' any younger, and you're not gettin' anywhere by drinkin'."

Before they opened their theme park, George asked Nancy to marry him, and they were joined in holy matrimony during a simple ceremony in his sister's living room. Their honeymoon was a trip to a nearby burger joint. Then it was back to work at their theme park, "Jones Country." They couldn't afford to take any time off — they were down to pocket money and a bag of beans. But people came to their park and Jones sang and time passed. And finally the gorillas left him alone.

In April 1984 the UK magazine *Country Rhythms* magazine sent a reporter and a photographer to the opening of Jones Country. "On Sunday, April 1st, Grammy and CMA award winning singer, George Jones, celebrated the official

1984 opening of Jones Country," the reporter wrote in an upbeat article that never mentioned George's past indiscretions, "his 95-acre music park and recreational and entertainment complex, located in Tyler County in East Texas.

"The recent park opening also gave Jones an opportunity to show off his new 3700-square-foot pine log home, which was completed just a few days before opening day. His sprawling new two-story house features a jacuzzi, cathedral ceiling rooms, a huge fireplace, a large kitchen, and will soon have a guitar-shaped swimming pool out back. It is located in the shady East Texas piney woods, just on the edge of his fence-enclosed music park.

" 'I've wanted to come back to East Texas, where I'm from,' explained Jones, who was born in adjacent Hardin County in 1931. 'I've always been familiar with this area. I like the rolling hills. We've had our things stored all over the country, it seems. It's good to get it all in one place again.'

"On hand to help Jones celebrate the seasonal opening of his park were more than 6,000 enthusiastic friends, family members, fans and well-wishers. For those of you who couldn't make it to the official opening, here's a special *Country Rhythms* tour!" The five-page photo-spread printed in the magazine shows several pictures of George and Nancy in various rooms of their new home, obviously in good health and a positive state of mind.

The following June, *Country Rhythms* reporter Lenny Kaye interviewed Nancy Jones for an article entitled "My Life With George." " 'Where's George?' might be one of those perennial Nashville questions," Kaye playfully begins, "but if you want the answer, you could look on 170 acres of piney woods about 60 miles north of Beaumont, Texas, around 100 miles northeast of Houston. There, just down the road from where George was born, you stand a good chance of finding one of the reigning kings of honky tonk music clearing land and waving to visitors as he moseys by on his four-wheeler. Combining his public and private lives, George Jones has opened a country music vacation campground with a humongous stage that this year will feature performers like Willie Nelson, Reba McEntire, Hank Williams Jr., and Merle Haggard. There's a newly opened grocery store on the property, a five acre lake, and next year George and his wife, Nancy, will be building cabins, a motel, rides for the kids . . .

" 'George did all this himself,' enthuses Nancy, her soft Southern accent emphasizing her own nearby roots in Shreveport, Louisiana. 'When we moved here, it was so thick the only way we could get through the brush was on four-wheelers. He planned the whole thing, and laid it out, and figured out where to put the stage and everything. It was nothing but these old pine trees and oaks when we started. I think he did a fantastic job.'"

Nancy continues on the subject of her relationship with George. "'We've been married two years as of March 4. And I knew him two years before that. It took me two years to get him straightened out,' she laughs. 'I was never the goin' out type, I was married before, and I've got two daughters, and I was pretty much already settled down. We became a team quite quickly. When I first got with George, I had to learn the hard way, because I never met the kind of people I met when I first met him. They were after everything they could get. I think with me not bein' in the music business, I was able to spot 'em a lot faster than George spotted them. I think that after he got his confidence in me he began to listen to me and kind of thin those people out. I think that got him a whole new look on life. There's times when George — and the fans never knew — would go out and do shows and a manager would skip with the money or tell him he didn't get paid and really he did. We don't have a manager now, we don't need one. George is 53 years old, and I think he's old enough to manage his own life. George's boys can pick up the money, make out the road reports, keep all the boys straight. There's nothing to it.' "

Nancy also offers a rare view of George's domestic life. " 'He's a television freak," Nancy told Kaye. 'He would put a satellite on top of his car if he could. His favorite shows are *Sanford & Son* and *The Jeffersons*. And he loves John Wayne. Good westerns and scary movies, that's what he likes. He's a pretty good cook, too. He cooks beef stew and chili and vegetable soup. He's got one fantastic recipe. He takes chicken breasts, and then he puts all these vegetables in there — corn, peas, the whole works — and he bakes it in the oven. That one is delicious. And as for me, I love to cook for him, 'cause he loves to eat.' "

" 'George's family life is very important,' Nancy says. "He loves his family and he's a family man. These grandkids running around hollerin' 'mama' and 'papa' . . . I think it thrills him to death. He is very much a family man and we always have a houseful."

George seldom expressed his deeper feelings about Hank Williams to journalists, but he did tell Dolly Carlisle while she was working on his biography that he felt that Hank had been "put here for a reason. . . . "I think he died of heartbreak. He died of worshiping the wrong love. As he told Minnie Pearl a few weeks before he died, 'That's just it, Minnie,' he says, 'it just ain't no light. There is no life.' But there was. He just saw the wrong light. He saw the light bulb burn out. 'I Saw The Light. I Saw The Light.' Hank saw the light about those things, those loves . . . too strong. Life itself will make you a dopehead, a drunkard. He was a real involved person. That's why he stayed so dumb of the facts. . . . He got so involved in something like his music, like I feel I have, that he was happy all the time, blind to the other things in life. You don't have time to be bothered. There's a song going 'round in there all the time."

George's insight into his own single-minded concentration and the problems he had over the years in his relationships was also beginning to come into focus. "Once you've gone that low, how in the hell can you think?" he told Mark Rose in *Village Voice*. "You've got to see that dark side to know what I'm talking about. Everything's so wrong you can't think. That's the reason we went in the hospital. That's the reason we got our thinkin' a little clearer." As George explained to Rose, "All I can say is that I put it all, everything, into one thing, singin'. . . . Then again maybe my singin' might be a lot of cause for my problems . . . I don't show a lot of affection. I have probably been a very unliked person among family, like someone who was heartless. I saved it all for the songs. I didn't know that you're supposed to show that love person to person. I guess I always wanted to, but I didn't know how. The only way I could would be in a song." With Nancy, George would get over that hurdle. And he wouldn't lose his ability to show his love abundantly to his show audiences.

Back in 1980, George had confessed his feelings of guilt about disappointing his fans in an article in *Music City News* called "George Jones: Making It Up To the Fans," written by William Rector. "With all the problems that I've had," Jones admits, "this, that and the other, I've let down a lot of fans. The main thing that I've been interested in is just to sing, to be able to perform and sing for the people. I feel like I've really let them down . . . Now, I just want to make it up to them." And so he would.

⊶⇒2⇐⊷
She's My Rock

I f Nancy Sepulvado had not come into George Jones' life, he might have
come to a sudden and final end far sooner than later, leaving this world before
recording some of his greatest songs in the 1980s and '90s. But even with
Nancy at his side, dispelling the myth of his no show reputation was not easy.

Putting his years of substance abuse behind him was one thing, but living
without the twin crutches George Jones had propped himself up with whenever
things got him down was another. To begin with, George had to face an audience sober for the first time in years. Nancy Jones told Nick Tosches how it
went on that first mid-1980s comeback night in Birmingham, Alabama. "It was
terrible. He was like a scared puppy. 'I can't do it,' he said. 'I can't go on.' He
was begging and breaking down and dying for a drink. And when he got out
there on that stage, and after the first song, he looked out to me in the audience, and he seemed like such a poor, lost, wounded soul that I burst into tears."

Needless to say, as soon as he began to sing, the fans loved him. Where, in
times past, Jones would have had no one to stand by him, no one to calm his
nervous fear and send him out onto that stage with a hug or a smile, as so many
of the top entertainers in the world have needed — and gotten, from time to
time — he now had Nancy. She was his rock.

> She's the rock that I lean on
> She's the sunshine of my day
> And I don't care what you say about her
> Lord, she took me and made me everything I am today
> She's my rock and I ain't a-goin' to throw her away

She's My Rock (S.K. Dobbins)

At least one music critic heard a new depth in George's singing of these
apparent tribute songs to Nancy, including (I Put A Golden Ring On) The Right

Left Hand (Today), a song that Littleton felt must be a tribute to Nancy Jones. In "The George Jones Enigma" published in the May 1987 issue of *Performance* magazine, Bill Littleton wrote, "There are singers who 'made it' with a lot of support from a small core of fans who saw the potential and persisted in requesting records and generally elevating that act's visibility until it all caught on. There may be some detached observers who look at the George Jones' career and say that's essentially what happened with him. With George, it was more a matter of people growing into an emotional capacity to understand what it is that he is doing with some writer's lyrics. It helps if the lyrics are great to start with (and most have been), but the man's tonality and phrasing become a communication mode almost unto themselves and picking up on the subliminal level is something a listener grows into, not at all unlike learning a new language."

To get Jones back working regularly, Nancy called Tony Conway at Buddy Lee Attractions. If Nancy were going to get her husband's career back on track, George needed a booking contract with a reliable agency. "I was sitting in my office . . . and got a call from Nancy Jones," Conway told *Performance* magazine writer Debi Moen in 1987. "And she introduced herself to me and said, 'We're in Nashville today and would it be all right if George and I came up to talk to you? George wants Buddy Lee Attractions to represent him.' That about knocked me out of my chair. He came up and Buddy Lee and I met with him and negotiated a deal and he's been here ever since."

The meeting with Buddy Lee and Tony Conway lasted for several hours and resulted in a working agreement. The agency believed that George was over his no show days, and they began to book him, instigating what turned out to be a winning formula. "George Jones is the greatest country music singer, ever," Conway told Moen. The agent was a huge Jones fan himself and he understood what it would take to turn things around in 1986. "He's a living legend. We feel that the true country music fans can find no better act to go see in concert. And if you take somebody like a Conway Twitty and Loretta Lynn or Randy Travis, who's a real traditional country newcomer, it rounds off the package nicely and makes it great. They get an evening of pure country in the truest sense of the word."

In that same issue of *Performance* magazine, nestled in box advertisements next to the text of Moen's article, are testimonials congratulating George Jones for his recent performances at the Coliseum Theater in Latham, New York; the Panhandle-South Plains Fair in Lubbock, Texas; the Big Valley Jamboree in Craven, Saskatchewan; and a half-page advertisement taken out by Bob Kelley and Jim Holt of Mid-South Concerts that depicts the new George in a photo with the caption, "*Nobody* could fill your shoes! Thanks George."

Moen also pointed out that Conway Twitty, Loretta Lynn, and George Jones had recently sold out a show (11,266 tickets) at the Biloxi, Mississippi Coliseum, and the next evening entertained 8,575 fans at the Pensacola, Florida Civic Center. Considering that these shows took place in the pre-Garthmania era, the numbers are impressive. Jones' newly-joined agency was rewarded for their belief in their singer, and Jones was on his way back to credibility. There had been minor hesitations at first, but by 1987 Tony Conway was confident enough to declare that "the 'No Show Jones thing' is out the window. That's back history. There have been dates that either we or the promoters have canceled but not because of George."

Counteracting this 'No Show' reputation was easier said than done, for the media seemed to have a vested interested in perpetuating George's bad boy reputation. Even his biographers, Dolly Carlisle and Bob Allen, seemed to like George better bad than good as they worked on their books during the early 1980s. To those writers, just like the management gorillas he fell in with, Jones was an industry, a way of making money.

When George Jones really needed a publicist, he never hired anyone to airbrush his image, not until he got himself straight in the 1980s, and by that time a *whole* lot of water had flowed under the bridge. For a while in Houston, Starday Records' head honcho Pappy Daily had hired Gabe Tucker to hype his young singer, Jones, to the world at large. With Daily out of the equation, there was no focus, no spin-doctoring — not even a comfortable buffer between the artist and the press. Jones' private life became public during the ongoing soap opera role he found himself playing as Tammy's husband and then her ex. In the 1970s, when a little publicity was needed, one of Jones' managers would call a press conference in an attempt to set some spin of their own on what was happening. Often, those media schmoozes failed to put across the intention of either the singer or the manager. Other times, George participated in press conferences organized by Tammy Wynette and George Richey, where his best interests were not always front and center. No matter what George Jones said in these organized events or in one-on-one interviews, some journalists had their own agenda, fitting Jones' quotes into that agenda, going so far as to predict his imminent death. When you throw all the rules of journalism out the window, you can toss some fairly nasty spitballs.

While Dolly Carlisle seems the least knowledgeable of the two authors who came up with unauthorized biographies during the 1980s, and even though her book *Ragged But Right: The Life and Times of George Jones* is riddled with hearsay and outright mistakes, she is a benevolent biographer, not prone to the melodramatic exaggerations and fabrications that mar Bob Allen's work. In *George Jones: The Saga of an American Singer*, Allen is not only quick and loose with the facts, he writes fiction in order to create a dramatic rendering of George Jones' life, which seems to have pleased reviewers at the time but certainly upset George. Allen focuses attention on the reports and opinions of ex-lovers, disgruntled recording artists, and a raft of people who had their own axes to grind when it came to telling George Jones stories.

Allen seemed to have a personal vendetta against Jones. "The Decline and Fall of George Jones" was the title of the article published in the Jan / Feb 1979 issue of *Country Music* magazine that preceded the release of his book. In that article, Allen asked such clearly antagonistic questions as, "George, you seem to be having more than your share of troubles lately. Just how have all these events in your life managed to get so out of hand?" Another question was phrased, "Several weeks ago, you were arrested for assault with intent to murder down in Florence, Alabama. Supposedly, you shot at your friend, Earl 'Peanut' Montgomery's car, and nearly hit him. What is the story behind that incident?" Addressing his drinking problem, Allen asked, "George, your drinking is said to be of monumental proportions. People have described you as a sort of Jekyll and Hyde character. People who know you say that when you're not drinking, you're one of the nicest people in the world. But when you start drinking, you sometimes change completely and things get out of hand. . . . When you drink, does it sometimes go on for long periods of time? For weeks and weeks? . . . Would you actually drink so much sometimes that you would stop eating for long periods of time?" In his book, whenever Allen reported that George bought a house, it was a "fancy" house, when he bought a car, it was a "fancy" car. When Allen described the Tammy Wynette kidnaping incident, he indicted George by association. Although George was never a suspect in the matter of Tammy's Wynette's highly publicized "kidnaping," not to the extent that he was even questioned by the police, Allen comments, in parenthesis, "(Jones was later cleared of any involvement in the incident)." But more distastefully, in a comparison of Hank Williams' father and George Jones' father, Allen denigrated both men, again in a parenthetical aside. "Both had fathers who were — each in his own way — rather weak and shiftless characters. (Williams' father's 'disability' was said to have resulted from shell shock he'd sustained in World War I, whereas George

Washington Jones' 'shell shock' seemed to come in a quart and pint bottles.)"

For the 1994 reissue of his biography, Bob Allen changed the title to *George Jones: The Life and Times of a Honky Tonk Legend*. In the preface, he writes that he has chosen not to change any of the text except to update it at the end, thus foregoing the chance to correct errors and adjust his opinions, so that new readers to country music history will still be told that Hank Williams' first national hit was *Lovesick Blues* (not the number 4 charted *Move It On Over* in 1947, or the number 14 *Honky Tonkin'* and the number 6 *I'm a Long Gone Daddy* in 1948). And they would be led to believe that George Jones was inducted into the Country Music Hall of Fame for his bad boy antics and not for being the greatest living country singer.

Nancy and George worked hard recording and touring in the 1980s to dispel this no show myth. One of the first moves took place when George recorded A TASTE OF YESTERDAY'S WINE with Merle Haggard. The sessions went so well that George and songwriter Glenn Martin, who had written *It's Not Love (But It's Not Bad)*, a number one for Merle in 1972, sat themselves down and wrote *No Show Jones*, a novelty tune that took full advantage of the nickname, which the hostile critics had labeled him with, and turned it around to good advantage. The song turned out to be a hoot for Jones and Haggard when Sherrill had them record it as duet. If he was stuck with the label, why not make it pay for itself? The song wasn't a giant single, but it became his new set-opener, and his fans loved it. They were also tickled when the title track, *Yesterday's Wine*, written by Willie Nelson, went number one in 1982. *C.C. Waterback* from the same duet album also made it into the Top 10. The duet album with Merle climbed to the number 4 position on the *Billboard* country chart and hung around for a full 52 weeks.

Later that same year, Epic released ANNIVERSARY – TEN YEARS OF HITS. The compilation album went gold. The next four years would see Jones and Sherrill pump out a total of eight more albums, two a year on the average. SHINE ON, released in August of 1983, yielded three Top 10 hits: *Shine On (Shine All Your Sweet Love On Me)* (number 3), *I Always Get Lucky With You* (number one), and *Tennessee Whiskey* (a number 2 hit at the end of the year.) JONES COUNTRY was issued in November. The next June YOU'VE STILL GOT A PLACE IN MY HEART was released. The singles *You've Still Got A Place In My Heart* and *She's My Rock* both hit into the Top 10. *We Didn't See A Thing*, the marvelous duet featuring George with Ray Charles, rose to the number 6 position on the chart. Next came BY REQUEST, which has been certified gold, and then LADIES

CHOICE, an album of duets with Deborah Allen, Lacy J. Dalton, Janie Fricke, Terri Gibbs, Emmylou Harris, Brenda Lee, Loretta Lynn, Barbara Mandrell, and Leona Williams. These duets are ragged but they're right in quite a few of the grooves.

FIRST TIME LIVE! followed in early 1985. It was good but not an overwhelming performance, and critics would later point to LIVE AT DANCETOWN USA, a bootlegged compact disc release by Ace Records in 1987 in the U.K., recorded in 1965, as supposed proof that the 1985 album had been misnamed. But in September 1985, the release of WHO'S GONNA FILL THEIR SHOES convinced both fans and critics alike that George Jones was back in top form. The album went Top 10 and sold well. It spent a total of 54 weeks on the chart and yielded three more Top 10 hits, including the superb title track.

Who's Gonna Fill Their Shoes was written by Troy Seals and Max D. Barnes, who was on a roll during the mid-1980s, penning hits like Chiseled In Stone, a number one hit for Randy Travis and the CMA Single of the Year in 1987, and Vince Gill's Look At Us, the '92 CMA Song of the Year. Once again the song seemed perfect for George Jones, embodying much of what he believed in and ringing true when he sang it as a tribute to his personal heroes and friends. The video for Who's Gonna Fill Their Shoes won the CMA Award for Best Video. People took the lyrics of the tribute to country legends like Hank Williams, Lefty Frizzell, and Marty Robbins to heart.

You know the heart of country music
Still beats in Luke the Drifter
You can tell it when he sings I Saw The Light
Old Marty, Hank, and Lefty
Why, I can feel them all here with me
On this Silver Eagle rolling through the night

Who's Gonna Fill Their Shoes (Troy Seals & Max D. Barnes)

Seals and Barnes' lyrics included hip references to Willie Nelson, Johnny Cash and Merle Haggard, too, as well as an oblique reference to Roy Acuff, George's first country music hero, whose signature tune on the Opry was Wabash Cannonball.

No there'll never be another red-headed stranger
A man in black and Folsom Prison Blues
The Okie from Muskogee, or 'Hello Darlin'

Lord, I wonder who's gonna fill their shoes . . .
Who's gonna fill their shoes
Who's gonna stand that tall
Who's gonna play the Opry
And the Wabash Cannonball
Who's gonna give their heart and soul
To get to me and you
Lord, I wonder who's gonna fill their shoes

Jones' rehabilitation was well on its way by this time and he seemed to be addressing everyone who had ever loved country music with *Who's Gonna Fill Their Shoes.*

WINE COLORED ROSES was released a year later, reaching into the Top 5 on the album chart and selling more than half a million copies. But the first signs of the trend toward youth at the "new country" formatted radio stations could be seen in the weaker performance of the singles at radio: *Wine Colored Roses* (10), *I Turn To You* (26), and *The Right Left Hand* (which peaked at the number 8 position). WALKING THE LINE, a collaboration with Willie Nelson and Merle Haggard, which featured duets and solo efforts recorded between 1976 and 1986, wasn't especially well received. SUPER HITS, though, went platinum the following year.

In July 1986 — the same year that Nancy arranged that meeting with Buddy Lee and Tony Conway — George Jones used an article written by Neil Pond for Music City News entitled "George Jones Talks (About his music, his reputation, life out of the fast lane & how a good woman turned him around)" to express his mature opinions about these many subjects, one of his first efforts to set the record straight which would culminate in his autobiography published in 1996. There is a minimum of editorial from Pond and a maximum number of quotes from Jones, each quote set out under its own headline. Pond describes the 55-year-old Jones as "a man who wears his legend as casually as his Polo shirt."

On his life story, Jones commented, "I'm really hoping to write my own book, with the help of my wife Nancy, and do it right for a change. I didn't authorize the other books, and all they did was gather up hearsay information and 90 percent of the stuff in there was not even factual. I think they just did it to make a dollar. Anybody can write anything they want about anybody, and there's really no privacy left in people's lives anymore."

On his reputation as country music's "bad boy," George admitted, "I got myself into all that. I think everybody has made their mistakes and I've surely had my share. But experience is the best teacher and a lot of us have to learn things the hard way. Yeah, I've done those things and I'm not proud of them, but I'm certainly not going to be ashamed of them. When they call me No Show Jones and this and that and the other . . . they can't do that anymore. In the last four years I've been straight. I see the light of day and I enjoy it a lot more."

On his wife Nancy, and how she turned his life around, he recognized, "I was pretty far gone, you might say, and then she came along. Without her help, there's no telling where I would be today. I've got a good wife, a very understanding wife. I think that anybody that's in this business has to have a partner that understands you fully before they fly into marriage or spend the rest of their life with you. And Nancy does that." On their homelife in Colmesneil, Texas, he continued, "I fuss at her and make her cook pies. No, I'm basically like anybody else . . . I love to get out and fish, I like to go into the woods. I don't care about shooting a bunch of animals or anything like that, I just like to get out and walk and fish and play with my dogs."

Assessing his own singing ability, he observed, "I just see myself as a singer, but I think my success lies with loving country music like I do and as deeply as I do. Ninety percent of it I owe to other artists that I was raised up listening to: Hank Williams, Roy Acuff, Bill Monroe, Lefty Frizzell. I got a little bit of them in my phrasing and in my style of singing, and about the other 10 percent I just quit trying to whine like them and put in some of me. And it all comes out George Jones. That's the best I can explain it." On singing duets, he continued, "People enjoy duets and I enjoy doing them, but they're the worst thing you can do for your career."

On the subject of country radio, he probably surprised a few folks by observing, "Some of the music they play on the radio stations, I just really don't enjoy listening to it that much any more. I'm disgusted with the trend and the way music is going. You turn on your radio and you hear all these pop arrangements and middle of the road pop/rock, and stuff that's *supposed* to be country, and it's not. They don't have enough of the George Straits and Merle Haggards and George Joneses and Gene Watsons, and some of the real good traditional country artists like we used to have. I'm hoping that one day they'll get tired of this mess and send that stuff back over to the regular pop stations and let us get back to the basics of country music."

This traditional country philosophy went back to Waylon Jennings's

Luckenbach Texas, recorded in 1977, a philosophy that had been echoed in George's own 1985 release of *Who's Gonna Fill Their Shoes*, but it did not endear Jones in radio programmers' hearts when they read his words. When newly-created high-powered, high fidelity, stereo country stations began to steal the country audience from the AM stations in the 1980s, FM music directors wanted a seamless sound as their program of hits and commercial jingles rolled out onto the airwaves. Consequently, records made before 1975 were seldom heard on these FM stations, and by the mid-1980s when new country became the rage, few of the pioneers were ever heard on the radio. For the first time since 1947, you couldn't hear Hank Williams on the radio when deejays reached for classic cuts or golden oldies — certainly not every day of the week as had been the norm for so long.

As the 1980s wore on, the country radio and recording industry fell into dire straits. In 1988, the year before George Jones and Epic Records parted ways, CBS Records, the parent company, was bought up by the Sony corporation. The transaction was so huge that few common people contemplated what effect it might have on their lives and on country music at that time. At the same time, there was a grand jury investigation already underway which had turned up considerable evidence of influence-peddling. An alleged network of pro-moters who used illegal practices to influence radio had been identified. "The record business was jolted awake on February 26, 1988," *Hit Men* author Fredric Dannen wrote, "less than two months after the Sony deal closed. That day the payola grand jury returned its first four indictments. Ralph Tashian, who for years had been Joe Isgro's chief liaison to Top 40, was charged with bribing men at three pop stations with cash and cocaine, distributing the drug, tax evasion and obstruction of justice." In 1989, independent record promoter, Isgro, was also indicted by the grand jury investigating payola on 51 counts of payola, drug-trafficking, racketeering, obstruction of justice, and tax fraud. This time, however, the indictment included record executive Ray Anderson, former head of Epic Records who had at one time also been head of CBS Records' promotion department.

In the shadow of this scandal, country radio continued to grow away from its roots. For a few years, hard-core country artists like George Jones, Dick Damron, and Johnny Cash were the only voices speaking out against this waste-land in country radio programming. By the end of the '90s, George Jones emerged as a champion for real country music. George had his health, his remarkable voice, and a ton of songs that served to remind people what country music was really all about. All along George *had* been doing it Hank's way. Jones was not a burned-out, over-the-hill country singer at all. No way, Jose. And even though most record label execs continued to spout their theory that people didn't want to hear old men on the radio, Jones just wouldn't go away. In fact, he sounded better than ever. And he was still singing about Luke the Drifter.

3
The King Is Gone

Billy Sherrill could be called Nashville's Phil Spector for the way he quarterbacked sessions and built tracks rather than letting the musicians run with the ball on their own — as Owen Bradley and Chet Atkins had done. He also had the show business sense that Pappy Daily possessed. Sherrill had seen the potential to mine gold in exploiting the George & Tammy soap opera on record. While George and Tammy were together, Sherrill also continued to come up with hit records for both Wynette and Jones that eerily echoed their private lives in the public arena long after the two artists had parted ways. Sometimes, these were outright schmaltz like the duet on *The Ceremony*, and sometimes the songs cut deeper like *The Door*, a solo cut for Jones, which juxtaposed the social milieu of a soldier conscripted into service during the Vietnam war and the hurtin' ethic of a straight-ahead Nashville ballad. In the late 1990s, George again showed concern for Vietnam vets when he made his video for *Wild Irish Rose* featuring an unfortunate former soldier and listed the 1-888 number vets could call to get help. Nancy Jones has stated that they were both aware that 40 percent of homeless Americans were Vietnam vets. *Golden Ring* featured the already estranged couple singing the high lonesome harmonies of a bluegrass act on choruses that Sherrill then nestled comfortably into his trademark lush string production. This recording stands the test of time, a marvelous creation, when the song comes up on a George Jones compilation.

Sherrill also put Jones together with artists like James Taylor, Elvis Costello, Emmylou Harris, Brenda Lee, and Willie Nelson. He knew when it was time to drop some of the lush production and get back to basics. In the late 1980s, when the sparkling acoustic tracks of the new traditionalists like Randy Travis were doing so well, Sherrill knew that Jones could appeal if he reached back into his own past, all the way back to the 1950s era when he had recorded *Why Baby Why*. So, Sherrill dug up Johnny Horton's 1956 hit, *I'm A One*

Woman Man, and crafted tracks that recreated that twangy guitar, honky tonk man appeal for George's 1989 version of the song. The cut went all the way to number 5 on the surveys. Patty Loveless had also resurrected George's earlier hit *If My Heart Had Windows* the previous year for her first MCA Top 10 hit. Sherrill followed up the Johnny Horton 'blast from the past' with a song for Jones that was, once again, more than just a novelty tune.

The King Is Gone (So Are You) combined the popular TV cartoon character Fred Flintstone and Elvis Presley in a very strange set of lyrics that turned out to be an effective vehicle for Jones, though not a Top 10 hit for a 'legal' reason. Walt Trott, in an article published in *Country People Today*, notes that when *The King Is Gone* was first released in 1989 under the title *Ya Ba Da Ba Do (So Are You)*, the song was climbing fast on the charts until a legal injunction halted its momentum. Seems the Hanna-Barbara cartoonists charged copyright infringements on their character Fred Flintstone's famed spiel, *Yabba Dabba Do!* The title was changed to *The King Is Gone (So Are You)*, which meant recalling records and altering publicity releases, leaving the single stalled at number 26 on the chart.

George might have dried out, but his fans were still willing to buy into a drinking song, especially one as weirdly sentimental and tragi-comic as this.

Last night I broke the seal
On a Jim Beam decanter
That looks like Elvis
I soaked the label off
A Flintstone jellybean jar . . .

I pulled the head off Elvis
Filled Fred up to his pelvis
Yabba Dabba Do . . .
The King is gone and so are you . . .

Round about ten we all got to talking
About Graceland, Bedrock and such.
Our conversation finally turned to women
But they said they didn't get around too much.
Elvis said, "Find 'em young."
And Fred said, "Old fashioned girls are fun."
Yabba dabba do . . .
The King is gone and so are you.

Later on it finally hit me
That you wouldn't be a-coming home no more
'Cause this time I know you won't forgive me
Like all of them other times before
Then I broke Elvis's nose
Pourin' the last drop from his toes
Yabba dabba do
The King is gone and so are you

— *The King Is Gone (So Are You)* (R. Ferris)

The King Is Gone (So Are You) is usually viewed as a novelty song, a light bit of comic relief, but the inclusion of Fred Flintstone in the scenario puts this lovesick, lonesome, drinking man's hallucinations into the context of George Jones' Deedoodle Duck cartoon-like delirium tremens and his often sorry domestic world. It's the end, alright, Elvis *is* dead and she's *not* comin' back. As the gently acoustic track ends, Jones is faded out singing, "Last night I broke the label off / A Jim Beam decanter that looks like Elvis . . ." If you're in the mood to be serious at all or on a whiskey-swilling bender, these lyrics grow sadder with tears in your beer potential. Few drinking songs provide so little hope.

The King Is Gone seemed to continue a dialog George had opened up with some of the disturbed spirits who dwell on life's other side, first begun with his tributes to Hank Williams and picked up on *Who's Gonna Fill Their Shoes*, where Jones includes Charlie Rich among the "boys from Memphis." Rich had been a rockabilly session piano player on Sun Records sessions in the late '50s and had first hit the pop charts in 1960 with *Lonely Weekends* a decade before he became a major country star with his countrypolitan hits like *Behind Closed Doors*.

God bless the boys from Memphis
Blue Suede Shoes and Elvis
Much too soon he left this world in tears
They tore up the fifties
Old Jerry Lee and Charley
And Go Cat Go still echoes through the years

You know the heart of country music
Still beats in Luke the Drifter . . .

The lyrics of *The King Is Gone (So Are You)* eerily recreate the days when the King and the Possum were running neck and neck in the race to see who would be the next singer to join ole Hank in Hillbilly Heaven. As the singer of the song drowns his sorrow, pouring the antidote from the Elvis decanter into the Fred Flintstone jellybean jar, the saddest aspects of Hank's legacy seem to drain away and fade along with Jones' vocal. Vocal fades on George Jones' records were not the usual endings used by Billy Sherrill, but here the fade is the message. Here, on record, Jones achieves a closure of sorts with the specter of Elvis. When George recorded Hank's *A Picture From Life's Other Side*, he came to grips with Williams as well. Singing the songs sober must have been a trip and a half but it was a strong message to Elvis and Hank — who surely checked in on the situation down here on earth every once in a while during those days — a message that said that ole George was alive and well and carrying on the tradition.

Other members of the Class of '55 had climbed that spiral staircase to Hillbilly Heaven, while some had revived their careers during the 1980s. In 1981, country singer turned rock & roller Bill Haley, according to his biographer, John Swenson, died "a broken, insane man . . . tortured by confusing specters of his past. He was the product of an essentially rural upbringing and as such was completely unprepared for the show business sophistication he would encounter as a rock & roll star." Near the end, when Haley would be found wandering aimlessly along country roads near his adopted home in Harlingen, Texas, police officers who found him there would testify that he truly "didn't know where he was." In these same years, George Jones had been living in a fantasy world dominated by Deedoodle duck and a mysterious old man . . . wandering aimlessly through Printers Alley, parking his Lincoln behind Jimmie Hill's barbershop in Alabama where he lived on a diet of sardines, peanuts, and whiskey, or driving a never-ending loop that took him from Florence, Alabama to Tammy Wynette's curved Nashville driveway . . . and back again.

Carl Perkins was still playing that 'feel good music' on his rockabilly guitar, touring with Johnny Cash from time to time. Their friendship outlasted their excesses and led to some triumphs, too, notably when Carl wrote *Daddy Sang Bass*, a number one hit for six weeks for Cash in 1969. In 1964 on a British tour with Chuck Berry, Carl met George Harrison who asked Carl to show him how to play the intro to *Honey Don't*. Carl found himself at the Abbey Road studio where The Beatles recorded three of his tunes: *Honey Don't*, *Matchbox*, and *Everybody's Tryin' To Be My Baby*. Over the years, Carl Perkins continued to be acknowledged by his peers, recording with Paul McCartney, touring with Ringo Starr, and in 1986 for the Cinemax production *A Rockabilly Session: Carl Perkins & Friends*, he was joined by Paul, Ringo, Eric Clapton, Rosanne Cash, and Dave Edmunds. A year later, Carl was inducted into the Rock and Roll Hall of Fame. His last record to chart was in 1986, *Birth Of Rock And Roll*, peaking at number 31 on the *Billboard* country chart. By the 1980s, rock and roll was country once again; mainstream rock had lost its "roll." Carl Perkins had always felt comfortable with country music, even though that "feel good music" he'd played in Memphis helped give birth to rock and roll. Among the many honors showered on Carl Perkins, his induction into the Nashville Songwriters Hall of Fame was one he cherished most before his death in 1998 at the age of 66.

In the late 1980s, Roy Orbison was enjoying the comeback of a lifetime, working with Bob Dylan, George Harrison, Tom Petty, Jeff Lynne, and Jim Keltner as a member of the Traveling Wilburys, the surprise supergroup success of 1988. But he did not live to accept his Grammy for his duet of *Crying* with cowpunker K.D. Lang or to see his final single, *You Got It*, climb into the Top 10 on the country charts. Roy died of a heart attack on December 6, 1988 in Hendersonville, Tennessee, and an empty rocking chair was used to represent his presence in the 1989 video for the Wilbury's *Handle With Care*. The posthumous release of his final album, MYSTERY GIRL, in 1989 was his first gold-selling release. Roy Orbison had only one hit for Sam Phillips at Sun Records, *Ooby Dooby*, in 1956, but as the creator of *Only The Lonely*, *Crying*, *Running Scared*, and *Oh, Pretty Woman* he lives on past his demise in the hearts and memories of his fans as a member of the Rock and Roll Hall of Fame. Country fans have always loved his music, too.

In 1987, Hank Williams Jr. recorded an ultimate tribute to his father. *There's A Tear In My Beer* featured Hank Jr. and Hank Sr. dueting together courtesy of a vocal that was dubbed in from a single copy of a recording that Hank Williams had made before he died. Utilizing some vintage live performance film footage of Hank Williams & The Drifting Cowboys, the music video for the release juxtaposed the two singers each in their separate time-frames. Then, through post-production digital editing magic, the son walked into his father's world to join his daddy in song. For the first time in quite a few years, ole Hank's fluid vocalizing was heard once again in the Top 40. Hank Jr. had won the first-ever CMA Video of the Year award in 1985 for *All My Rowdy Friends Are Coming Over Tonight*, a truly innovative production where the singer's pals come floating out of a TV set to join him. George Jones had won the video award in 1986 for *Who's Gonna*

Fill Their Shoes where Hank Sr. was once again acknowledged along with other country legends. Hank Jr. won the video award in 1987 with *My Name Is Bocephus,* and (along with his daddy) he repeated again in 1988 when *There's A Tear In My Beer* was named Video of the Year. This was a happier Hank Jr. than people had seen before, and, although he was not heard much on the radio in the 1990s, he was heard every Monday night during football season on network TV. He has become an American institution in his own right. And his son, Hank Williams III, has hit the tour circuit, a third generation rebel rock presence on Music Row.

Johnny Cash was just too tough, ornery, honest, and kind to die. With help from June Carter and her father Ezra, Cash had emerged from his own personal hell to help fellow addicts, finding his faith in his God that he had lost along the way. Cash had been associated with Bob Dylan, the Stones, and The Beatles as one of the superstars of the late 1960s and early '70s, but never gave up his country roots. Only Eddy Arnold, George Jones and Conway Twitty had been played on country radio more than the Man in Black. And he kept coming back — as a Highwayman in the '80s, as an actor on the TV series *Doctor Quinn, Medicine Woman* in the '90s — while still recording very good albums.

Jerry Lee Lewis was still alive and kicking, but not in the best of health. His marriage to his 13-year-old cousin had sabotaged his career, not that any of that dimmed his enthusiasm. Jerry Lee just didn't give a shit about what anyone thought. But he'd hurt himself nearly every day of his life and you could see the results in his skinnier-than-a-rail frame as he stepped up the ramp from his limousine to the country festival stages in the 1980s and '90s. Jerry Lee was a walking, talking shadow of his former self. Still, Joel Whitburn listed "the Killer" at number 42 on his list of the Top 100 country stars of all time in the *Billboard Book of Top 40 Country Hits (1944-1996).*

Waylon Jennings was hanging in there, too, but still haunted by the memory of his friend Buddy Holly who had died when the plane they were both flying in crashed during their Winter Dance Party tour of 1959. In 1996, Waylon told songwriter Billy Joe Shaver, who wrote *Honky Tonk Heroes* and *Old Five And Dimers* for Waylon, and *No Depression* magazine interviewer Grant Alden about one weird flight in New Zealand that brought that era back to mind.

"Well, we're out there on the runway, fixin' to take off in this big plane, 747. Take off down the runway and Mantovani's playing. And they pull down, there and then, and stopped. Just shut the sumbitch down. And they backed up, turned it around this way and come back up there, and then they turned it

THE KING IS GONE

around like they was going to go up again, and Buddy Holly started singing *Peggy Sue*. And so Kris Kristofferson and John Cash, and all of 'em looked at me. And I says, 'We ain't goin' on this sumbitch.' So, we made 'em take us back to the gate and got us another airplane . . . It's crazy to go from Mantovani to Buddy Holly. Not a chance. I still don't like airplanes."

All these memories come alive in *The King Is Dead (So Are You)*. Billy Sherrill's restrained production, beginning with just a strummed acoustic guitar and voice, then and building with drums, bass, dobro, piano to the point where harmony vocals enter on the "Yabba dabba do's," confirms George's comments in the liner notes to COLD HARD TRUTH that Sherrill was a genius. Sadly, the sessions for the ONE WOMAN MAN album marked the end of the collaboration between the two men.

The last four albums George recorded for Epic also marked the transition from vinyl to digital. By 1991, vinyl was dead, too, and the increasing popularity of the new format CDs was already beginning to push cassettes from the music mart shelves. The sound that had once been "warm" in the analog format was colder in the digital format, brittle. Sherrill had left CBS Records before Jones to work as an independent producer, but he still had a better sense than anyone else about who George Jones was. The veteran producer was also aware of the youth movement being pushed by the purveyors of "new country." There was little he could do as he watched *The King Is Gone (So Are You)* and then *Writing On The Wall* stall in the 20s and 30s on the survey. *A Few Ole Country Boys*, a duet with Randy Travis culled from FRIENDS IN HIGH PLACES, an album patched together from duet recordings with Charlie Daniels, Vern Gosdin, Ricky Van Shelton, Buck Owens and other artists made between 1984 and 1990 and released on the Epic label in 1991, was the last Sherrill-Jones collaboration to chart.

In 1990, Garth Brooks hit with *Friends In Low Places*, a reverse tribute to Jones, which stole everyone's thunder and became the CMA Single of the Year while launching a new generation of 'hat acts', most of whom emulated George Jones as they sat in the national spotlight. *Rockin' Years*, a duet with Dolly Parton written by Randy Parton, never saw the light of day, though George believed the song "could return him to the top of the chart," Walt Trott reported. "Epic dismissed the song as inferior. Shortly after Jones departed Epic for MCA, superhot Ricky Van Shelton was substituted as Dolly's duet partner and their single shot to number one in 1991."

Singing with current country superstar Randy Travis put Jones in the Top

10 again, but it would also be his final chart success in the 20th century. It truly was the end of an era. For the first time since he'd cut *No Money In This Deal* in Jack Starnes' living room and been signed by Pappy Daily to that first Starday contract, George Jones was without a record deal. When George and Nancy went label-shopping, they soon discovered that his past reputation was a liability, not so much his bad boy behavior as his traditional country roots. Label executives riding the wave of new country popularity were wary of signing anyone who was older than a teenager. "I mean, there wasn't a label down here," Jones told David Gates, "that was willing to take a chance on George Jones."

MCA's Bruce Hinton came to the rescue. Hinton signed Jones to the label and turned him over to Nashville producer Tony Brown who had played piano for Elvis and worked on the west coast in Emmylou's Hot Band and Rodney Crowell's Cherry Bombs. He was viewed as the hottest country producer in the 1990s. Tony had first cut his teeth on Music Row working with Joe Galante at RCA and had then come over from RCA to head up MCA's country division. At MCA he brought in new blood like Patty Loveless. He had inherited Reba McEntire. Inherited George Strait whose career was red hot. And Tony had been making headway with his pals Vince Gill, Marty Stuart, and Rodney Crowell, turning so-so careers into marquee stars. Tony had an ally in Bruce Hinton, his superior at MCA, who felt that if they did not give Jones — who they both knew full well everyone was referring to as "the greatest living country singer" — a chance, well, it would be difficult to live with their consciences.

Putting Jones back into the Top 10 was a challenge, though, and for several years Tony gave it his best shot, pairing George with producers like Kyle Lehning, Kelso Herston, Buddy Cannon, Norro Wilson, and Brian Ahern. Between 1991 and 1996, George made six albums for MCA. For the initial project, AND ALONG CAME JONES, Brown assigned Kyle Lehning to work with Jones. The album's singles didn't light any fires at radio, but continued the groundswell of critical acclaim and career acknowledgment building day-by-day in the trades and dailies. In 1992, Jones' second album for MCA, WALLS CAN FALL, went gold, largely on the interest generated by *I Don't Need Your Rockin' Chair* and the push that Bruce Hinton was able to provide at the promotional level. The song didn't hit the Top 10, but album sales were the bottom line, and, for Jones, touring the album proved lucrative, as well. The supporting video featuring Jones and boxer George Foreman helped immensely when it thrived on CMT. The single won George and his collaborators a CMA award for Vocal Collaboration of the Year in 1993. By that time he had already graciously accepted his induction into the Country Music Hall of Fame at the 1992 CMAs. Well, he was grateful enough and gracious enough to attend, so most folks were pleased. But when George made his acceptance speech, he took it upon himself to speak out against the deplorable conditions at country radio. That brief tirade, while applauded by some, once again did not endear him to the radio folks. Some association members felt it was just ungrateful to use their podium for such an exercise. HIGH TECH REDNECK (1993) sought to repeat the success of WALLS CAN FALL but failed to capture the same magic.

No one, it seemed, could convince country radio music directors to put Jones back in the Top 10. The jukeboxes had been stored in some lost warehouse somewhere. The slick new country cabarets were now filled with the amplified shouts of deejay fever and dance track versions of new country radio hits that were designed for line dancers and the designer jean crowd who were the paying customers. They were the patrons who now inhabited what were once called honky tonks, who had never heard *Why Baby Why*, *White Lightning* or *She Thinks I Still Care*, and thought that *Achy Breaky Heart* was the number one country song of all time simply because corporate executives had poured millions of dollars into promoting the release through legitimate channels, along with a line dance that was based on it, and millions more into the pockets of outside record promoters who were no more than the cleaned up payola merchants of the music industry's dark and deceitful past. That dubious moment in country music history was a successful promotion that sold more than eight million albums for Billy Ray, but the song became so overexposed before it was done on the radio that it spawned a parody, *Kiss My Achy Breaky Ass*, which was also got quite a bit of airplay on many stations. It was not exactly the way Hank had done it.

During his years of excess, George Jones had become aware that he was in danger of succumbing to a drug-induced heart attack, just like ole Hank. After Elvis Presley's death in 1977, he began to worry more, although at first he reacted by making an obsession of death rather than cleaning himself up. When he kicked his habits, he finally had peace of mind. But in August 1994, he was not influenced by either drugs or alcohol when he punched out a soundman at the Opryland theater. His sudden flare of temper came from a physical cause.

The technician had fouled up George's monitors, and feedback had snarled up his opening two numbers for a convention audience of talent-buyers Jones felt he needed to impress. Something snapped and there was Jones up to his old tricks, back there in the wings scrabbling with his techie. During the previous five months of playing two shows a night at Opryland and traveling to Las Vegas for other shows, George began to suffer from fatigue, as Nick Tosches reported in his *Texas Monthly* article "The Devil in George Jones." Tosches took in George's show at Bally's Casino Resort in Las Vegas, from backstage, first in George Jones' dressing room suite, then in the wings. "When it was time for him to go on," Tosches writes, "he slapped his gut — that symbol of his return from the dead — and smiled once, his attitude changing from one of playfulness to one of tired resignation. 'Let's get this over with,' he said." George sang only seven songs, staying on stage for only 23 minutes.

A few weeks later, in September, George left the company of 300 guests who had come to his home to celebrate his upcoming 63rd birthday and simply went to bed to sleep. Nancy had begun to notice his condition, but George wasn't eager to seek medical help. When Nancy finally got George to take some tests, an EKG revealed that he was in pretty bad shape. He was admitted to Baptist Hospital in Nashville, scheduled for triple-bypass surgery in a few days. A phone conversation with Waylon Jennings helped out some since Waylon had undergone the same operation; in fact, Waylon and Johnny Cash had undergone heart surgery in the same hospital at the very same time. As fate would have it, George went into surgery on the day of his 63rd birthday, September 12, 1994. Before he was wheeled into the operating room, Waylon showed up to provide support, along with Connie Smith, Jimmy Dickens, and other close friends. Merle Haggard, Alan Jackson, Doug Stone, and others were in touch with Nancy by telephone. Garth Brooks and Reba McEntire sent a truckload of flowers. And the vigil began. Gospel songs were sung as folks opened their hearts, raised their voices in song, and joined hands, and said prayers. Fans were gathered in a separate waiting room. A deluge of cards began to arrive — more than 10,000 before the ordeal was over.

Jones came through surgery. His daughter, Tamala Georgette, a registered nurse, was there to greet him when he opened his eyes. After five days of recovery in intensive care, Jones went home. Nancy received helpful advice from Jessi Colter and Charlene Sherrill who had both been through this same tense period of recuperation with their own husbands. At first, George found some of the adjustments he was forced to make were tough. Tough quitting smoking. Tough eating a less fatty diet. And tough realizing he needed to take things at an easier pace. In October, while George was still in his convalescence, MCA Records released their fourth George Jones album. It had been recorded during the early months of 1994 at Owen Bradley's Barn during some of the worst weather conditions to ever hit Nashville.

4
The Bradley Barn Sessions

"I wanted to re-visit George Jones' old hits in a time machine charged with superstars whose purpose was to motivate this great artist, described by Sinatra as the second-best singer in America," producer Brian Ahern declares in the liner notes to this unique recording. The man who had so successfully produced Anne Murray, married and worked with Emmylou Harris, and had been at the core of some of the very best country music put on record during the past three decades couldn't help but add, "Frankie was wrong. The deer doesn't say, 'I think I'll run pretty today, it just runs.' " THE BRADLEY BARN SESSIONS, an album of duets with superstars from all walks of life, is a marvelous creation inspired by Ahern's genius.

Concept albums have nearly always generated initial enthusiasm, but few of them have delivered the goods on vinyl or CD. Some of the best ones like The Beatles' SERGEANT PEPPER'S LONELY HEARTS CLUB BAND have clicked because of one song that provided a unifying theme. Some have told stories as does Emmylou and Paul Kennerly's THE BALLAD OF SALLY ROSE. Brian Ahern had put together the remarkable traditional gem ROSES IN THE SNOW in 1980, bringing Emmylou together in the studio with singers like Dolly, Linda, Ricky Skaggs, and Johnny Cash in what *Music Hound* critic Elizabeth Lynch calls "Harris' valentine to old-timey music." Sometimes it has been the combination of singers that made a concept album work, as in the case of the 1985 album HIGHWAYMEN that brought Waylon, Willie, Johnny Cash, and Kris Kristofferson together for sessions that resulted in a number one radio hit and a spinoff tour. Sometimes the location has helped provide the ambience and inspiration, something Johnny Cash discovered when he went into Folsom Prison to record live.

To realize his goal, Brian Ahern chose Owen Bradley's studio located just outside of Nashville on farming land in Mount Juliet, Tennessee. Bradley had moved his operation there after selling his Music Row Quonset Hut studio to

Columbia Records in 1966. Originally, Owen had set up his son, Jerry, with a demo facility that over the years had developed into one of the most comfortable settings for laying down real music tracks. To this rural studio Owen Bradley had brought K.D. Lang for the SHADOWLAND recordings in the late 1980s, inviting Kitty Wells, Loretta Lynn, and Brenda Lee along to record a concept medley that became known as the *Honky Tonk Angels Medley*.

Brian Ahern had his own vision of what would work with George Jones. And he had the nod to go ahead with this project from MCA where Tony Brown and Bruce Hinton were at the helm. He also had Nancy Jones to work with, not any one of a long line of former handlers of Jones whose practices had often gotten in the way of the music-making. And he had a George Jones, who could truly be said to be a happy guy these days, someone who was sure to show up ready to sing and not half-zipped on speeders, powders, or whiskey, and sipping from an old fruit jar between takes. The cast of players and singers invited to the sessions were people who respected George Jones at least as much as Brian did. This was almost a sure thing, as sure as any event involving the Possum could ever be.

Of course, none of the label execs, technicians, pickers, or singers had consulted the weather man as the ice storm that hit Nashville that winter nearly shut the sessions down before they got started. "Power poles and ancient trees were exploding throughout Nashville," Ahern remembers. "My control room was in a lead-lined 40-foot semi and was locked in ice like some high-tech trapper's cabin. We were drawing life through massive cables connected to Owen Bradley's studio . . . The worst storm in a hundred years had scattered the cast and their families to hotels with electricity, but they kept coming to the Bradley Barn Sessions."

Thirty miles from the barn, on the eve of the first scheduled session, the power went out in George and Nancy Jones' home. To keep George from catching cold, Nancy bundled him beneath a pile of blankets and checked on him several times during the night to make sure that he was doing all right. Then they climbed into their car and drove those 30 miles over dangerously icy roads. George was determined he wasn't going to be a no show this time, not with all the care that MCA Nashville division chairman Bruce Hinton had gone to setting up the situation. Jones credits Hinton for supporting several seniors like himself with recording contracts at a time when radio had abandoned them altogether. The reward both Jones and Hinton have shared is that, in a decade where he had little air-play, George Jones' albums sold very, very well. The

Bradley Barn Sessions was a bit of a departure from the routine procedure of creating hits, in that Ahern deliberately set out to create what he called an "anti-radio" album, giving George a chance to make the record he never made, so to speak.

Despite the conditions, people honored their commitments. Emmylou, Dolly, and Trisha showed up to record Earl "Peanut" Montgomery's *Where Grass Won't Grow*. Travis Tritt dropped in to lay down *The Race Is On*. Mark Knopfler brought new enthusiasm to *White Lightning*. Marty Stuart was perfect for *One Woman Man*, as was Ricky Skaggs when he and George laid down the ultimate take on *Why Baby Why*. George Jones was there on every track, coming in for second verses with powerful lower register vocals, which picked up the energy every time he made an entry, and picked it up again when he came back to harmonize and trade phrases.

There is this look that comes over Jones' facial expression when he sings harmonies with someone. You can see it in his live shows and in videos like *Same Ole Me*. George seems happier at those moments than most people can ever hope to be. If there had ever been any doubt that George Jones was back, the music made in the barn during those sessions testified to the truth of it. This wasn't George Jones and George Foreman in some video being macho, this wasn't some "hi-tech redneck" label attached to Jones with velcro — *this* was the real deal.

James Taylor's *Bartender's Blues* has become a fixture in George Jones' live shows. Like many of his best records, the lyrics ring true to his personal life experiences. Trisha Yearwood surprises you the first time you hear her begin the opening phrases of that song on THE BRADLEY BARN SESSIONS. Her vocal on this traditional yet hip melody seems to soar and carry you away even before George Jones joins in. Together, in harmony on the choruses, their two voices lift your spirit to heavenly heights.

> I need four walls to hold my life
> To keep me from going astray
> I need a honky tonky angel to hold me tight
> And keep me from slipping away
>
> *Bartender's Blues* (James Taylor)

Tammy Wynette and George were reunited for an update on *Golden Ring*, which inspired them to record another album of duets, ONE, the following year, and to go on a brief tour together.

Vince Gill showed up to record George's *Love Bug*, bringing his guitar along with him and a whole lot of good energy that sprung the novelty tune free from a time warp and made it real, once again. Vince plays the twangy guitar part from *Act Naturally* into the *Love Bug* track and the effect is electrifying.

Keith Richards put in an appearance to record *Say It's Not You* with Jones. Ahern's liner notes acknowledge that "our most famous guest was also our most humble. In contrast to his rocker friends, Keith Richards described our musicians as quiet, powerful angels and himself as a . . . pig in shit." But that track worked, too, and it served to point out that George's fan base reaches far beyond the rank and file of country fans and recording artists into the rock world's baddest band.

Reporter David Gates was at the barn when Keith Richards arrived for the afternoon session and chronicled the event for an article printed in the March 14, 1994 issue of *Newsweek* magazine. "He'd flown in overnight from L.A.," Gates wrote, "where he'd been mixing the Rolling Stones' new album, telling the band, 'Hey, don't ruin the record while I'm away.' Jones, meanwhile, was driving around the neighborhood, putting off the encounter. 'I dreaded that session,' Jones said later. 'I thought, We're going to go together here like a club and clawhammer. We're not going to rhyme, you know?' Finally, Jones nerved himself up enough to come in and was led over to the bar. Richards turned, beamed, and said, 'What can I get you, sir?' " With the ice broken, "two of popular music's most passionate performers and most legendary overindulgers" went to work.

In his autobiography, Jones would later remember that the Rolling Stones who had borrowed band equipment from the Jones Boys back in the 1960s and blown a speaker in one of their guitar amps. And he has said that he sometimes will listen to a Stones cut, just to hear Keith Richards play his guitar. It is a rare indulgence for someone who maintains he seldom listens to nothin' but country music. The camaraderie that afternoon grew when Marty Stuart handed Keith Richards a vintage guitar that had at one time been played by none other than Hank Williams. "No wonder Richards says he was in pigshit heaven," Gates adds. "Jones, in turn, called Richards: 'a character. I mean he could care if the sun come up tomorrow or not. Lord, we just — we just had a ball. I can't get over it yet.' "

Gates was also present when Mark Knopfler laid down his track with Jones. "Mark Knopfler, by contrast, didn't crack a smile for the first hour, and seemed painfully conscious of being out of his depth. 'You're kinda cutting your words just a little bit short,' said Jones. 'That's because I can't sing,' said Knopfler. But their session yielded what may be Jones' hottest-ever version of *White Lightning*. The whole studio broke into applause. 'I need something to rest on,' Jones told the room. 'Where's my lawnmower?' "

The crowning achievement of everyone pulling together under some of the worst conditions ever dumped on recording sessions came when George and Alan Jackson recorded Jerry Chesnut's *A Good Year For The Roses*, a cut that won the pair a TNN/Music City News award for Vocal Collaboration in 1995. With players like Ricky Skaggs on fiddle, Marty Stuart on mandolin, Jerry Douglas on dobro, Paul Franklin on pedal steel, and Vince Gill, James Burton, Mark Knopfler, and Brent Rowan on electric guitar, joined on piano by Leon Russell and Hargus 'Pig' Robbins (who played on the original *White Lightning* session back in the Qonset Hut in 1958), and a rhythm section anchored by bassists Glenn Worff and David Hundgate and drummers Harry Stinson and Eddie Bayers — well, the credits for Bradley Barn Sessions reads like a "who's who" of the best Nashville Cats of all time. As good as this music was, and you have to split hairs to find a better album in the 1990s, it didn't inspire country radio programmers to rediscover George Jones.

George Jones' most unique duet of all came in 1994 when some executives high up in the MCA organization decided to listen to Ray Charles when he said, "Muddy Waters, George Jones — we own that music! We can go to the *bank* with that." The MCA project became known to the public as the *Rhythm, Country & Blues* album, a collection of duets featuring country and R&B artists. Ray Charles' favorite country singer has always been George Jones, and the two men had a ball recording *We Didn't See A Thing* together with Chet Atkins in 1984 for Ray's album FRIENDSHIP. For this summit recording of blues and country artists, George was paired with B.B. King.

MCA Entertainment Group Chairman Al Teller saw both commercial and artistic potential in a project that brought together American music's two root forms. "The idea had been swirling around in my head for a while," Teller said at the time of the album's release. "And it focused itself basically because our company has such strong country and R&B operations. I've always loved both forms; they're alternate versions of American soul music. I had been thinking of how to pull them together. It occurred to me to bring them home on one song." Teller began to work with MCA Soundtrack Department Head Kathy Nelson and Tony Brown, then President of MCA/Nashville, hammering out song selections and possible pairings of the artists who would record with producer Don Was. When you first hear the names, some of the choices seem surprising; when you hear the music — it all works really well. Gladys Knight teams up with Vince Gill for a smooth *Ain't Nothin' But The Real Thing*. Tanya Tucker and Little Richard click together on Eddie Cochran's *Somethin' Else*. Conway Twitty and Sam Moore have a ball with Tony Joe White's *Rainy Night In Georgia*. Chet Atkins and Allen Toussaint create a little magic on Allen's *Southern Nights*. Aaron Neville and Trisha Yearwood come up with a whole new version of Harlan Howard and Hank Cochran's *I Fall To Pieces*. This stand-out cut turned out to be a Grammy Award winning performance. Marty Stuart and the Staple Singers wail on the Band's *The Weight*. Patti LaBelle and Travis Tritt re-invent the Sam & Dave classic *When Something Is Wrong With My Baby*. Lyle Lovett and Al Green find a commonality on Willie Nelson's *Funny How Time Slips Away*. And Reba teams with Natalie Cole for a superb *Since I Fell For You*. All in all, it's a marvelous album. All 11 cuts.

George Jones, teamed with B.B. King, represented one of the most significant of all of these recordings. Both artists were equal to the challenge. The back-up players included Kenny Aronoff on the drumkit, Willie Weeks on bass, Steve Nathan on pedal steel, Reggie Young and Don Potter on rhythm guitar — plus a string section and *both* Barry Beckett on piano and Benmont Tench on Hammond B-3 — the sort of band I imagined ole Hank might put together in Hillbilly Heaven — if angels have bands, that is. "The dynamics of family relationships, life and death, and the passage of time assume center stage," liner-note author James Hunter comments, "as B.B. King and George Jones enact the transcendent melodrama *Patches*. As the background chorus of soul men and country women fortifies the arrangement, King's nuanced solos and long narrative raps combine with Jones' magisterial voicings of the dying father's last words, demonstrating the unusual depths of Clarence Carter's hit." Of all the duets George Jones has sung, this one stands tall as his most heartfelt. I thought of George and his own father while listening to the song for the first time and realized that he may very well have had his own daddy in mind as he put his heart and soul into each chorus. *Patches* seemed to bring him full circle, healing something that had been broken.

—5—
I Lived To Tell It All

In 1992 when Jones had needed a hit on the radio, Garth and Emmylou, along with Vince Gill, Mark Chestnutt, Travis Tritt, Joe Diffie, Alan Jackson, Pam Tillis, T. Graham Brown, Patty Loveless, and Clint Black joined in on *I Don't Need Your Rockin' Chair*, which won a 1993 CMA Award for Vocal Event of the Year. Sadly, country radio programmers only saw fit to playlist this great song and vocal effort, recorded by an undeniable pantheon of the best country stars, for a mere five weeks in the Top 40.

By the time George had gone on to record I LIVED TO TELL IT ALL, there was still no change in the stonewall at radio. George parted ways with MCA. Once again, it was a duet, this time with Patty Loveless, that did put him back on the radio in a big way. Their vocal collaboration on *You Don't Seem To Miss Me* won them a 1998 CMA Award for Vocal Event of the Year. The cut was produced by Patty's husband Emory Gordy Jr. and released on her label. No doubt, it helped George out some when Asylum Records signed him. By 1999, George was making a comeback with a new record out on a new label, encouraged by Evelyn Shriver at Asylum Records, who was actively lobbying on his behalf. Although he wasn't exactly hitting into the Top 10 with his single releases, there was one bright spot on the horizon. His album COLD HARD TRUTH had passed the 300,000 mark in sales, steadily climbing toward becoming yet another gold record. As the new millennium approached, George was back on the radio, along with Hank Jr., on Chad Brock's novelty tune, A *Country Boy Can Survive (Y2K Version)*. The three singers had a whole lot of fun with the lyrics and celebrated the new era country style, though the release died away once the Y2K bug was no longer front page news.

Despite a lot of bad luck and some no luck at all over the years, George Jones had started to look lucky again. It had been a long haul, beginning back in Texas when he had married Nancy and built Jones Country in the Big Thicket.

I've had good luck and bad luck
And no luck it's true
But I always get lucky with you . . .

I keep two strikes against me
Most all of the time
When it's down to just a phone call
I'm minus a dime
There's been good days and bad days
But when the day is through
I always get lucky with you

I *Always Get Lucky With You* (T.Whitson, F. Powers, G. Church
& M. Haggard)

Life was good for George Jones. After enjoying a good long run with their
shows at Jones Country, they moved back to Tennessee, settling on a rural
property where the living was easy. George Jones had become pretty much your
average everyday guy. His private life was no longer a spectacular series of
death-defying acrobatics performed on the high trapeze above hushed crowds
of spectators who waited with drawn breath for the long predicted moment the
press had promised. Without their usual No Show Jones stories to write, some
of the journalists hung in there to take little pot shots at the Possum while
grudgingly writing accounts of how his music was better than ever. Others
would wangle an interview, view his home and daily habits, then struggle with
the reality that Jones had settled into a graceful existence in his golden years.
They reported on the herd of cows he doted over. They reported that Nancy
called them 'Bub' when they visited. She called her husband Possum. She doted
on the man. They reported that George had a haircut just about every day. They
reported that his favorite pastime was mowing the extensive lawns on his 150-
acre estate seated on one of those lawnmowers he had sometimes used to advantage in the past when no other vehicle was available to take him to liquor
outlets. They reported that he stocked the waterways of his estate with trout and
went fishing, like a page out of the original script for *The Andy Griffith Show*,
only no one mentioned any whistling. They reported that he was a pitch man for
a brand of dog food. They reported that he built squirrel-feeding stations . . . and
so on. Only a few Nashville writers remained oddly vindictive. This wasn't the
god or devil of a man they wanted to encounter, so they wrote him up as the

opposite. Some called him a brilliant singer but "vacant" as a person, refusing to believe what George had been telling them all of these years — he was a simple man.

One such journalist was Nicholas Dawidoff who attended a soiree where Jones was hawking his new line of dog food to the press and who wrote that experience up into a full-length feature for his book *In the Country of Country (A Journey to the Roots of American Music)*. "At the time I met him," Dawidoff writes, "he was just finishing his autobiography, *I Lived To Tell It All*. The book turned out to be a massive chronicle of vile behavior related with brutal candor. If you picked it up without knowing that Jones was a famous singer, however, the book could be read as the confessions of almost anyone who spent much of his life throwing drinks in other people's faces. Next to nothing revealing is said about the art of singing. As Jones presents it, his life is the story of a nuisance." Dawidoff continues, incredulously, "these recurrent struggles make Jones seem a lot like Johnny Cash, but the differences between them are considerable. Cash is a highly intelligent and witty man, a gifted artist struggling with demons, who turns to narcotics in an effort to distract himself from the very keenness of his worried mind. Jones clearly had plenty of demons too, but the truth was that he was dynamic only when he was drunk or stuffing his anger and misery into a microphone." Old myths die hard, but fortunately the critical consensus on George's *I Lived to Tell It All* autobiography contradicted Dawidoff. Music critics in *Newsweek, The Washington Post, L.A. Times, USA Today* and many other publications raved about the book, and the buying public kept the book on the bestseller lists for ages, listed as high as number six in New York.

I Lived To Tell It All is honest, riotously funny in places, though maudlin in others, yet as tragic as anything ever written about Jones. The one thing that George Jones does consistently show for the people that he speaks about is respect. On stage, George was making it up to the fans for all of the disappointments he'd handed them over the years, and off stage, he was healing as much of the hurt he had caused with as many people as he could. Writing his autobiography helped gain a measure of closure with nearly everyone he'd alienated over the years.

George Jones had become known to the world at large first through Tammy Wynette's biography *Stand by Your Man* in which she had been unforgiving and relentless when she blamed Jones' drinking and alleged violence for the failure of their marriage. Both Dolly Carlisle and Bob Allen had bought into most of Tammy's assertions, especially the alleged violence. By the time Tom

Carter and George Jones got around to straightening out the record, the die had been cast, so to speak, and it almost seemed that George Jones must be lying simply because he'd done a whole lot of drinking. Jones and Carter do some detective work of their own and point out the discrepancy between two separate "guns" in Tammy's description of the time Jones is supposed to have threatened her with a shotgun that becomes a rifle that becomes a . . . ?

Not that George remembered things that way. For George, his years with Wynette had been the happiest he had known, and he seldom spoke her any ill. During their marriage, he made a supreme effort to cut down his drinking and, for the first time in his adult life, had long periods of sobriety. Tammy may have been close to the truth of it when she later said that their marriage failed because of her "nagging" and George's "nipping." But George has said, several times, "I don't think she tried to understand me and help me to understand about her and the things goin' on between us. I think she took the quick way out."

When Tammy Wynette died in the winter of 1998, George had come to terms with her. Revered by the CMA in 1998, now that she had passed away, Wynette was finally inducted into their Hall of Fame in the fall of the year. She was paid tribute to with an album featuring the top female vocalists of the day *and* Sir Elton John. But then her name was sadly back in the tabloids as subject of a scandal that reached beyond the grave as her children sued George Richey and Dr Willis Marsh. Their lawsuit sought to have her body exhumed so that the coroner could determine whether her death had been nudged along. At issue was a vast inheritance and a certain insurance policy. Tammy had once been cast in a TV soap, but the show had folded soon after she taped her first few episodes. She had joked with journalists like Alanna Nash that her whole life seemed like a soap opera. Now, her death was turning out to that way, too. Those who actually knew Tammy felt her loss, as did her fans, no matter what had gone on. Everyone missed her, including George and Nancy Jones, who helped George Richey with the funeral arrangements and stood by him in his moment of grief.

Our golden years are best spent with a measure of peace in our hearts. George has found that. They are best spent with someone that you love. And George has found that love, too. Now that he has found his higher ground, George seems willing to forgive any and everyone he once felt had wronged him or he felt were opposed to him. In *I Lived To Tell It All*, he is not merely counting the notches on his gun, tallying up his successes, trophies, conquests, and he is not merely refuting others or bringing them down. Instead, he is down on his knees, laboring to tell it all as honestly as he can, working to reconcile all conflicts. He seems to have done so with Tammy — even with Shug Baggott — though it may take him a while to get around to making his amends with every single one of the Jones Boys. There have been more than 200 of them and we're still counting. George may have started on his road to recovery a little too late to make amends with his father, George Washington Jones, and his mother, Clara, but he has stated that he wants to make those amends in heaven when he gets there. In his heart I wager he has already done that.

A few years ago, there would not have been many who would have laid any bets on that happening — George Jones going to Heaven. Today, it looks like a sure thing. Of course, there are a few more tomorrows before that day. And, no doubt, there will be a few more records and performances, too. If God is willing, more than a few. Roy Acuff lived a good long life, during his final years in a house on the Opryland grounds where he was never far from the mother church of country music he helped build and maintain. George Jones is just stretching out into his own golden years. There are a whole lot of country singers who are doing their level best to follow in his footsteps. Nowadays, that doesn't seem like such a bad thing to do.

There have been several tributes to George Jones that playfully touch on his volatile career. One of the best is the 1989 recording *They Don't Play George Jones On MTV*, a light-hearted novelty number released by bluegrassers Byron Berline, Dan Crary, and John Hickman. George is also mentioned on Tim Wilson's comedic 1998 release *GEORGE is On My Mind* along with a whole lot of other Georges. James O'Gwynn, the smiling Irishman of country music, was more serious in the lyrics to his *If I Could Sing A Country Song (Exactly Like George Jones)*. Canadian songwriter Larry Coad, who hung with George at times during his wild and crazy days, penned two tunes for Canadian country artist Harold MacIntyre; both *Possum* and *George* display a measure of hero worship that was deeply felt throughout the Canadian scene during the early 1980s. Longtime Jones Boy Ron Gaddis put out an album titled A CHIP OFF THE OLD BLOCK. The tongue in cheek lyrics to *I Fell Off The Wagon* provide a perfect forum for Gaddis and Jones to duet while the session players tear up the recording studio with one of the hottest country tracks ever recorded. Becky Hobbs was inspired to cut one of her best tracks when she recorded *Jones On The Jukebox*.

At the turn of the century, George Strait and Alan Jackson recorded their version of bluegrass singer-songwriter Larry Cordle's *Murder On Music Row*, where the two current country stars duet on lyrics that satirize the damage that has been done to country music by pop music trends, singing lines like "someone killed country music, cut out its heart and soul . . . they got away with murder down on Music Row . . ." with gusto and enthusiasm. Cordle and co-writer Larry Shell also mention ole Hank and identify the two remaining country legends who continue to champion hard core country in the song lyrics:

> *The Hag wouldn't have a chance on today's radio*
> *Since they've committed murder down on Music Row*
> *Why they'd even tell the Possum to pack it up and go back home*
> *There's been an awful murder on Music Row*

> Murder on Music Row (Larry Cordle and Larry Shell)

While this novelty tune got airplay for Strait and Jackson, it didn't place the Hag and the Possum back in the Top 10, though the influence of George Strait and Alan Jackson made it more difficult for music row power-brokers to sweep Haggard and Jones under the rug, especially when they were nominated in 2000 by the CMA for Vocal Collaboration, with Cordell and Shell among the five finalists in the Song of the Year category. Writing and singing about George Jones had become a ticket to ride.

Back in March 1999, George crashed his car into a bridge abutment near Franklin, Tennessee, nearly killing himself, and the tributes poured in again, except from the Country Music Association. Although CMA members had nominated George Jones' single *Choices* (despite its lack of Top 10 status) for the 1999 awards, the show programmers asked the Possum to sing only a shortened version on the CBS network show after his recovery. George declined their offer. Then Alan Jackson made a politically incorrect but endearing gesture by tagging his own CMA awards' show performance of *Pop-A-Top* with a chorus from Jones' *Choices*. "Had George Jones died," Jackson later told Walt Trott, "there would've been a 10-minute standing ovation salute to him on the show. But he lived and they wouldn't give him three minutes!"

While commenting on the state of contemporary country radio in the George's authorized video biography, Alan observes, "It's like the old country sound is kind of disappearing. I hate to see that. Not everybody needs to sound like a George Jones' record. But that's what I've always done and I'm going to keep it that way — or try to." Way back in 1981, George had told Marina Nickerson, author of *Country Music: A Look At The Men Who've Made It,*

"What you hear on the radio nowadays isn't exactly what I call country music. I sing country music. So does Merle Haggard and Moe Bandy. We don't have too many more cuz all the good ones went pop." In his 1996 autobiography, he comments, "I don't care much for many of today's young country singers. They're not country — they're clones. Many got their contracts because they sound like someone else . . . today's country music is a lot like the television industry. It's in love with reproducing itself. . . . I look at the shape of contemporary country music and I'm saddened. There never has been a time when country radio was so disrespectful of its elders." George wonders what today's Music Row execs will do and how they will feel when they, too, are cut because they have grown older. Regarding LeAnn Rimes' debut *Blue*, he writes, "People make a big deal about her young age. I think they should make a bigger deal about her singing. That child is brilliant for ANY age. I saw Patsy Cline live. I worked with her. Not since Patsy have I heard such a no-bluff voice." And upon hearing that some country programmers would not playlist her debut single because there was a yodel in it, he exclaimed, "A 14-year-old who didn't fit a 'young country' format? What a crock of shit! I hope LeAnn becomes a billionaire, buys up all of those stations, and fires their program directors."

When Alan Jackson made reference on record to George in *Don't Rock The Jukebox*, George returned the compliment when he made an appearance in Alan's video for the song. There was Jackson on CMT, evoking memories of Hank Williams with his big white stetson, and, when his name came up in the lyrics, there was George leaning on the juke box in the shadows with a warm smile on his face.

Country radio and music associations might have tried to put George Jones out to pasture, but the testimony of his peers identifies Jones as the number one pure country artist of the century. In the video biography *Same Ole Me*, Johnny Cash, when asked who his favorite country artist is, answers, "You mean other than George Jones?"

Waylon Jennings says, "If we all could sound like we wanted to, we would all sound like George Jones."

"It's almost like he's lived every minute of every word that he sings," says Randy Travis, "and there's very few people that can do that."

Loretta Lynn, who has never stopped being a hillbilly from the hollers, says, "Man, he stoled everybody's heart! He stole my heart."

Conway Twitty once noted, "He can stroll out on that stage, strap on that guitar, and knock you right out of your seat."

"George puts so much emotion, so much feeling, into his songs," Ricky Van Shelton observes. "And that's what it's all about."

"Every note of his voice pierces my heart," says Patty Loveless. "He moves every emotion in my soul. He is my hero!"

"When you hear George Jones sing, you are hearing a man who takes a song and makes it into a work of art — always," Emmylou Harris once said. At her first Nashville press conference, she added, "My idea of the perfect voice would be a blend of George Jones and Carter Stanley."

"He's messed up a million times in his life," says Vince Gill, "but people just idolize that voice."

"There's really no describing the voice of George Jones," Mike Greenblatt comments in a special tribute issue of *Modern Screen* magazine. "A lowball swoon with the wiggly soul antics of an R&B singer is woefully inadequate, but when George sings, it connects bigtime. It's the universal clarion call to emotion and understanding. You don't need to love country to instantly react when George sings. His voice is a multi-layered instrument that's as expressive and passionate as it is commanding, warm, macho, humorous and quixotic. You can hear Jones a mile away, that's how distinctive his voice is."

"Jones' voice, when he unleashes it, has the power of a great primal scream of sorrow," Billy Sherrill, who knows that voice better than anyone, states in the authorized video biography, "conjuring up a bottomless pit that is the essence of honky tonk desperation. In more restrained musical moments, he can emote, with similar ease, all the softer emotional shades of tenderness and devotion with a voice that is as pure and soothing as mother's milk. Then, in the next breath, singing through clenched teeth, he can insinuate into even the most mundane of melodies, a compelling sense of sadness, rage and confusion that is as piercing as a cold wind blowing on a dark night."

George does often sing through clenched teeth, which some critics have seen as an expression of emotion, but this gesture has more to do with vocal technique than body language. In an article called "The Mask of the Face" published in *Canadian Musician* magazine, Brian Vollmer offered advice to singers for improving their technique. "Imagine that you have an upside down or inverted triangle in the center of your face," Vollmer writes. "This wide part of the triangle is across your cheek bones and the point of the triangle is on your upper lip. This area is known, in singing, as the mask of the face. Within this area you are going to concentrate, vocally and mentally, the whole range of the voice. Low sounds, because they are produced by slowly vibrating vocal chords and very little breath, have a weak sound wave. In order for the low sounds to have enough resonance to project as far as the higher notes, it is essential to focus your thoughts of the low notes between the lips, ahead of the front teeth. By doing this, you are ensuring that the low notes will not resonate in the back of the throat. The back of the throat contains several soft surfaces that soak up the sound, causing the low sounds to lose their projection. The low notes must be focused in the point of the imaginary triangle, in front of the face." George Jones never was a theoretical person, but the technique he developed on his own simply meant that, in order to achieve this power in the lower register, he clenched his teeth at times and sang through this embouchure with considerable power.

When he sang those words to *Who's Gonna Fill Their Shoes* about the legendary vocal power of his favorite country singers, George might have been singing about himself.

> *You know this old world is full of singers*
> *But just a few are chosen*
> *To tear your heart out when they sing*

Sometimes, for an artist who was breaking on the scene, merely singing a George Jones' song was a ticket that led toward success. Dolly Parton, for example, chose George's 1956 hit *You Gotta Be My Baby* for her debut on Ralph Emery's radio show during the 1960s. Singing for the first time face-to-face with George has proven to be intimidating for a number of singers, including Tammy Wynette. In her autobiography, she recalls singing *My Elusive Dreams*, the hit duet she had recorded with David Houston, on stage with George for the first time, after Houston had refused to do so during a dispute. "I was shaking so hard the fringe on my gold dress was in constant motion. I stood there with my hands behind my back, fidgeting, too scared to speak a word." When Jones, not Houston, sang the first line of the song, the audience went bananas. "It was the most exciting moment that had ever happened to me as a performer," Tammy declared. "George didn't know all the words to *My Elusive Dream*, so I had to whisper his lyrics while I sang my own. We kept getting tickled and breaking up, but the audience loved it." Melba Montgomery has similar memories of the thrill of performing with George and his role in helping her step into the country music spotlight, as does Lorrie Morgan, a generation later.

When Lorrie auditioned for a spot on George's touring show in the early 1980s, she chose to sing a duet with Jones, rather than sing something like *Stand*

By Your Man on her own to impress George, as several of the other girl singers had done that afternoon during the audition. Lorrie remembers the incident in her autobiography, Forever Yours, Faithfully, which she co-wrote with George Vecsey. "George was staring at me with those piercing eyes that can scare you half to death, but I was not about to back down. My competitive nature kicked in. Plus, I needed the job. I stared right back at him, jaw to jaw, eyeball to eyeball, and we sang the song. He gave me the job, right then and there." Lorrie began touring with Jones while he was still a mess in more ways than one, but she stands by George. "For all of that, I loved George Jones. You had to. He wasn't deliberately being a jerk. He was hurtin'. Something inside him made him act that way." This was an insight that Tammy Wynette never had.

Despite all of the opposition George Jones has faced from the music industry, some well deserved, he has become the all-time most-played country singer on radio, though strangely, he's logged few number one hits (nine as a solo artist and four as a duet partner), far fewer than artists like Conway Twitty (40), Merle Haggard (38), Ronnie Milsap (35), and even the current King of Country, Garth Brooks. But since that first Top 40 hit, Why Baby Why, George has logged 144 more Top 40s, more than any other country artist, and, according to Joel Whitburn's "Top 100 Country Artists of All Time" listed in the Billboard Book of Top 40 Country Hits, by 1996 George Jones was already the second-most played country singer in the history of country radio — second only to Eddy Arnold. By the time you read these words, he's passed Eddy, too.

The British magazine Country Music People was the first publication to come out with the results of a poll that had been conducted to determine the all-time top country acts at the end of the 20th century. The magazine named George Jones its Country Artist for the Millennium, while Hank Williams was named Country Songwriter for the Millennium. He Stopped Loving Her Today, written by Bobby Braddock & Curly Putman and performed by George Jones, was named Country Song for the Millennium, while BITTER TEARS by Johnny Cash was named Country Album for the Millennium. Hank Williams and Johnny Cash were second and third in the artists list. Harlan Howard and Dolly Parton were second and third songwriters. Your Cheatin' Heart was named second in the song category. Dolly Parton's I Will Always Love You and Kris Kristofferson's Sunday Morning Coming Down were tied for third. JOHNNY CASH AT SAN QUENTIN was second in the album list. There was a four-way tie for the third position among NIGHT LIFE by Ray Price, STORMS OF LIFE by Randy Travis, WANTED: THE OUTLAWS by Waylon, Willie, Jessi & Tompall, and HONKY TONK HEROES by Waylon

Jennings, featuring the songs of Billy Joe Shaver. The editorial announcing the winners was tagged with a short statement: "Even though current favorites like George Strait, Alan Jackson, Garth Brooks, Reba McEntire, Dwight Yoakam, Vince Gill and Billy Ray Cyrus were heavily voted, the winning nominations show that readers gave careful consideration to the most influential figures in country music this century."

As the results of other magazine polls continued to filter in, *100 Years of Country Music*, a special edition of *Modern Screen* magazine, named Merle Haggard, George Jones, Willie Nelson, Hank Williams, Johnny Cash, Jimmie Rodgers, Lefty Frizzell, Marty Robbins, and Vince Gill as the leaders on their Top 20 Male Country Singers of All Time. Johnny Cash topped the album poll with JOHNNY CASH AT FOLSOM PRISON. Ray Charles was a pleasant surprise at the number 2 position with MODERN SOUNDS IN COUNTRY & WESTERN MUSIC. Hank Williams topped the Top 25 Songwriters list ahead of Kris Kristofferson, Harlan Howard, Cindy Walker, Roger Miller, and 20 others. Tammy Wynette topped the Female Country Singers list ahead of Loretta Lynn, Kitty Wells, Patsy Cline, Emmylou Harris, and 15 others.

In 1999, before *Choices* and *Cold Hard Truth* were released, Asylum Records' Evelyn Shriver noted that overall George Jones had charted a grand total of 158 singles in the Top 100. Along the way Jones has blazed unlikely trails and become a living legend. His reputation as a honky tonk singer who has lived the lifestyle to the max has added considerably to that legendary status, but Jones has shown remarkable resilience. He is a survivor of a cyclonic tour of duty as a road warrior in an industry that has eaten up many of the most talented country singers well before they became senior citizens. Yet, today, George is still performing and making records. His steadfast loyalty to the roots and traditions of country music shines as a beacon that can still be seen and heard by both contemporary country artists and the Music Row power-brokers who have abandoned those roots, with the result that sales for country records were at a new modern era low percentage of total record sales in 1999.

In the summer of the year 2000, SONY re-issued George's classic 1980 album, I AM WHAT I AM, featuring the original art work, as part of their Epic/ Legacy "American Milestones" series. "What makes this CD version so extra-special for fans and collectors," Larry Delaney noted in *Country Music News*, "are the four bonus tracks. A gift indeed. All four are knockout hurtin' tunes — *I'm a Fool For Loving Her*, the Wynn-Stewart penned *It's All In My Mind*, and uncredited *Am I Losing Your Memory Or Mine*, and *The Ghost Of Another Man*."

Over the years, George's record labels have issued some 450 albums in North America and Europe. Sure, many of these are reissues with new titles or a song or two added that were often released separately in the United States, Canada, and the U.K., making it difficult for record collectors to complete their libraries of his material. But any which way you slice it . . . 450 albums is one heck of a lot of albums. George has been called the "Rolls Royce of Country Singers," a tribute to his unique vocal style and rich sincere vocal delivery, and the "King of Country Music," a title first claimed by the late, great Roy Acuff, one that George has not actively encouraged himself. When George toured with his third wife, Tammy Wynette, the two were known as "Mr & Mrs Country Music" and the "First Couple of Country." But many country disc jockeys and true country fans fondly call George "the Possum." George Jones continues to provide inspiration to new singers of country music, proving that if you really want to you *can* record country music that is honest and true to the tradition, true to its roots.

George has carried on the tradition of Jimmie Rodgers, Hank Williams, Lefty Frizzell, Marty Robbins, Roy Acuff and Bill Monroe. He has walked through the years alongside his friends and fellow singers Johnny Cash, Waylon Jennings, Merle Haggard, and Buck Owens. He has sang duets with the greatest women country artists — Deborah Allen, Melba Montgomery, Tammy Wynette, Loretta Lynn, Brenda Lee, Emmylou Harris, Dolly Parton, Lacey J. Dalton, Terri Gibbs, Barbara Mandrell, Lorrie Morgan, Patty Loveless, and Trisha Yearwood. True to form, George has handed us a perfect anthem, country music's own *Auld Lang Syne*, in *Who's Gonna Fill Their Shoes*. It may never become as familiar as *White Lightning* or *The Race Is On* or bring as many people to a full-stop as often as *She Thinks I Still Care* and *He Stopped Loving Her Today*, but *Who's Gonna Fill Their Shoes* gives us occasion to draw a deep breath and cast a glance back through the wonder of it all, all of the great country singers who have entertained us with their records over the years. To think that nobody is likely to fill their shoes is wrong, though, for the beat goes on. And just as trees have roots, they also blossom forth in the spring season, so country music seems to be doing once again with the very young singers who have moved into the spotlight. Not just singing in churches or in their family homes but on records and television. Some of those young singers, like LeAnn Rimes, are supremely talented.

George's roots reach back into the gospel music he learned from his grandfather, Uncle Litt Patterson, and they reach back to the times he listened to the

Carter Family on the battery operated family radio in the Big Thicket. His roots still curl around the people who helped him learn his craft like Brother Burl & Sister Annie and Eddie & Pearl. The people who helped him make his music like Pappy Daily, Billy Sherrill, Norro Wilson, Keith Stegall, and Brian Ahern. The times he spent on the road with Patsy Cline, Faron Young, Johnny Cash, and Little Jimmy Dickens; Hank Snow, Carl Perkins, Johnny Horton, and Stonewall Jackson. His memories embrace guitar players he worked with in his earliest days like Dalton Henderson, session players like Floyd Robinson who played on *White Lightning*, road musicians like Sonny Curtis, Charlie Justice, Wayne Kemp, Freddie Haws, James Hollie, Hal Rugg, Tom Killen, Ernie Rowell, Ralph Land, and Ron Gaddis, and the times he recorded with Chet Atkins, Mark Knopfler, Ricky Skaggs, Brent Mason, Hargus "Pig" Robbins, James Burton, and even Keith Richards. And his memories include the time he met Hank Williams on a radio show where he forgot to play along. The time he was on the *Louisiana Hayride* with Elvis. The time he shared a date with the Rolling Stones. The times he played Willie Nelson's July 4th Picnic and Farm Aid benefit shows. And the times he gathered up his courage and took his hill-billy honky tonk music to Madison Square Garden in New York City and came away a winner. The times he entertained in Las Vegas and traveled overseas to play the great Wembley International Country Music Festival in England. The times he sang with Gene Pitney and the great Ray Charles, B.B. King, Johnny Paycheck, Merle Haggard, Elvis Costello, and Vince Gill. And the time that Garth Brooks joined a choir of voices to sing on George's *I Don't Need Your Rockin' Chair*. The times he has sung with Alan Jackson, Marty Stuart, Clint Black, Travis Tritt, Sammy Kershaw, and Joe Diffie. And each time he has raised his voice in song with all of those talented artists, the harmonies have sounded sweet, and the legend has been passed on and shared. No Show Jones has shown up a whole lot of times when the chips were really down. And he shows up in the hearts of country music fans everywhere whenever his music comes to their ears. *When That Final Curtain Falls*, as it must for every soul that is born to this life, George Jones will live on in his music here on Earth. His spirit will enrich the heavenly choir. The circle will be unbroken.

6
Live with the Possum

GEORGE JONES: LIVE WITH THE POSSUM begins with an introduction by Alan Jackson speaking casually but with a nervous edge as he refers to the Possum — "George Jones . . . legend, singer . . . I mean what could I say about him that hadn't already been said a thousand times and all of it's true. To meet somebody like that and still realize they are just a good ole human being and they just love singing, that's what George does, and he sings better'n anybody. I can't think of anything that can say any more than his songs and music has said for the last 30 years." Jackson strums his acoustic guitar as he sings, "Don't rock the jukebox, I want to hear George Jones!" As the audience applause swells up into your stereo system speakers, an announcer declares: "Here's country's living legend . . . George Jones!" The initial thunder of applause continues to grow as the Jones Boys launch into the familiar opening bars of the Possum's set opener, *No Show Jones*.

George greets his audience warmly. "How we doin'? Ah, bless your hearts. I want to welcome Knoxville, Tennessee to our video tonight, and to our great big show. We're gonna have a great big time, I can see that already . . . We love you. Here we go!" When George mentions Knoxville a second time, you realize he's recording live right there in the same city where Hank Williams climbed into his big old Cadillac for the last time on that fateful night of December 31, 1952.

The audience response is enthusiastic as Ron Gaddis leads off the novelty number *No Show Jones*: "Hey, George . . . did you know Waylon and ole Willie are the outlaws, did you know that?" Jones' response sets the tone, ironic, tongue-in-cheek. They are having fun with it. "I didn't know that at all, son . . ." Gaddis continues the tributes. "Did you know that Roger is the King of the Road . . ." with George answering, "Uhuh." When George leads off, he adds his own twists. But when he sings, "Everyone knows Hank's been in prison . . ." he raises a question in everybody's mind. In prison? Is that what he's been doing since he wrote this song and began to celebrate Hank's legend rather than let it get him down — setting ole Hank free? Gaddis quips, "We didn't *know* that . . ." George appears to be on top of it all, now, adding, "and Dolly's got two big reasons why she's well known . . ." As George and Ron step into the chorus singing harmony on, "They call me no show Jones . . . I'm hardly ever on . . ." it's a frolic in the woods. They are two young boys off with their fishing poles, just passing the time of day on their way to their favorite trout stream . . . just a hop-step and a-jumpin' along. When Ron says, "Tell me about Tammy, George," Jones draws an appropriate swell of audience response with his line, "Tammy had some kind of scheme, she divorced George Jones . . ."

At the end of *No Show Jones*, as the band ends with a flourish and begins to segue into the next number, George swears that this is the very last time they are ever going to do this stupid song. Gaddis quips, "Hey George, somebody told me you wasn't going to show up tonight." And Jones answers, "Oh, I quit that years ago."

By this stage in his career, George has completely dispelled the myth that he could only sing when he was drinking. In fact, some folks think he's better than ever. Walt Trott provided a well-rounded picture of the situation in the December 1999 edition of the British magazine *Country Music People,* where he reports that "Ron Gaddis has sung harmony and fronted Jones' shows for nearly 20 years, harking back to the scary days when irate fans rocked their Silver Eagle bus back and forth because the headliner failed to show. Ron recalled, 'People around Nashville gave up on Jones. They thought he was pretty much doomed. It's such a thrill to be up there with him now. He's really pounding it!' "

And there you have it in a nutshell, everything that needs to be said about ole No Show George Jones' past on a night like this. There's so much energy and emotion in this living legend's show that you forget for a moment that George Jones is 68 going on 18. You forget everything except the words he is singing to you. The lucky people in the theater seats in Knoxville respond with thunderous applause to *Once You've Had The Best*. When the Jones Boys begin *The Race Is On*, everyone begins clapping and keeping the beat. By the time George has begun *Bartender's Blues*, he has us all under his spell. The producer listed on LIVE WITH THE POSSUM for this "great big show in Knoxville, Tennessee" is not Billy Sherrill, Pappy Daily or even Brian Ahern or Norro Wilson. The producer is George Jones. It's his show. All the way.

The first time I listened to LIVE WITH THE POSSUM, I was struck by the sincere personal relationship George offers to each individual who has shown up to hear him sing. And I was drawn into believing that he was welcoming me, personally, too, into his heart and his life during the between-song patter. And when he sings it is as if he enters each and every soul and gathers each one of us to himself, creating a glow that includes all and everyone forevermore. Reluctantly, you realize that each of these harmonic moments of honeyed joy and sorrow must end, as all things must, and when the music dies away you realize that the old man up there on the stage, and in your eyes-closed headset imagination, really is still a small shy boy with a battered guitar and a naughty grin of a smile. He really is touched that you like him. He really is. He's tickled half to death.

And proud he should be. Half a century after Hank Williams made his last exit from that lost highway leading out of Knoxville into West Virginia, George Jones is alive and well and on the road again at the beginning of a whole new millennium. Tonight and every night country music beats in the heart of George Jones.

REFERENCES

Books

Alden, Grant and Peter Blackstock, eds. *No Depression: An Introduction to Alternative Country Music (Whatever that Is)*. Nashville, TN: Dowling Press, 1998.

Allen, Bob. *George Jones: The Saga of an American Singer*. New York, NY: St Martin's Press, 1984, 1996.

Bedwell, Randall, ed. *Unbroken Circle: A Quotable History of The Grand Ole Opry*. Nashville, TN: Cumberland House, 1999.

Brown, Peter Harry and Pat H. Broeske. *Down at the End of Lonely Street: The Life & Death of Elvis Presley*. New York, NY: Penguin-Putnam; Dutton-Signet Edition, 1997.

Carlisle, Dolly. *Ragged But Right: The Life & Times of George Jones*. Chicago, IL: Contemporary Books, 1984.

Cash, John R. *Johnny Cash: Man in Black*. New York, NY: Zondervan Books, 1978.

Cash, John R. (with Patrick Carr). *Johnny Cash: The Autobiography*. New York, NY: Harper Paperbacks, 1997.

Cooper, Daniel. *Lefty Frizzell: The Honky Tonk Life of Country Music's Greatest Singer*. New York, NY: Little, Brown & Co., 1995.

Corvette, Nick. *Rock 'n' Roll Heaven*. New York, NY: Boulevard Books, 1997.

Cusic, Don. "Willie Nelson: His Lyrics." Introduction to *Willie Nelson: Lyrics 1957-1994*. New York, NY: St. Martins Press, 1995.

Damron, Dick. *The Legend and the Legacy*, Kingston, ON: Quarry Music Books, 1997.

Dawidoff, Nicholas. *In the Country, Of The Country: A Journey to the Roots of American Music*. New York, NY: Random House Ltd., Vintage Books Edition, 1998.

Dannen, Fredric. *Hit Men*. New York, NY: Vintage Books, 1991.

Dellar, Fred and Richard Wooton. *The Country Music Book of Lists*. New York, NY: Times Books, 1984.

Ellison, Curtis W. *Country Music Culture: From Hard Times to Heaven*. Oxford, MI: The University of Mississippi Press, 1995.

Emery, Ralph (with Tom Carter). *Memories: The Autobiography of Ralph Emery*. New York, NY: Simon & Schuster Inc., 1992

Emery, Ralph (with Patsy Bale Cox). *The View From Nashville*. New York, NY: William Morrow & Co., 1998.

Escott, Colin (with Martin Hawkins). *Good Rockin' Tonight: Sun Records and the Birth of Rock 'N' Roll*. New York, NY: St. Martins Press, 1991.

Escott, Colin. *Tattoed on Their Tongues: A Journey through the Backrooms of American Music*. New York, NY: Schirmer Books, 1996.

Faragher, Scott. *Music City Babylon: Inside the World of Country Music*. New York, NY: Birch Lane Press, 1992.

Feiller, Bruce. *Dreaming Out Loud*. New York, NY: Avon Books, 1998.

Flint, Country Joe (and Judy Nelson). *The Insider's Country Music Handbook*. New York, NY: Peregrine, 1983.

Greenwood, Earl (with Kathleen Tracy). *Elvis: Top Secret*. New York, NY: Penguin Books, Signet Edition, 1991.

Guralnick, Peter. *Last Train To Memphis*. New York, NY: Back Bay Books; Little, Brown & Co., 1994.

Hagan, Chet. *Grand Ole Opry: The Complete History of a Great American Institution and Its Stars*. New York, NY: Henry Holt & Co., 1989.

Hall, Doug. *The Real Patsy Cline*. Kingston, ON: Quarry Music Books, 1998.

Hume, Martha. *Martha Hume's Guide to the Greatest in Country Music: You're So Cold I'm Turnin' Blue*. New York, NY: Viking Press, 1982.

Jennings, Waylon (with Lenny Kaye). *Waylon: An Autobiography*. New York, NY: Warner Books, 1998.

Jones, George (with Tom Carter). *I Lived To Tell It All*. New York, NY: Bantam, Doubleday, Dell, 1997.

Jones, Nancy (with Tom Carter). *Nashville Wives*. New York, NY: Cliff Street Books, 1998.

Kosser, Michael. *Country Music '88*. New York, NY: Paperjacks, 1988.

Killen, Buddy (with Tom Carter). *By the Seat of My Pants: My Life in Country Music*. New York: Simon & Shuster, 1993.

Linedecker, Cliff. *Country Music Stars and the Supernatural*. New York, NY: Dell Publishing Co. Ltd., 1979.

Lynch, Elizabeth, Contributing Reviewer. *MusicHound: Country – The Essential Album Guide*. New York, NY: Visible Ink Press, 1997.

McCabe, Peter (photos by Raeanne Rubenstein). *Honky Tonk Heroes: A Photo Album of Country Music*. New York, NY: Harper & Row, 1975.

McCall, Michael, Dave Hoekstra and Janet Williams, Contributing Writers. *Country Music Stars: The Legends and the New Breed*. Lincolnwood, IL: Publications International Inc., 1992.

McLaurin, Melton A. and Richard A. Peterson, eds. *You Wrote My Life: Lyrical Themes in Country Music*. Cultural Perspectives on the American South, Volume 6. Montreux, Switzerland: Gordon & Breach Science Publishers, 1992.

Malone, Bill C. and Judith McCulloh, eds. *Stars of Country Music (Uncle Dave Macon to Johnny Rodriguez)*. Urbana, IL: University of Illinois Press, 1975.

Marcus, Greil. *Mystery Train*. New York, NY: Penguin Books, Plume Edition, 1997.

Moore, Thurston, ed. *The Country Music Who's Who*. Cincinati, OH: Cardinal Enterprises, 1960.

Morgan, Lorrie (with George Vecsey). *Forever Yours, Faithfully: My Life Story*. New York, NY: Ballantine Books, 1998.

Morthland, John. *The Best of Country Music: A Critical and Historical Guide to the 750 Greatest Albums*. New York, NY: Doubleday, 1984.

Nash, Alanna. *Behind Closed Doors*. New York, NY: A Borzoi Book, Alfred A. Knopf, 1988.

Nickerson, Marina (& Cynthia Farah, photographs). *Country Music: A Look at the Men Who've Made It*. El Paso, TX: C.M. Publishing, 1981.

Pierce, Jennifer Ember. *Breakin' into Nashville*. Lantham, MD: Madison Books, 1994.

Presley, Priscilla Beaulieu (with Sandra Harmon). *Elvis and Me*. New York, NY: G.P. Putnam's Sons, 1985.

Pugh, Ronnie. *Ernest Tubb: The Texas Troubadour*. Durham, NC: Duke University Press, 1996.

Riese, Randall. *Nashville Babylon: The Uncensored Truth and Private Lives of Country Music's Stars*. New York, NY: Congden & Weed, 1988.

Shestack, Melvin. *The Country Music Encyclopedia*. New York, NY: KBO Publications, 1974.

Shestack, Melvin. "Hank Williams: He Had Country Soul." Introduction to *The Songs of Hank Williams*. Nashville, TN: Acuff-Rose International, 1974.

Swenson, John. *Bill Haley*. London, UK: W.H. Allen, 1982.

Tosches, Nick. *Country (The Twisted Roots of Rock 'n' Roll)*. New York, NY: Da Capo Press, 1998.

Whitburn, Joel. *The Billboard Book of Top 40 Albums*. New York, NY: Billboard Books, Watson-Gupthill Publications, 1995.

Whitburn, Joel. *The Billboard Book of Top Country Albums*. New York, NY: Billboard Books, Billboard Publications, 1996.

Whitburn, Joel. *The Billboard Book of Top 40 Country Hits*. New York, NY: Billboard Books, Billboard Publications, 1996.

Whitburn, Joel. *The Billboard Book of Top 40 Hits*. New York, NY: Billboard Books, Billboard Publications, 1996.

Williams, Hank, Jr. (with Michael Bane). *Living Proof*. New York, NY: Dell / James A. Byrans, 1983.

Wynette, Tammy (with Joan Dew). *Stand by Your Man*. New York, NY: Simon & Schuster, 1979.

Newspaper & Magazine Articles, Album Liner Notes

Ahern, Brian. Liner Notes: GEORGE JONES: THE BRADLEY BARN SESSIONS, MCA Records, 1994.

223

Allen, Bob. "The Decline and Fall of George Jones." *Country Music*. Jan-Feb, 1979.

Anonymous. "The Stars Paid Off for George Jones." *Country Song Roundup*. June, 1956.

Anonymous. "George Jones: A New Home, A New Club, A New Life." *Nashville Sound*. January, 1976.

Anonymous. "George & Tammy at The Holler." *Nashville Sound*. May, 1976.

Anonymous. "Welcome to Jones Country." *Country Rhythms*. August, 1984.

Anonymous. "George Jones 'Totals' Auto; Hit With DIU." *The Tennessean*. March 31, 1982.

Anonymous. Reuters Newswire Service: "George Jones Critical After Crash." May 7, 1999.

Anonymous. Record review: MY VERY SPECIAL GUESTS. *People*, January 21, 1980.

Albrecht, Jim (with Stacy Harris and Bob Battle). "George & Tammy Du-et Again — A Soap Opry." *Country Style*. June, 1980.

Bolsom, Rick. "George Jones: I'll Never Do Anything But Country Music. Part I." *Country Song Roundup*. March, 1977.

Bolsom, Rick. "George Jones: I'll Never Do Anything But Country Music. Part II." *Country Song Roundup*. April, 1977.

Carlisle, Dolly. "Barely Afloat in a Sea of Troubles, C&W Star George Jones Plots His Own Rescue." *Today*. January 15, 1979.

Carr, Patrick. "Stand by Your Fans: A Review of George & Tammy's First Concert After Their Reunion." *Country Music*. June, 1980.

Cramer, Richard Ben. "The Strange and Mysterious Death of Mrs. Jerry Lee Lewis." *Rolling Stone*. March 1, 1984.

Cramer, Richard Ben. (On the writing of: "The Strange And Mysterious Death Of Mrs. Jerry Lee Lewis.") *Rolling Stone: A 25th Anniversary Special, 1967-1992*. June 11, 1992.

Daily, Pappy. Liner Notes: I'LL SHARE MY WORLD WITH YOU, Musicor Records, 1969.

Dawidoff, Nicholas. "Just Put that Sad Back in The Bottle." *New York Times*. June 15, 1995.

Gates, David. "George Is on Our Mind." *Newsweek*. March 14, 1994.

Greenblatt, Mike, ed. "100 Years of Country Music," Special Edition of *Modern Screen*, 2000.

Haggard, Merle (with Peggy Russell). "Me and Elvis Presley, George Jones, Johnny Cash and Little Richard: Some Fond And Bitter Remembrances." An excerpt from *Sing Me Back Home*, in *Honky Tonk: The Magazine Of New Country*. February, 1979.

Hitts, Roger. "Tammy Wynette Was Beaten and Given Drugs." *Star*. May 4, 1999.

Hunter, James. Liner Notes: COUNTRY RHYTHM & BLUES. MCA Records, 1994.

Kaye, Lenny. "My Life With George: Nancy Jones Talks Candidly about Life with Country Music's Most Famous Singer." *Country Rhythms*. June, 1985.

Kienzle, Rick. Boxed Set Liner Notes: THE ESSENTIAL GEORGE JONES, Columbia/Legacy "Country Classics," Sony Music, 1994.

Littleton, Bill. "The George Jones Enigma: Writer's Memories Enliven Jones' Chemistry." *Performance*. May 29, 1987.

Moen, Debbi. "'No Show' Jones Nickname Is 'Yesterday's Wine'." *Performance*. May 29, 1987.

Pond, Neil. "George Jones Talks (About His Music, His Reputation, Life Out of the Fast Lane & How a Good Woman Turned Him Around.)" *Music City News*, July 1986.

Rector, Lee. "George Jones Determines to Make It Up to the Fans." *Music City News*. March, 1980.

Rose, Mark. "George Jones: Last Exit Off a Dark Highway." *The Village Voice*, September 23-29, 1981.

Schriver, Evelyn. Liner Notes: "The Making of COLD HARD TRUTH Was a Little Miracle," Asylum Records, 1999.

Sullivan, Robert, ed. Collector's Edition: *Life: The Roots of Country Music*. September, 1994.

Tosches, Nick. "The Devil in George Jones." *Texas Monthly*. July, 1994.

Trott, Walt. "Country Artist for the Millennium." *Country Music People*. December, 1999.

Vollmer, Brian. "The Mask of the Face." *Canadian Musician*. April, 1996.

Wood, Gerry. "Record Review: *George Jones: LIVE with the Possum*." *Country Weekly*. October 28, 1999.

Wynette, Tammy. "An Interview with George Jones by Tammy Wynette." *Country Music*. June, 1980.

Other Media

The George Jones Show. TNN. Produced by Billy Galium and Nancy Jones.

Same Ole Me. The Authorized Video Biography of George Jones. Nashville, TN: Hallway Productions, 1989.

ACKNOWLEDGEMENTS

The author would like to thank the following people. Larry Delaney at *Country Music News* for the research, support, and insight without which this book could not have seen the light of day. Bob Hilderley, my editor at Quarry Music Books, for forbearance and a sense of direction. Lauren Bufferd at the Country Music Foundation Library & Media Center for her assistance. Dee Lippingwell and the Merritt Mountain Music Festival. Cathy Taylor for the research in Nashville. And George Jones for the great music.

Photo Credits

Cover Photo: Hope Powell/Archive Photos
p. 2   Frank Driggs Collection/Achive Photos
p. 28   Frank Driggs Collection/Archive Photos
p. 29   Frank Driggs Collection/Archive Photos
p. 30   Tony de Nonno/Globe Photos
p. 31   Tony de Nonno/Globe Photos
p. 32   Reuters/Fred Prouser/Archive Photos
p. 153   Frank Driggs Collection/Archive Photos
p. 154   Lynn McAfee/Globe Photos
p. 155   Fritz Hoffman/Globe Photos
p. 156   Andrea Renault/Globe Photos (top)
         Lisa Rose/Globe Photos (bottom)
p. 157   Andrea Renault/Globe Photos

Lyrics

Every effort has been made to provide complete and correct copyright publishing information for the lyrics quoted in the text.

Choices. By Mike Curtis & Billy Yates. Music Corp. of America / Hillbillion Music / So Bizzy Music (BMI) / Boondocks Music / Makin' Friends Music, Inc. / Mack Loyd Wadkins Publishing (ASCAP).

Where Grass Won't Grow. By Earl Montgomery. Glad Music Co.

Good Ones & Bad Ones. By Joe Chambers & Larry Jenkins. Universal MCA Music Publishing / MCA Music Canada.

No Money In This Deal. By George Jones. Fort Knox Music Inc. / Trio Music Co. Inc.

Why Baby Why. By George Jones & Darrell Edwards. Fort Knox Music Inc./ Trio Music Co. Inc.

Just One More. By George Jones. Starrite Publishing Co.

A Picture From Life's Other Side. By Hank Williams. Acuff Rose / Hiriam Music / Seven Shooter Music.

White Lightning. By J.P. Richardson. Fort Knox Music Inc. / Trio Music Co. Inc. / Glad Music Co.

She Thinks I Still Care. By D.L. Lipscomb. Dickey Lee / Glad Music (BMI).

The Race Is On. By Don Rollins. Glad Music Company / Sony ATV Songs LLC (BMI).

I'll Share My World With You. By Ben Wilson. Glad Music Co.

If Drinkin' Don't Kill Me (Her Memory Will). By H. Sanders & R. Beresford. Careers / BMG Music Publishing / Warner-Tamerlane Publishing Co.

The Door. By Billy Sherrill & Norris Wilson. EMI Algee Music Corp.

He Stopped Loving Her Today. By Bobby Braddock & Curly Putman. Sony ATV Songs LLC.

She's My Rock. By S.K. Dobbins. Chappell & Co./ Famous Music Corp.

Who's Gonna Fill Their Shoes. By Troy Seals & Max D. Barnes. Published by Sony/ATV Songs LLC (BMI)/WB Music Corp. Two Sons Music (ASCAP).

The King Is Gone (So Are You). By R. Ferris. BMG Songs.

Bartender's Blues. By James Taylor. Country Road Music Inc (ASCAP).

I Always Get Lucky With You. By T. Whitson, F. Powers, G. Church & M. Haggard. Sony ATV Songs LLC.

Murder On Music Row. By Larry Cordle & Larry Shell. Wandachord Music, Shell Point Music, Pier Five Music / BMI.